Study Guide: Tools for Success

Principles of Macroeconomics

Fourth Edition

Fred Gottheil
University of Illinois

Prepared by

David M. Wishart
Wittenberg University

THOMSON

Study Guide: Tools for Success to accompany *Principles of Macroeconomics, 4e,* by David M. Wishart

Vice President: Dreis Van Landuyt
Marketing Manager: Sara L. Hinckley
Director of Product Creation: Becky Schwartz
Manufacturing Supervisor: Donna M. Brown
Pre-Media Supervisor: Christina Smith
Graphic Designer: Krista Pierson
Rights and Permissions Specialist: Kalina Ingham Hintz
Project Coordinator: Brian Schaefer
Technology Coordinator: Wendy E. May
Internal Design: Tim Flem/Publishware
Project Editor: James Reidel

Printed in the United States of America.

1 2 3 4 5 07 06 05 04

Thomson Publishing
5191 Natorp Blvd.
Mason, Ohio 45040
USA

International Headquarters
Thomson Learning
International Division
290 Harbor Drive, 2nd Floor
Stamford, CT 06902-7477
USA

For information about our products, contact us:
1-800-355-9983

0-324-26004-0

TABLE OF CONTENTS

Preface

My first contact with Fred Gottheil came some 35 years ago when my Dad enlisted my aid typing a long, long book review as part of Professor Gottheil's graduate level History of Economic Thought course that he was taking at the University of Illinois. Typing was one of the more useful things I learned in junior high school, and my Dad, no slouch of an economist, knew how to exploit cheap labor. Fifty cents per page was the going rate. Either that or mow the yard. Never in my wildest, 13-year-old imagination did I dream that I'd go on to major in economics after having taken Fred's Principles course in economics at Illinois (mainly to defend myself in arguments with my Dad), become good friends with Fred, write a Ph.D. thesis under his supervision, and be involved in this textbook/study guide project through four editions. Working with Fred has been one of the joys of my life. I owe him a debt of gratitude for teaching me about economics and much more. That Fred is a wonderful soul comes through in his text.

Writing this study guide has been fun and rewarding. I haven't done it alone. Hundreds of my students at Wittenberg University have been subjected to dozens of questions and problems, variants of which appear in this book. My students have been quick to point out flaws in the questions, doing a first round of editing for me. Especially helpful in this regard for the first edition were Deborah Goldstein, Ed Hasecke, Chris Murray, Kristen Neubaurer, Ryan Terry, Steve Valenti, and Bethany Young. Mojca Fink read the entire first edition and pointed to many corrections that were necessary. Mojca's eye for detail was a great help.

For the second edition, Chris Taendler and Javier Herrera helped with editing and locating Web sites for the Economics Online segments in each chapter. Thanks guys. Javier read the entire manuscript, some of it twice, and checked answers carefully. He was a tireless worker, always willing to challenge me. Professor Gottheil offered feedback on many of the chapters. There was no shortage of red ink from Fred's pen, all of it constructive. Margaret Landman edited the entire manuscript and helped write some of the Chapter in a Nutshell and Graphing Tutorial/Pitfalls segments. Her help sharpening the questions and the prose throughout has been invaluable. For the third edition, another of my students, Wendy Hanson, was enormously helpful checking out Web sites. Colin Zink performed the same task for the fourth edition in his usual careful and efficient manner. Thanks also go to the editorial staff at South-Western/Thomson — Jack Calhoun, Dennis Hanseman, and Rebecca Robey on the first edition. Thomas Sigel's editorial help on the second edition was terrific. Tom deserves credit for many of the features in the second edition. On the current edition, James Reidel has been extremely helpful going through the manuscript, pointing up errors, and making certain that the study guide is consistent with the new edition of the text. Any questions about the study guide can be addressed to me by e-mail, *dwishart@wittenberg.edu*.

Finally, my wife Jo Wilson gets special thanks for her patient support over many months of writing. My sons Tony and Jacob have put up with a distracted parent for too long. We're overdue for a fishing trip.

David M. Wishart
Wittenberg University
February 2004

CHAPTER 1

INTRODUCTION

Chapter in a Nutshell

Economics is an important branch of the social sciences where study is focused on three critical areas of human behavior. First, economists study the problems that arise because **resources are scarce and people's wants are insatiable.** If resources are scarce and human wants are unlimited, then it makes sense that **choices have to be made.** It's the making of these choices that forms the other two areas of human behavior that economists study. Choices have to be made about **allocating scarce resources to produce goods and services to satisfy insatiable wants.** The third area of human behavior that economists study is **distribution.** Once goods and services are produced, they have to be distributed to people. The way goods and services are distributed is crucial to understanding how an economy performs. In our society, **consumer sovereignty** drives the production of most goods and services, meaning that consumers are free to decide what they want to purchase in the marketplace. Consumers form households that supply renewable and nonrenewable resources to firms that produce goods and services. Firms are guided by the market, just as if they were being led by an **invisible hand,** to produce exactly the goods and services that consumers want.

Production and distribution are complicated social processes. Economists use **models to help simplify the study of real-world economic relationships.** These models help economists to understand cause-and-effect relationships in the economy. Economists use models to study microeconomic and macroeconomic relationships. **Microeconomics** focuses on **individual economic relationships. Macroeconomics** studies the **behavior of the economy as a whole.** Economists use **positive analysis — the study of the economic relationships that exist** in the economy and **normative analysis — the study of what ought to be** in the economy. Economists have made substantial progress toward a better understanding of the economy due to the collection of better economic data over the last 50 years and the use of new statistical methods to test the accuracy of economic models. **Econometrics** is the branch of economics that deals with the **use of statistical methods to analyze economic data.** Even though economists' predictions aren't perfect, they are improving as economic knowledge advances.

After you study this chapter, you should be able to:

- Describe the finite character of the earth's **resources.**
- Distinguish between **renewable and nonrenewable resources.**
- Discuss people's **insatiable wants.**
- Connect Adam Smith's idea of the **invisible hand** to the way markets work
- Tell how **scarcity** and choice are related to each other.
- Explain why **economic models** are used.
- Define and contrast **microeconomics** and **macroeconomics.**
- Compare **positive** and **normative economics.**

1

Concept Check — See how you do on these multiple-choice questions.

All of our resource supplies are finite. And, for practical purposes, human wants can be described as insatiable.
Do you see a problem here?

1. The **finite character of resource supplies** combined with **insatiable wants** results in
   a. normative economics
   b. *ceteris paribus*
   c. the problem of scarcity
   d. the circular flow model
   e. consumer sovereignty

Economic analysis can be carried on at the level of households and firms, or it can be done at the level of the
economy as a whole. What are these types of analysis called?

2. Economists who study **microeconomic questions** focus on
   a. national saving and investment
   b. unemployment and inflation
   c. the economy as a whole
   d. individual economic behavior
   e. circular flows

Positive economics describes what exists in the economy.

3. Which of the following statements makes a **positive economics** statement?
   a. Greenhouse gas emissions should be cut by 10 percent from 1990 levels
   b. Carbon dioxide emissions contribute to global warming
   c. A tax should be placed on gasoline to decrease carbon dioxide emissions
   d. Developing countries ought to limit their greenhouse gas emissions
   e. Slowing down global warming should be a top priority for the United States

Economic models are used to simplify real-world economic relationships in order to understand them better.

4. A major advantage of using **economic models** is that they
   a. allow us to focus on only the most important variables
   b. are expressed algebraically and not in words
   c. are able to capture all the elements in economic relationships
   d. force us to use econometric methods
   e. emphasize the role played by scarcity and insatiable wants

Can cause-and-effect economic relationships be identified if all variables change simultaneously?

5. The primary reason for using the *ceteris paribus* assumption is that it allows us to
   a. examine a relationship where all variables change together
   b. predict economic changes with nearly perfect accuracy
   c. examine the impact of changes in variables one at a time
   d. distinguish between microeconomics and macroeconomics
   e. hold stocks of nonrenewable resources constant

Am I on the Right Track?

Your answers to the questions above should be **c**, **d**, **b**, **a**, and **c**. It's very important that you appreciate how scarcity forces people in a society to make choices about what is produced and how the output is distributed. Scarcity and choice are at the heart of economic analysis. You should also have an appreciation for the ways that economic analysis is conducted. For example, the distinction between microeconomics and macroeconomics should be clear. Positive economic analysis and normative economic analysis are also easily distinguishable. Try using the *ceteris paribus* assumption in a conversation with one of your friends. If you can explain it to them after they give you a strange look, then you are probably on the right track.

Key Terms Quiz — Match the term on the left with the definition in the column on the right.

1. natural resources	_____	a. social science that studies scarcity and choice
2. macroeconomics	_____	b. statistical methods for testing economic models
3. insatiable wants	_____	c. what ought to be
4. positive economics	_____	d. free choice in the market on what to buy
5. scarcity	_____	e. simplification of real-world economic relationships
6. normative economics	_____	f. unlimited desires for goods
7. economics	_____	g. the study of individual economic behavior
8. econometrics	_____	h. the study of human behavior generally
9. consumer sovereignty	_____	i. other things being equal
10. social sciences	_____	j. exchange relationships between households and firms
11. economic model	_____	k. what is
12. *ceteris paribus*	_____	l. people living under one roof with a source of income
13. circular flow model	_____	m. an enterprise that produces goods and/or services for market
14. household	_____	n. renewable and nonrenewable gifts of nature
15. firm	_____	o. market guides firms to produce goods and services people want
16. microeconomics	_____	p. finiteness of resources relative to unlimited wants
17. invisible hand	_____	q. the study of the economy as a whole

True-False Questions — If a statement is false, explain why.

1. Economists regard natural resources as gifts of nature. (T/F)

2. The main difference between renewable and nonrenewable resources is that we will never run out of renewable resources, but we will someday exhaust our nonrenewable resources. (T/F)

3. Because human wants are insatiable, scarcity would be a problem even if resources were found in unlimited supplies. (T/F)

4. Economic models are simplifications or abstract representations of economic reality. (T/F)

5. In the resource market depicted in the circular flow model, wages, rent, interest, and profit flow toward firms and labor, land, capital, and entrepreneurship flow toward households. (T/F)

6. Adam Smith's idea of the invisible hand suggests that by pursuing their self interest in everyday economic behavior, people will fail to serve the interest of society as a whole. (T/F)

7. The circular flow model would better represent the real world if flows of money, resources, goods, and services to and from government were included. (T/F)

8. The *ceteris paribus* assumption is often used to simplify economic analysis. (T/F)

9. Economics is one of the social sciences because it examines individual and social behavior. (T/F)

10. Microeconomics is more useful than macroeconomics because it gives a more detailed picture of the economy. (T/F)

11. Macroeconomic analysis focuses on economic activity at the level of the whole economy rather than at the level of the individual. (T/F)

12. Positive economics analyzes the way the economy actually operates. (T/F)

13. Normative economics is free from value judgments. (T/F)

14. An economist hired to formulate economic policies for a presidential candidate would never engage in positive economic analysis. (T/F)

15. Because social scientists work with models that are precisely accurate in their predictions, they can develop policies that will solve any social problems we face. (T/F)

Multiple-Choice Questions

1. The difference between a renewable resource and a nonrenewable resource is that
   a. a renewable resource can never be depleted while a nonrenewable resource is depleted as it is used
   b. a nonrenewable resource can never be depleted while a renewable resource is depleted as it is used
   c. the stock of a renewable resource can be maintained forever
   d. conservation efforts cannot save renewable resources
   e. renewable resources are liquids and nonrenewable resources are solids

2. Economics is a social science that explores the problem of
   a. how society transforms scarce resources into goods and services
   b. persuading people to limit their wants
   c. scarcity in poor countries but not rich countries
   d. what ought to be done to make the world a better place
   e. circular flows within the family unit

3. Economists use the *ceteris paribus* assumption in their analysis because it
   a. converts positive economic statements to normative ones
   b. converts normative economic statements to positive ones
   c. is the only way to move from theoretical model building to the real world
   d. allows us to develop one-to-one, cause-and-effect relationships
   e. broadens the scope of analysis, creating a social science approach to the subject

4. Positive economics deals with _____ while normative economics considers
   _____.
   a. what ought to be; what is
   b. what is; what ought to be
   c. good policies; policies for normal times
   d. improvements in living standards; how to keep the economy steady over time
   e. a positive approach to economic problems; a normal approach to problems

5. Microeconomics is the branch of economics that analyzes _____ while macroeconomics
   is the branch of economics that analyzes _____.
   a. the behavior of individual economic units; how national economies work
   b. how national economies work; the behavior of individual economic units
   c. positive questions; normative questions
   d. historical issues on a micro scale; contemporary issues on a large scale
   e. economic details; broader aspects of economic issues

6. In the circular flow model, households furnish labor, capital, land, and entrepreneurship to businesses for
   which they are paid _____, _____, _____, and _____, respectively.
   a. profit, interest, rent, wages
   b. wages, interest, rent, profit
   c. wages, interest, profit, rent
   d. wages, profit, interest, rent
   e. wages, rent, interest, profit

7. If we accept the assumption that people have insatiable wants and that the resources available to satisfy
   these wants are finite, then
   a. misery is guaranteed for all
   b. the economy is easy to model
   c. because of scarcity, people are forced to make choices
   d. consumer sovereignty can be invoked to eliminate scarcity
   e. firms and households will cooperate to decrease wants and increase resource supplies

8. An economist who is attempting to accurately estimate the unemployment rate for a national economy is
   practicing
   a. microeconomics
   b. normative economics
   c. positive economics
   d. consumer sovereignty
   e. sociology

9. Microeconomics is a subarea of economics that focuses on
   a. the economies of smaller countries
   b. the behavior of the economy as a whole
   c. the use of statistics to quantify and test economic models
   d. the product market loops in the circular flow model
   e. the market behavior of individual households and firms

10. Models that economists use are
    a. perfect representations of the real world
    b. typically useless oversimplifications of the real world
    c. abstractions of an economic reality
    d. exempt from *ceteris paribus*
    e. applicable only to macroeconomics

11. Money flows in resource markets represent payments to _____ whereas, money flows in product markets represent payments to _____.
    a. business firms; workers
    b. natural resource owners; banks
    c. the government; private businesses
    d. property owners; only the most productive individuals
    e. households; firms producing goods and services

12. The circular flow model is an abstraction from economic reality because
    a. it includes so many details of economic life
    b. it clearly shows money flows and flows of goods and services between households and business firms
    c. the real economy is much more complicated than the model portrays it to be
    d. government and the financial sector are unimportant in the economy
    e. the *ceteris paribus* assumption applies in the model

13. Which of the following statements **is not** a positive statement?
    a. Taxes on the rich should be increased.
    b. Poverty in America is increasing.
    c. The poor receive larger amounts of government aid than they did 10 years ago.
    d. Price ceilings are used to keep the prices of necessities low.
    e. Subsidies to farmers in America are a cause of surplus production.

14. Because it is impossible to run controlled experiments in economics so that only one variable is changed at a time, economists
    a. create extremely complex economic models
    b. create very simple models
    c. use the *ceteris paribus* assumption in their analysis
    d. focus on demand and supply
    e. cannot hope to improve their understanding of the economy

15. All of the following are examples of nonrenewable resources **except**
    a. forests
    b. iron ore
    c. coal
    d. oil
    e. natural gas

16. All of the following are examples of renewable resources **except**
    a. the sea
    b. fish in the sea
    c. gold used to make earrings
    d. labor used to grow corn
    e. corn used to feed cattle

17. Although scarcity exists today, it is not nearly as severe as it was in ancient times. Looking to the future, economists believe that societies will better cope with scarcity
    a. by developing new technologies that create greater supply to satisfy human wants
    b. by producing enough to completely satisfy human wants
    c. by doing better positive economic analysis
    d. by doing better normative economic analysis
    e. with more accurate economic models

18. Using the *ceteris paribus* assumption to study the effect of an increase in the price of mustard on the amount of ketchup that is purchased requires that
    a. the price of mustard be held constant
    b. both the price of mustard and the amount of ketchup purchased be held constant
    c. everything except the price of mustard and the amount of ketchup purchased be held constant
    d. nothing should be held constant
    e. econometrics be used

19. Consumer sovereignty is a term used to describe the way
    a. voters choose their leaders at the ballot box
    b. consumers determine which goods and services are produced with their purchases
    c. scarcity ultimately controls the consumption patterns of households
    d. the invisible hand leads people to help others
    e. consumers decide what to purchase

The following questions relate to the historical and theoretical perspectives presented in the text.

20. Stanley Jevons's prediction in 1865 that England's economic power would collapse because of the depletion of coal has proven to be
    a. true because so few workers mine coal in England today
    b. true because coal is a nonrenewable resource
    c. false because coal reserves are renewable to some extent over long periods
    d. false because England has switched to oil and natural gas as substitute energy sources
    e. false because productivity growth in the British coal industry has been high

21. After the price of oil soared in the late 1970s, one of the economic responses was
    a. a dramatic shift to the use of more abundant coal supplies as an energy source
    b. a decision to leave the remaining oil in the ground as part of a conservation effort
    c. a decrease in drilling for oil since little was left to be discovered
    d. the widespread adoption of solar energy
    e. an increase in the number of active drilling rigs to the highest level since 1940

22. Adam Smith's idea of the invisible hand as it is applied to the circular flow model links
    a. wages with households furnishing labor to firms
    b. flows of renewable and nonrenewable resources
    c. consumer sovereignty with the pursuit of self-interest by firms in the product market
    d. consumer sovereignty with the pursuit of self-interest in the resource market
    e. microeconomics with macroeconomics

Fill in the Blanks

1. Resources that are _____ can be maintained forever with properly managed conservation.

2. Examples of disciplines that are part of the social sciences include _____, _____,

   _____, _____, and _____.

3. In order for an economist to make the statement that as its price increases, the quantity demanded for filet

   mignon will decrease, the _____ assumption will have to be introduced.

4. Households _____ land, labor, capital, and entrepreneurship to firms in return for

   _____ that they use to _____ goods and services produced by firms.

5. Economists who make normative statements concerning economic issues apply their own personal and

   social _____ to make these statements.

Discussion Questions

1. What do economists study? Identify the main branches of economics and the types of analysis that are
   used.

2. How do social values and responsibilities influence economic behavior?

3. Can you imagine scarcity becoming a thing of the past? Think about what was available to your
   grandparents compared to what you have at your disposal. What does it tell you?

4. Why aren't economists' predictions perfect?

5. Suppose that you were to make the circular flow model more detailed by including banks and the government. How would the addition of these groups change the model?

Everyday Applications

1. Go to the business pages of a newspaper and survey the content of the articles there. How many of the articles are about microeconomic topics? How many are about macroeconomics? Can you pick out any predictions that economists or business analysts are making in these articles? What sort of economic models seem to be the basis for their predictions?

2. Watch the Jim Lehrer News Hour on PBS some evening and analyze the discussions between interviewers and guests for positive and normative content. How do the people being interviewed use positive analysis to support their normative arguments? Can you see how the two types of analysis can work together?

Economics Online

For a peek into the wild and wonderful world of econometrics, visit the SHAZAM homepage (*http://shazam.econ.ubc.ca/*). SHAZAM is an econometrics computer program. You probably won't understand many of the technical terms on this homepage, but if you continue with your study of economics, you'll come to appreciate how useful econometrics can be. Better yet, it can be fun, especially with the computer technologies now available.

Answers to Questions

Key Terms Quiz

a. 7	**f.** 3	**k.** 4	**p.** 5
b. 8	**g.** 16	**l.** 14	**q.** 2
c. 6	**h.** 10	**m.** 15	
d. 9	**i.** 12	**n.** 1	
e. 11	**j.** 13	**o.** 17	

True-False Questions

1. True
2. False. Renewable resources may run out if society consumes them more rapidly than they are renewed.

Nonrenewable resources may never run out if they can be replaced by renewable substitutes.

3. True
4. True
5. False. In the circular flow model, wages, rent, interest, and profit flow toward households and labor, land, capital, and entrepreneurship flow toward firms.
6. False. Smith's concept of the invisible hand suggests that by pursuing their self interest in the market, people will be led, as if by an invisible hand, to serve the interest of society at large.
7. True
8. True
9. True
10. False.   Whether micro or macroeconomics is more useful depends on what problems are under consideration.
11. True
12. True
13. False. Positive economics is free from value judgments.
14. False. The economist would certainly want to understand how the economy works to draw cause-and-effect conclusions.
15. False. The social sciences use models that are not perfect representations of the world.

Multiple-Choice Questions

1. c	**6.** b	**11.** e	**16.** c	**21.** e
2. a	**7.** c	**12.** c	**17.** a	**22.** c
3. d	**8.** c	**13.** a	**18.** c	
4. b	**9.** e	**14.** c	**19.** b	
5. a	**10.** c	**15.** a	**20.** d	

Fill in the Blanks

1. renewable
2. economics, sociology, anthropology, political science, psychology
3. *ceteris paribus*
4. supply, payments, purchase
5. values

Discussion Questions

1. Economists study how societies cope with the problem of scarcity. For example, economists study the allocation of scarce resources for production of goods and services. Distribution of these goods and services is also a focus of analysis. Economists develop theoretical models to help them sort out the core issues in economic questions. It is possible to test these theoretical models against real-world data. The main branches of economics are microeconomics and macroeconomics, while econometrics is also an important field. Economists pursue both positive and normative analysis in their work.

2. Even though consumer sovereignty guides what we buy and, therefore, what we produce for the market, our economic choices are nonetheless constrained by social values and responsibilities. For example, most cultures find extremely excessive and wasteful behavior to be inappropriate. Certain types of drugs are illegal in most cultures, though this varies from society to society. We feel a responsibility to pay taxes even though we would prefer not to. So, even though the consumer is mostly sovereign, limits are placed on economic behavior by our shared cultural values and responsibilities.

3. We will always have scarcity because of unlimited wants. However, the advances of the industrial

revolution in recent history have helped to diminish the severity of scarcity. Pick up a 1950s Sears catalog and look at the mix of goods that was available to American consumers then. Or read the opening pages of Dickens's *A Tale of Two Cities.* Imagine yourself using these goods to satisfy your wants. Would you trade places with these earlier consumers?

4. Economists' predictions aren't perfect because it is impossible to control for changes in the myriad variables that may affect the variable being predicted. Sometimes the data used by economists turn out to be flawed.

5. Households contribute savings to banks, which, in turn make loans to firms and to households. Households also furnish resources to banks, as they do to other firms, and banks make payments to households for supplying resources. Households pay taxes to the government and, in return, receive payments such as Social Security from the government. Moreover, government makes payments to business firms for products that they supply to government. Also, households supply resources to government and the government makes payments for these resources in return.

APPENDIX

ON READING GRAPHS

Appendix in a Nutshell

The appendix acquaints you with some of the techniques that economists use in translating economic concepts to mathematical and graphical forms. Remember, anything that is expressed mathematically or graphically can also be expressed in words. The reason we use math and graphs in economics is because they simplify discussions. The intention is not to make life more difficult for those trying to do economics but, rather, to make concepts that would be difficult to express in prose more easily understandable. Graphs in economics are a classic case of pictures being worth a thousand words. None of the mathematics and graphs in this text are terribly difficult. So, relax, graphing can be fun.

After you study this appendix, you should be able to:

- Find the **origin** of a graph.
- Measure distances on graphs.
- Graph relationships between **independent and dependent variables**.
- Connect points representing data from a table to form a graph.
- Explain what is meant by the **slope of a curve**.
- Describe various shaped curves by their slopes.
- Measure the **slope at a point on a curve**.

Concept Check — See how you do on these multiple-choice questions.   ✔

What are the *x* and *y* coordinates that we associate with the origin?

1. The **origin** of a graph is
    a. the end of the line that describes the independent variable
    b. the slope of the curve
    c. the graph's point of reference
    d. the sum of the horizontal and vertical distances on the graph
    e. where one starts to connect points to form a curve

Typically, economists work with **relationships that express dependence.** For example, the amount of a good that people are willing to buy depends on its price.

2. The **independent variable** and the **dependent variable** in a relationship reflect a linkage between them such that
    a. changes in the dependent variable depend on changes in the value of the independent variable
    b. the dependent variable always has a larger value than the independent variable
    c. the dependent variable is always some multiple of the independent variable
    d. as the independent variable increases, so does the dependent variable
    e. as the independent variable increases, the dependent variable decreases

Slopes can be either positive or negative, and they can be either constant or changing.

3. The **slope** of a curve measures the
    a. ratio of the change in the variable on the horizontal axis to the change in the variable on the vertical axis
    b. ratio of the change in the variable on the vertical axis to the change in the variable on the horizontal axis
    c. rate of decrease in the dependent variable
    d. rate of increase in the independent variable
    e. percentage change in the dependent variable divided by the percentage change in the independent variable

Sketch a U-shaped curve and a hill-shaped curve and use the definition of slope to determine the correct answer for this question.

4. Curves that are **U-shaped** have slopes that are first _____ and then turn _____, while curves that are **hill-shaped** have slopes that are first _____ and then turn _____.
    a. decreasing; increasing; increasing; decreasing
    b. negative; positive; positive; negative
    c. positive; negative; negative; positive
    d. rising; falling; falling; rising
    e. zero; infinite; infinite; zero

Measuring the slope at a point on a curve is necessary if the slope is not constant. If the slope of a curve is constant, then it is a straight line.

5. In order to measure the **slope at a point on a curve**, one should
    a. find the x and y values of the point
    b. divide the x value of the point by the y value
    c. draw a line from the origin to the point and find the slope of the line
    d. divide the y value of the point by the x value
    e. draw a tangent through the point and find the slope of the tangent

Am I on the Right Track?

Your answers to the questions above should be **c**, **a**, **b**, **b**, and **e**. Some of the terms used in the concept check show up in the key terms quiz below. Make sure you clearly understand their meanings.

Key Terms Quiz — Match the terms on the left with the definitions in the column on the right.

1. origin   _____ a. a variable whose value influences the value of another variable
2. independent variable _____ b. a straight line that touches a curve at only one point
3. dependent variable   _____ c. the slope of a curve at its point of tangency
4. slope of a curve   _____ d. a graph's point of reference
5. tangent   _____ e. a variable whose value depends on the value of another variable
6. slope of a tangent   _____ f. the slope of the tangent to the curve at a point

Graphing Tutorial

The best way to learn to read graphs is to construct a few of them and begin to interpret them. This tutorial is far from exhaustive. However, it will show you how to construct a graph from values that are listed in a table. The graph will be interpreted. Then, the problems below will help you apply different concepts relevant to reading graphs.

Suppose you are operating a lemonade stand during the hottest part of the summer and you vary the price of lemonade from day to day to see how changes in the price affect the amount of lemonade purchases. The data from your experiment on changing the price are shown in the table below.

Price per Cup ($)	Quantity Demanded
2.50	0
2.00	3
1.50	5
1.00	8
0.50	12

Each of these pairs of price and quantity demanded values can be translated into a point on a graph. Then the points can be connected to form a curve. In this case, the curve that is formed is called a demand curve because it reflects the quantity demanded of lemonade at different prices. You will learn more about demand curves in Chapter 3. The curve constructed from the table is shown on the following page, with the price measured along the vertical axis and the quantity demanded measured along the horizontal axis.

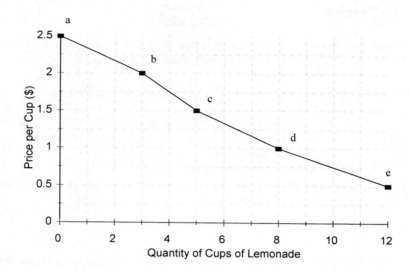

Each of the points shown in the table is labeled with a letter in the graph. Point a in the graph corresponds to a price of $2.50 and 0 cups of lemonade purchased. Points b, c, d, and e correspond to the other pairs of values listed in the table. What can be said about the slope of this curve? Clearly, the slope is negative because the curve is downward sloping. That is, as price decreases, the quantity demanded increases. For every decrease in value of the variable measured on the vertical axis, there is an increase in the value of the variable measured along the horizontal axis. Furthermore, the slope of this curve is not constant. Look at what happens as we decrease the price by $.50 from point to point along the curve. The quantity demanded increases by 3 cups, then 2 cups, then 3 cups, then 4 cups.

By working through the problems that follow, you will improve your ability to interpret graphs.

Problems

1. Using the example in the graphing tutorial, compute the slope of the curve between the following prices:

   a. From a price equal to $2 to a price equal to $1.50

   b. From $1.50 to $1.00

   c. From $1.00 to $.50

d. What happens to the value of the slope over this range of prices? How does this influence the shape of the curve?

2. Consider the graph shown below and explain how the slope changes along the graph by drawing tangent lines at various points along the curve.

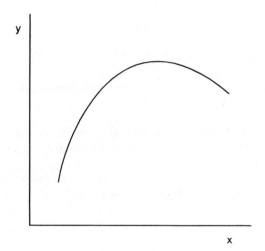

3. Explain the changes that occur in the slope along this curve from the origin to point A, then from point A to point B.

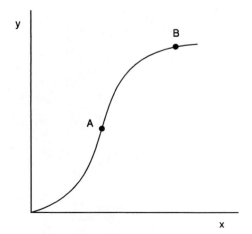

Answers to Questions for the Appendix

Key Terms Quiz

a. 2   d. 1
b. 5   e. 3
c. 6   f. 4

Problems

1. a. The slope between prices of $2 and $1.50 is (2 − 1.50)/(3 − 5) = −.5/2 = −.25

   b. The slope between prices of $1.50 and $1 is (1.5 − 1)/(5 − 8) = −.5/3 = −.167

   c. The slope between prices of $1 and $.5 is (1 − .5)/(8 − 12) = −.5/4 = −.125

   d. The value of the slope is negative but increasing over this range, meaning that the slope becomes less negative and the curve is becoming flatter.

2. Starting at the point on the curve closest to the origin, the slope is positive but decreasing until it becomes zero at the peak of the curve beyond which the slope becomes increasingly negative.

3. From the origin to point A, the slope is positive and increases as the curve gets steeper. From point A to point B, the slope is positive and decreases as the curve becomes flatter.

Homework Questions

True-False Questions — If a statement is false, explain why.

1. The circular flow model is a detailed representation of a modern economy. (T/F)

2. Consumer sovereignty suggests that the individual choices of consumers in product markets ultimately determine the kinds of goods and services that are produced. (T/F)

3. Macroeconomics is the branch of economics that examines individual economic behavior. (T/F)

4. Labor, land, capital, and entrepreneurship are the resources supplied by households to firms in resource markets. (T/F)

5. Advances in the field of econometrics have made economic predictions virtually perfect over the last fifty years. (T/F)

Multiple-Choice Questions

1. Scarcity will continue to be a problem for human societies as long as
   a. renewable resources are poorly managed
   b. some resources are nonrenewable
   c. wants are insatiable
   d. consumer sovereignty fails to result in the correct combination of goods being produced
   e. people are not frugal enough to make the available resources last

2. Which of the following statements is not related to macroeconomics?
   a. IBM is expecting lower profits in the next year.
   b. Consumption spending in the European Union is increasing.
   c. Inflation is a looming problem for the United States economy.
   d. Economic growth in Asian countries is accelerating due to technological progress.
   e. Investment in new machinery in the United States will likely decline due to higher interest rates.

3. Economists use abstractions in their analysis of the economy because
   a. information is insufficient to allow for detailed consideration of any economic problem
   b. abstractions are useful when economic model building is inappropriate
   c. they want to reduce the complexity of the world to more manageable dimensions
   d. abstractions are used by all social scientists
   e. the real world they want to understand is itself an abstraction

4. The circular flow model presented in the text includes which participants?
   a. firms and the government
   b. households, banks, and firms
   c. households and the government
   d. firms, households, and the government
   e. firms and households

5. Which of the following statements in not a positive statement?
   a. The price of essential medical care should be set by the government.
   b. The number of oil drilling rigs has decreased since 1981.
   c. The amount of available resources is finite.
   d. Unemployment in December was 5.7 percent.
   e. Households purchase goods and services in product markets.

Discussion Questions/Problems

1. In the space below sketch the circular flow model and explain the flows between the product and resource markets. Label your sketch carefully.

2. Are we running out of natural resources? How does your answer differ depending on whether the resource is renewable or nonrenewable?

CHAPTER 2

PRODUCTION POSSIBILITIES AND OPPORTUNITY COSTS

Chapter in a Nutshell

This chapter considers how **productive resources** — **labor, capital, land, and entrepreneurship** — are combined to produce goods. A model is developed to represent an economy's **production possibilities**. Our model of production possibilities highlights the need for societies to make choices in the face of scarcity — a concept that was stressed in the first chapter. There is an **opportunity cost** associated with any choice that is made. For example, in order for an economy to produce more of one good, it will be forced to sacrifice units of production of other goods. Moreover, we will find that shifting resources from the production of one good to another involves increasing sacrifices of the first good in order to generate equal increases in the second good. This phenomenon is called **the law of increasing costs**.

Economic growth occurs in an economy where the supplies of productive resources increase over time. Economic growth is an expansion of an economy's production possibilities. Another source of economic growth is ideas that take the form of **new applied technologies** called **innovations**. Innovation allows a given quantity of resources to produce a larger output. **Division of labor and specialization** is yet another way that an economy can experience economic growth. As people specialize in specific tasks, they are able to produce more than if they spread their talents and energies over many unspecialized tasks. **Division of labor and specialization** occur at the international level. We will learn that economies specialize at the international level in activities for which they have an **absolute advantage** — that is, the country can produce a good with fewer resources than can other countries. Specialization also occurs according to **comparative advantage**. A country has a comparative advantage if it can produce a good at a lower opportunity cost than other countries.

After studying this chapter, you should be able to:

- Name the **factors of production**.
- Describe an economy's **production possibilities**.
- Distinguish between **capital goods** and **consumption goods**.
- Define **opportunity cost**.
- Explain the **law of increasing costs**.
- Show how new **technology** and **innovation** lead to **economic growth**.
- Explain how **specialization and division of labor** increases productivity.
- Account for international specialization according to **absolute and comparative advantage**.

Concept Check — See how you do on these multiple-choice questions.

Does the opportunity cost of producing a good change as more is produced given the law of increasing cost?

1. An economy that experiences **the law of increasing costs** and shifts resources from automobile production to computer production in order to increase computer output by fixed increments must
   a. be inefficient
   b. be shrinking
   c. be growing
   d. operate beyond its production possibilities curve in the impossibilities region
   e. give up increasing amounts of automobiles

Recall that an innovation is the introduction of a new applied technology to production that reduces the severity of scarcity.

2. An **innovation** is a change in the way that a good is produced such that
   a. economic growth decreases
   b. the amount of labor used increases
   c. the same amount of resources can produce a larger output
   d. computers are used in production
   e. scarcity is abolished

Economic growth is a shift to the right in the production possibilities curve. Which of the possible answers listed below would not result in a shift in the production possibilities curve?

3. All of the following except _____ will result in **economic growth**.
   a. growth in the labor force
   b. growth in the capital stock
   c. improvements in technology
   d. an increase in entrepreneurship
   e. an increase in the unemployment rate

A poor economy must necessarily devote most of its resources to the production of consumption goods just to provide for subsistence.

4. **Capital accumulation** is limited in poor countries because
   a. their citizens don't want to work
   b. most of their resources must be devoted to production for subsistence
   c. of the law of increasing costs
   d. people in these countries are quite satisfied to be poor
   e. wars in these countries have wiped out the advanced technology that used to exist

For this question, think about what is given up in going to see the movie?

5. The **opportunity cost** of going to see a movie is equal to
   a. the cost of the ticket
   b. the time lost while watching the show
   c. the value of the next best possible action
   d. five points that you missed on the economics quiz you could have studied for
   e. the pleasure you could have enjoyed watching TV instead

Am I on the Right Track?

If your answers to these questions were **e**, **c**, **e**, **b**, and **c**, then you are on the right track. Perhaps the best study hint for mastering this chapter (and one that applies to all subsequent chapters) is to learn the jargon used by economists. Economists use language that appears rather ordinary, but the meanings they attach to these words are often quite different from the ordinary meanings usually associated with them. So, learn the concepts of opportunity cost, law of increasing cost, technological change, innovation, labor specialization, among others. Progress will be much easier if we all agree on definitions to specific terms. The key terms quiz that follows should help.

Key Terms Quiz — Match the term on the left with the definition in the column on the right.

1. factors of production	_____ a. division of labor into specialized activities
2. labor	_____ b. manufactured goods used to make other goods and services
3. capital	_____ c. combinations of goods and services that can be produced
4. human capital	_____ d. the opportunity cost of producing a good increases as its output rises
5. land	_____ e. an idea that becomes an applied technology
6. entrepreneur	_____ f. producing a good with fewer resources than another producer
7. production possibilities	_____ g. resources that are less than fully utilized
8. opportunity cost	_____ h. producing a good at a lower opportunity cost than another producer
9. law of increasing costs	_____ i. physical and intellectual effort by people in the production process
10. innovation	_____ j. the quantity of goods that must be given up to obtain a good
11. underemployed resources	_____ k. land, labor, capital, and entrepreneurship
12. economic efficiency	_____ l. the knowledge and skills acquired by labor
13. labor specialization	_____ m. the maximum possible output with resources fully employed
14. absolute advantage	_____ n. a natural-state resource such as real estate
15. comparative advantage	_____ o. a person willing to assume the risks of a business

Graphing Tutorial

From a graphing perspective, this chapter is fairly straightforward. There is really only one type of graph presented in the chapter — the production possibilities curve (or frontier). The production possibilities curve is drawn bowed-out from the origin. The bowed-out shape of the curve reflects the law of increasing costs. However, the law of increasing costs is just one of many economic principles that can be illustrated with a production possibilities curve. The example presented below will help you appreciate the variety of applications for the production possibilities model.

Suppose an economy can produce pizzas or ovens in the combinations shown in the table below.

Pizzas	Ovens
0	10
5	9
10	7
15	4
20	0

This information is presented as a graph on the following page.

Production Possibilities Frontier for Pizza and Ovens

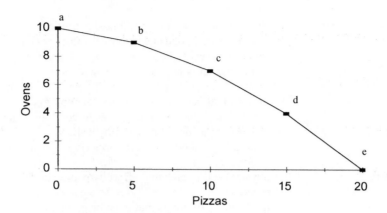

Note how the production possibilities frontier is bowed-out from the origin. Clearly, the law of increasing costs is at work in this case. Looking at the graph, let's start with 10 ovens and no pizza, at point **a**. To produce the first 5 pizzas, resources are shifted from oven making to pizza making. One oven is sacrificed. We move from the vertical intercept at 0 pizzas and 10 ovens toward the right on the curve to point **b** at 5 pizzas and 9 ovens. But look at what happens as we increase pizza production again. Resources must be shifted out of oven production, and we give up more ovens for each additional batch of 5 pizzas. Increasing costs show up as consecutive sacrifices of 2, 3, then 4 ovens as we increase pizza output from 5 to 20, finally ending up at point **e**.

The production possibilities table and curve assume full employment. Suppose this economy was producing only 10 pizzas and 4 ovens. Find this point on the graph. It lies inside the production possibilities frontier, indicating that resources are either unemployed or underemployed. Find the point represented by 15 pizzas and 8 ovens. This point lies outside the curve in what is termed the impossibilities region of the economy. Over time, with increases in the supplies of resources, new innovations, and greater labor specialization, we can expect the production possibilities for this economy to expand. The values shown in the table for pizza and oven output will increase, and the curve will shift to the right. This shift represents economic growth.

The questions and problems that follow will provide you with ample opportunity to develop your skills interpreting and drawing production possibilities frontiers.

True-False Questions — If a statement is false, explain why.

1. Factors of production include consumption goods. (T/F)

2. Slavery is a particular type of labor. (T/F)

3. When my hired housekeeper vacuums my home, he is performing labor. (T/F)

4. Human capital and labor are identical. (T/F)

5. The personal computer that my son uses to play games on is a capital good. (T/F)

6. An entrepreneur is a person who assumes the risks associated with undertaking a business venture. (T/F)

7. The opportunity cost of a bushel of wheat is the money that must be sacrificed in order to produce it. (T/F)

8. An economy that operates on its production possibilities curve is efficient. (T/F)

9. The production possibilities for an economy expand as the supplies of factors of production increase. (T/F)

10. An economy that is growing will display outward shifts in its production possibilities curve. (T/F)

11. A pair of countries where one has an absolute advantage over the other in all areas of production will find it impossible to benefit from trade. (T/F)

12. The richer the economy, the more easily it can grow because the opportunity cost of shifting resources to capital goods becomes less painful. (T/F)

13. An economy that has underemployed resources can still operate on its production possibilities curve. (T/F)

14. If Japan can produce more automobiles and more computers than the United States using the same amount of resources, then Japan has an absolute advantage in both activities. (T/F)

15. If the opportunity cost of producing one car in Japan is 10 computers and the opportunity cost of producing one car in the United States is 5 computers, then the United States has a comparative advantage in computer production. (T/F)

Multiple-Choice Questions

1. Lumber, used in the construction of a farmer's barn, is considered
   a. a consumption good because the farmer will use the barn
   b. entrepreneurship if the farmer is an independent operator
   c. capital because it is a good used to make other goods
   d. human capital because it contains labor that made the lumber from the tree
   e. neither a consumption good nor a factor of production because it is raw material

2. Points A and B on the production possibilities curve shown below represent combinations of consumption goods and capital goods produced in country A and country B, respectively. These positions suggest that in the future
   a. country A will grow faster than country B
   b. country B will grow faster than country A
   c. they will grow at the same rate because they are on the same curve
   d. neither will grow because both are producing fewer capital goods than consumption goods
   e. both countries will have unemployed resources

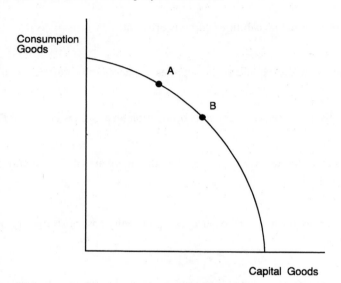

3. The production possibilities model applies
   a. only to economies that produce simple goods like the Crusoe economy described in the text
   b. to economies without labor specialization
   c. to economies without division of labor
   d. to economies whose factors of production are fully employed
   e. universally to all economies regardless of their differences

4. If an economy experiences unemployment, it would show up as a point
   a. on the production possibilities curve but on one of the axes
   b. outside the production possibilities curve
   c. inside the production possibilities curve
   d. on the production possibilities curve
   e. on a production possibilities curve that is shifting to the right

5. The opportunity cost of producing a good is
   a. the dollar amount paid to produce the good
   b. the quantity of other goods that must be sacrificed in order to produce the good
   c. the labor hours required to produce the good
   d. the amount of capital used to produce the good
   e. higher than most people realize because scarce resources are expensive

6. The law of increasing costs suggests all of the following **except** that
   a. resources, such as labor and land, are not of equal quality or fertility
   b. resources, such as labor and land, are of equal quality and fertility
   c. switching from producing one good to another involves increasing sacrifices of the first good
   d. the opportunity cost of producing a good is not constant along a bowed-out production possibilities curve
   e. the opportunity cost of producing more of a good increases as resources are shifted away from producing other goods

7. To economists, the term "capital" refers exclusively to
   a. goods used to produce other goods and services
   b. money used to purchase capital in the form of stocks and bonds
   c. savings accumulated by households to purchase capital
   d. money used by an entrepreneur to purchase capital
   e. real estate, forests, metals, and minerals

8. New bicycles that are maintained as inventory in a sporting goods store are
   a. consumption goods
   b. capital goods
   c. held at a high opportunity cost
   d. capital goods if they are intended for traveling to and from a job
   e. consumption goods if they are intended for recreation

9. New ideas that are used in production as applied technologies are called
   a. inventions
   b. entrepreneurship
   c. factors of production
   d. economic efficiency
   e. innovations

10. Capital accumulation (addition to capital) occurs in an economy when
    a. more inputs are used in production
    b. resources are shifted from the production of consumption goods to the production of capital goods
    c. new technologies are adopted
    d. workers work longer hours
    e. the economy operates at full employment

11. One of the reasons that poor economies tend to stay poor is that
    a. workers in these economies are not sufficiently motivated because their consumption goods are insufficient to satisfy their needs
    b. their governments tend to shift resources from capital goods to consumption goods
    c. most of their resources are devoted to consumption goods production so little capital accumulation occurs
    d. they are exploited by the industrially advanced economies
    e. they do not have a production possibilities curve

12. If an economy is operating along its production possibilities curve, then it is clear that
    a. all factors of production are fully employed
    b. poverty is eliminated
    c. technological change is assured
    d. some resources may still be underemployed
    e. economic growth must slow down

13. The most likely explanation for the shift in the production possibilities curve shown below is
    a. a decrease in the supplies of some inputs
    b. a decrease in the supplies of all inputs
    c. the adoption by the government of a full employment policy
    d. a shift from capital goods to consumer goods production
    e. technological change which occurs in the production of both capital and consumption goods

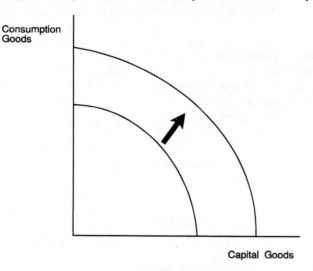

14. An entrepreneur _____ manager of a firm, but assumes _____ for the success or failure of the firm.
    a. is the sole; no responsibility
    b. may or may not be the sole; full responsibility
    c. cannot be the sole; full responsibility
    d. desires to be; full responsibility
    e. may or may not be the sole; partial responsibility

15. Specialization and division of labor take place at the international level according to the
    a. law of increasing costs
    b. principle of comparative advantage
    c. principle of economic efficiency
    d. rate of new innovation
    e. universality of the production possibilities model

16. Which of the following is a clear example of underemployment?
    a. a young man works as a carpenter
    b. a middle-aged man works as a bank manager
    c. a retired woman works as a hospital volunteer
    d. an African American man is not hired as a police officer because he lacks a high school diploma
    e. a young woman is denied a promotion only because she is a woman

17. Although countries may experience devastating losses of human life and physical capital during a war, their postwar economies typically recover quickly because
    a. citizens are motivated by patriotism to rebuild quickly
    b. the ideas on which production technologies are based are indestructible
    c. other countries will typically come to the devastated country's aid
    d. entrepreneurs usually find great investment opportunities right after a war
    e. political leaders use great care in planning for recovery

18. Given the following production possibilities frontier, the opportunity cost of increasing capital goods production from one to two is
    a. five consumption goods
    b. four consumption goods
    c. three consumption goods
    d. two consumption goods
    e. one consumption good

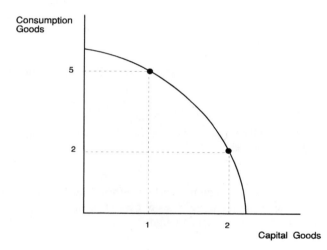

Questions 19 and 20 are based on the data in the following table. In one day, Mexico can use all of its resources to produce either 100 bushels of corn or 200 pounds of avocados. Similarly, the United States can use all of its resources to produce either 80 bushels of corn or 80 pounds of avocados in one day.

Quantities of Corn and Avocados Produced in Mexico and the United States
in One Day

	Corn (bushels)	Avocados(pounds)
Mexico	100	200
United States	80	80

19. Which country has an absolute advantage in what?
    a. Mexico in avocados; the United States in corn
    b. Mexico in corn; the United States in avocados
    c. Mexico in avocados and corn
    d. the United States in avocados
    e. the United States in corn

20. In the United States, the opportunity cost of one bushel of corn is _____ pound(s) of avocados while in Mexico the opportunity cost of one bushel of corn is _____ pound(s) of avocados so the United States has a comparative advantage in _____ production.
   a. one; two; corn
   b. one; two; avocado
   c. 80; 200; corn
   d. 80; 200; avocado
   e. 100; 200; corn

The following questions relate to the applied, theoretical, and historical perspectives in the text.

21. Steve is walking along 5th Avenue passing by a penny, a nickel, a dime, and a quarter along the way. He only bothers to bend down to pick up the quarter. We can infer that the opportunity cost to Steve of picking up a coin measured in monetary units is
   a. one cent
   b. five cents
   c. ten cents
   d. greater than ten cents but less than 25 cents
   e. at least 25 cents

22. For an economy that produces along its production possibilities curve, the opportunity cost of increasing the production of military goods is equal to the
   a. dollar amount by which the defense budget increases
   b. cost of the war in which they will be used
   c. nonmilitary goods sacrificed to produce the military goods
   d. capital goods sacrificed to produce the military goods
   e. consumer goods sacrificed to produce the military goods

23. Although the port city Rotterdam was destroyed by German bombs early in World War II, it was quickly rebuilt after the war so that the port could handle even greater volumes of cargo because the
   a. Germans spared most of the port facilities in their bombing campaign
   b. Dutch are thrifty, hard-working people
   c. British taught the Dutch how to build improved port facilities
   d. knowledge about how to build a port was not destroyed and new capital was more productive
   e. United Nations provided funds to rebuild the port with new technology

Fill in the Blanks

1. The _____ of producing more capital goods is the amount of _____ sacrificed.

2. As resources are shifted from producing one good to producing another, the opportunity cost of the second

   good _____, which illustrates the _____.

3. Because a poor society must devote so many resources to the production of _____ goods, it is very

   difficult for it to produce _____ goods in order to encourage faster economic growth.

4. If an economy operates inside its production possibilities frontier, it is an indication of _____ or

   _____ resources.

5. To say that the United States produces computer software at lower opportunity cost than does Great Britain suggests that the United States has a _____ in software production.

Discussion Questions

1. Does my son, who weeds the backyard because I insist, constitute labor? Does your answer change if my son and I agree that he will be paid $0.25 per bucket of weeds pulled? Explain.

2. What is the opportunity cost of your college education? How does the opportunity cost change if you had been offered a job paying $75,000 a year in a field you love at the beginning of this academic year? Would you still be in college this year?

3. Why do entrepreneurs hire specialists, sometimes at very high wage rates?

4. Carefully distinguish between the terms absolute advantage and comparative advantage.

5. How does specialization according to comparative advantage affect labor productivity?

Problems

1. The figures in the table below represent the production possibilities for a country that produces capital goods and consumption goods.

Capital Goods	Consumption Goods
1,000	0
800	400
600	750
400	1,000
200	1,150
0	1,200

    a. Sketch a graph with capital goods on the horizontal axis and consumption goods on the vertical axis and draw the production possibilities curve that corresponds to these data.

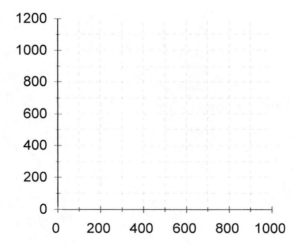

    b. Does the graph you have drawn exhibit the law of increasing costs? How do you know? Use the concept of opportunity cost and the data provided to explain the law of increasing cost.

2. The following table shows the amounts of apples or cheese that can be produced in Washington and Wisconsin in one day.

	Apples(bushels)	Cheese(pounds)
Washington	400	100
Wisconsin	400	200

If these two states specialize, what should each one produce? Why? Explain carefully using the concepts absolute and comparative advantage.

3. Return to the graphing tutorial presented on pages 19-20 above. Suppose that the resources available in the economy were to double, that is, twice as much labor, capital, land, and entrepreneurship. How would the economy's production possibilities change? Construct a table to show the new production possibilities and draw a graph to show how the production possibilities curve changes.

4. The following table shows the **labor time in hours** required to produce skis and chocolate in Switzerland and the United States.

	United States	Switzerland
One pair of skis	10	8
One pound of chocolates	2	1

a. Given this information, which country has an absolute advantage in skis? In chocolate? Explain.
   (Hint: Be careful because the units in this table are in hours of time required to produce each good, not in
   physical units.)

b. Which country has a comparative advantage in chocolate? In skis? Explain.

Everyday Applications

1. What was the opportunity cost of your working through these study guide exercises? Was it worth it? How
   will you know? Knowing the concept of opportunity cost won't necessarily make you a better decision
   maker, but it should change the way you evaluate the decisions you make.

2. North Korea is a desperately poor country right now. Will North Korea stay poor because it currently is
   poor? What would happen if North Korea were to allocate more of its resources to the production of capital
   goods rather than consumption goods?

Economics Online

Output tables were used in this chapter to illustrate the principle of comparative advantage. It is also possible to
see comparative advantage in real trade statistics. For example, take a look at U.S. trade with Japan in the year
2000 at *http://www.census.gov/foreign-trade/balance/c5880.html*. In which categories does the U.S. seem to
have a comparative advantage? In which areas does Japan seem to have a comparative advantage? (Hint: if a
country has a comparative advantage in a sector, what would be true of its exports versus imports?) Take a look
at some years prior to 2000. Is comparative advantage static or might it be changing over time?

Answers to Questions

Key Terms Quiz

a. 13	**f.** 14	**k.** 1
b. 3	**g.** 11	**l.** 4
c. 7	**h.** 15	**m.** 12
d. 9	**i.** 2	**n.** 5
e. 10	**j.** 8	**o.** 6

True-False Questions

1. False. Consumer goods are some of the final goods and services produced by factors of production.
2. False. Labor requires a voluntary agreement between an employer and employee. Slavery is involuntary.
3. True
4. False. Labor is the physical and mental exertion of people engaged in production. Human capital is the

knowledge and skills acquired by labor usually through education and training.
5. False. If my son is playing games on the computer it is a consumption good.
6. True
7. False. The opportunity cost is the quantity of other goods that must be given up to produce the bushel of wheat.
8. True
9. True
10. True
11. False. Trade can benefit both countries if comparative advantages exist.
12. True
13. False. Full employment of all resources in the economy is a requirement for its being on the curve.
14. True
15. False. The United States would have the comparative advantage in car production because the opportunity cost of producing cars in the United States is less than in Japan (5 computers compared to 10 computers).

Multiple-Choice Questions

1. c	6. b	11. c	16. e	21. d
2. b	7. a	12. a	17. b	22. c
3. e	8. b	13. e	18. c	23. d
4. c	9. e	14. b	19. c	
5. b	10. b	15. b	20. a	

Fill in the Blanks

1. opportunity cost; consumption goods
2. increases; law of increasing costs
3. consumption; capital
4. underemployed or unemployed
5. comparative advantage

Discussion Questions

1. My son will tell you that the only way he will weed the backyard without pay is if I coerce him. This is not labor. However, if we agree on a wage, then the work is labor.

2. The opportunity cost of going to college is the money you give up not working during the time you are in college. If the described job offer is better than your next best alternative now, then your opportunity cost has risen, and you are less likely to go to college this year.

3. Entrepreneurs hire specialists because these people are very productive. That is, a specialist can produce more in a given period of time than a nonspecialized worker. Because specialists produce more, they are paid a higher wage.

4. An absolute advantage exists if one country can produce more of a good than another country with the same resources. A country has a comparative advantage in the production of a good if it can produce the good at a lower opportunity cost than can another country. That is, the country with the comparative advantage gives up less to produce the good than does the other country.

5. Specialization according to comparative advantage will increase labor productivity because countries and their labor forces will be specializing in activities that they perform at relatively lower opportunity costs. For example, a country that begins to specialize according to its comparative advantage shifts its productive

resources into producing goods that have a lower opportunity cost to produce. If the country gives up less to produce these goods, it necessarily ends up with more output from its workers. Hence, labor productivity is higher.

Problems

1. a. Your graph should look like the one shown below.

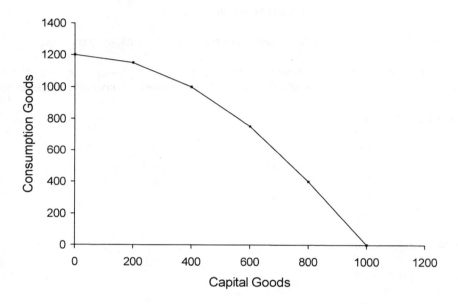

   b. This graph does exhibit the law of increasing costs because it is bowed-out from the origin. Furthermore, for each 200-unit increase in capital goods production, the sacrifice in consumption goods rises. These sacrifices, or opportunity costs, are 50, 150, 250, 350, and 400 for each additional 200 units of capital goods produced.

2. Washington will specialize in apple production because the opportunity cost of one bushel of apples is one-fourth pound of cheese. Wisconsin will specialize in cheese production because the opportunity cost of producing a pound of cheese is two bushels of apples whereas the opportunity cost of producing a pound of cheese in Washington is four bushels of apples. Wisconsin has an absolute advantage in cheese production while Washington has a comparative advantage in apple production.

3. All the numbers in the table would double and the production possibilities curve would shift out to the right so that all the values along the curve double too.

4. a. Switzerland has an absolute advantage in both activities because it does both in less time than does the United States.

   b. The opportunity cost of one pound of chocolates in the United States is one-fifth pair of skis. In the two hours it takes to produce one pound of chocolate in the United States, one-fifth pair of skis is given up. By similar reasoning, the opportunity cost of one pound of chocolates in Switzerland is one-eighth pair of skis. It takes one hour to produce a pound of chocolate in Switzerland and eight hours to produce a pair of skis. Therefore, Switzerland has a comparative advantage in chocolate production because the opportunity cost of producing chocolate is lower there.

Homework Questions

True-False Questions — If a statement is false, explain why.

1. Human capital and labor are identical. (T/F)

2. An entrepreneur is a person who assumes the risks associated with undertaking a business venture. (T/F)

3. An economy that is growing will display outward shifts in its production possibilities curve. (T/F)

4. If Brazil can produce steel at lower opportunity cost than can the United States, then Brazil has an absolute advantage in steel production. (T/F)

5. The law of increasing costs states that in order to produce additional units of one good, say consumer goods, constant amounts of capital goods must be sacrificed. (T/F)

Multiple-Choice Questions

1. If an economy is operating inside its production possibilities curve, then it is possible to
   a. increase the output of one good but not the other
   b. move to a point on the curve without any sacrifice of other goods
   c. experience the law of increasing cost by moving to the curve
   d. determine that the economy has an absolute advantage in one of the goods produced
   e. determine that the economy has a comparative advantage in one of the goods produced

2. Which of the following statements about technological change is **false**?
   a. an idea that eventually takes the form of newly applied technology is described as innovation
   b. technological change can shift the production possibilities curve to the right
   c. new technology reduces the severity of scarcity
   d. our grandchildren will no doubt regard our technology as rather primitive
   e. new technology shifts the production possibilities curve inward because it creates unemployment

3. The production possibilities curve is bowed-out from the origin because
   a. of the scarcity of productive resources
   b. of the law of increasing costs
   c. of inefficiency
   d. resources are unspecialized in most cases
   e. of a lack of technological change

4. The following table shows the amounts of chocolate and ice cream that Switzerland and the United States can produce in one day.

	Chocolate (tons)	Ice Cream (tons)
Switzerland	200	100
United States	300	900

All of the following statements are true *except*
a. the opportunity cost of 1 ton of chocolate in Switzerland is one-half ton of ice cream
b. the opportunity cost of 1 ton of chocolate in the United states is 3 tons of ice cream
c. Switzerland has an absolute advantage in both activities
d. Switzerland has a comparative advantage in chocolate production
e. the opportunity cost of one ton of ice cream in the United States is one-third ton of chocolate.

5. From the table above, we can conclude that
a. the United States has a comparative advantage in ice cream production
b. these two countries cannot benefit from specialization and trade in chocolate and ice cream
c. the United States is the low opportunity cost producer of chocolate
d. Switzerland is the low opportunity cost producer of ice cream
e. the price of ice cream is probably much higher in the United States than in Switzerland

Discussion Questions/Problems

1. Use graphs of production possibilities curves to show what happens to a country's economic capacity due to a war and during the ensuing recovery after a war. Why is it that countries typically recover rapidly after even the most devastating wars?

2. Use graphs of production possibilities curves to explain why it is relatively easier for rich countries to achieve economic growth than it is for poor countries.

CHAPTER 3

DEMAND AND SUPPLY

Chapter in a Nutshell

How are prices determined? This is the basic question we explore in this chapter. Let's conclude before we start our analysis of price determination: Price depends on **demand and supply**. That's it. But what's **demand** and what's **supply**? **Demand** represents people's **willingness to buy goods and services at different prices**. Price is a reflection of how willing people are to buy goods and services. Supply can be interpreted similarly. **Supply** represents the **willingness of producers to supply goods and services at different prices**. However, supply depends on the time frame being considered to a greater extent than does demand. Producers can better adjust to changes in the market given more time. We'll develop three time frames in which to consider supply — **the market day, the short run, and the long run.**

With an understanding of demand and supply, it is possible to describe how **equilibrium prices** are determined in markets for goods and services. The equilibrium price equates the **quantity demanded** and the **quantity supplied** in a market. **Changes in demand** and **changes in supply** cause changes in equilibrium prices and quantities demanded and supplied in markets. Prices effectively **ration goods and services** in our economy. Price increases ration the available supply of a good to those who can still afford it. A price decrease makes a good available to a wider segment of the market.

After you study this chapter, you should be able to:

- Discuss how **consumer demand** is measured.
- Describe the **inverse relationship** between price and quantity demanded.
- Discuss how **supply** is measured.
- Distinguish between **market-day supply, short-run supply, and long-run supply.**
- Explain how **equilibrium prices** are determined.
- Define **normal goods, substitute goods, and complementary goods.**
- Show how **changes in demand** and **changes in supply** cause changes in equilibrium prices.
- Give examples of **price as a rationing mechanism.**

Concept Check — See how you do on these multiple-choice questions.

With this question, be careful to keep separate in your mind the difference between a change in quantity demanded and a change in demand.

1. A decrease in price causes an increase in the **quantity demanded** because
   a. consumers cannot afford to buy as much
   b. consumers are willing to buy more at a lower price
   c. consumers' tastes change as the price decreases
   d. consumers' incomes increase as the price decreases
   e. the number of consumers increases as the price decreases.

What is the shape of the market-day supply curve?

2. One characteristic of the **market-day supply** is that
   a. the time period is too short to allow changes in the quantity supplied
   b. it applies in the short run
   c. it applies in the long run
   d. it depends on the demand
   e. it depends on the quantity demanded

Recall that a **change in demand** is different from a **change in quantity demanded**.

3. A **change in demand** can be caused by all of the following *except* a change in
   a. income
   b. the prices of other goods
   c. tastes
   d. population
   e. the price of the good being considered

Improvements in technology permit a larger quantity of a good to be produced with the same amount of resources.

4. An improvement in the **technology** for producing a good will cause
   a. an increase in the demand for the good
   b. a shift to the left in the short-run supply curve
   c. a shift to the left in the long-run supply curve
   d. an increase in the supply of the good
   e. an increase in the incomes of consumers

If wants are insatiable and resources are scarce, then a mechanism must exist for allocating products among the consumers who desire them.

5. To say that **price serves as a rationing mechanism** means that
   a. only those with the willingness to pay for goods in a market get them
   b. demand is limitless
   c. supplies keep dwindling
   d. wants are insatiable
   e. resources are scarce

Am I on the Right Track?

Your answers to the questions above should be **b**, **a**, **e**, **d**, and **a**. Understanding demand and supply is key to your understanding all that follows in this text. If the answers to the questions above weren't readily apparent to you, then you may want to return to the text and re-read some or all of the chapter. Be sure that you understand the difference between changes in demand and quantity demanded, the different time frames in which to consider supply, and the role that prices play in rationing goods and services in markets. Then come back and work carefully through the exercises that follow. This is an extremely important chapter!

Key Terms Quiz — Match the terms on the left with the definitions in the column on the right.

1. change in quantity demanded	_____ a. a curve that relates price and quantity demanded
2. law of demand	_____ b. the sum of all individual demands in a market
3. demand schedule	_____ c. quantity supplied greater than quantity demanded at a price
4. demand curve	_____ d. the price that equates quantity demanded to quantity supplied
5. market demand	_____ e. supplier can change all resources used in production
6. supply schedule	_____ f. a shift in the entire demand curve
7. market-day supply	_____ g. goods that can replace each other
8. supply curve	_____ h. a shift in the entire supply curve
9. excess supply	_____ i. a change in the amount purchased due to a price change
10. excess demand	_____ j. inverse relationship between price and quantity demanded
11. equilibrium price	_____ k. quantity supplied is fixed, regardless of price
12. short run	_____ l. a schedule of quantities of goods purchased at different prices
13. long run	_____m. a schedule of quantities of goods supplied at different prices
14. change in demand	_____ n. goods that are used together
15. normal good	_____ o. quantity demanded greater than quantity supplied at a price
16. substitute goods	_____ p. a curve that relates price and quantity supplied
17. complementary goods	_____ q. supplier can change some resources used in production
18. change in supply	_____ r. a good whose demand increases when income increases

Graphing Tutorial

Drawing and interpreting demand and supply diagrams is easy. Consider the data presented below for the market for brooms during a month-long period. The first column shows the price per broom in dollars, the second column shows the quantity demanded at each price, and the third column shows the quantity supplied at each price. The table combines information for the demand schedule and the supply schedule.

Price ($ per broom)	Quantity Demanded (per month)	Quantity Supplied (per month)
6	10	70
5	20	60
4	30	50
3	40	40
2	50	30
1	60	20

Note that the information contained in the table corresponds to the market for brooms. Therefore, the demand schedule represents the sum of all the buyers' individual demand schedules. Likewise, the supply schedule represents the total number of brooms put on the market by suppliers at different prices during a month. It is a simple matter to plot these data on a graph with quantities measured horizontally and prices measured vertically. The graph is shown below.

The demand curve is drawn as a downward-sloping line starting at the point 10 brooms per month and $6 per broom. At a price of $6, 10 brooms per month are demanded by consumers. The demand curve shows

that for each $1 decrease in the price of a broom, the quantity demanded increases by 10 brooms per month.
The supply curve is an upward-sloping line starting at the point 20 brooms per month and $1 per broom. For
each $1 increase in the price of a broom, the quantity of brooms supplied increases by 10 per month.

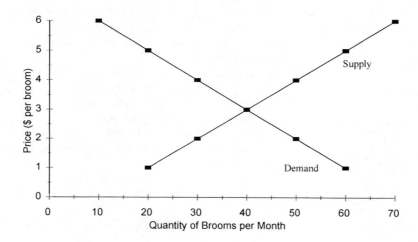

        Consider the point where the demand curve and the supply curve intersect. This point is 40 brooms per
month at a price of $3 per broom. At a price of $3 per broom, the quantity of brooms demanded is equal to the
quantity of brooms supplied. In other words, all the brooms that are offered for sale are purchased at this price.
In this example, $3 is the equilibrium price.

        Suppose the price were $2 per broom. At $2 per broom, the quantity of brooms demanded is 50 while
the quantity of brooms supplied is 30. There is an excess demand for brooms, represented on the graph as the
horizontal distance between the points on the demand curve and the supply curve at a price of $2, which is 20
brooms. Would the price stay at $2 per broom? Of course not. The excess demand for brooms will generate
competition between buyers that will push the price of brooms higher, causing the quantity demanded to
decrease and the quantity supplied to increase until equilibrium is reached at a price of $3 per broom.

        Consider a price above equilibrium at, say, $4 per broom. At $4 per broom, the quantity of brooms
supplied is 50 while the quantity of brooms demanded is 30. At this price, an excess supply of brooms exists,
represented by the horizontal distance between the points on the supply curve and the demand curve at a price of
$4 per broom, which is 20 brooms. Suppliers are trying to sell 20 brooms more than consumers are willing to
buy at $4 per broom. In this case, the price will begin to decrease as suppliers lower price, causing the quantity
demanded to increase and the quantity supplied to decrease until the equilibrium is reached at a price of $3 per
broom.

        What sort of supply curve have we drawn in this example? We know that it cannot be a market-day
supply curve because it isn't drawn vertically at a specific quantity level. This supply curve could either be a
short-run supply curve or a long-run supply curve, depending on how easily suppliers can adjust the quantities
of resources used to produce brooms.

        A variety of factors influence the position of the demand and supply curves we have drawn. These are
discussed at length in the text. Make sure you understand how demand and supply curves shift due to changes
in these factors. Any time there is a shift in one or the other or both curves, the equilibrium price will change, as
will the quantity demanded and supplied. The exercises below will give you the opportunity to practice drawing
and interpreting demand and supply diagrams.

Graphing Pitfalls

Consider the graph shown below. What is wrong with it? In a purely technical sense, nothing at all. The only difference between this graph and the one shown above is that price is measured along the horizontal axis and quantity is measured on the vertical axis in the graph below. The information conveyed by the graph is exactly the same. So, does this mean it doesn't matter which axis we label price and which we label quantity? No! By convention, economists measure price on the vertical axis and quantity on the horizontal axis. You'll decrease the level of confusion if you stick to this convention in drawing your graphs!

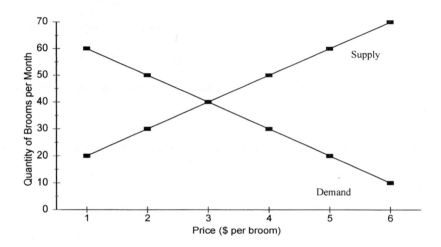

The axes are switched on this graph! Measure quantity on the horizontal axis and price on the vertical axis!

True-False Questions — If a statement is false, explain why.

1. The law of demand states that as price decreases, quantity demanded decreases. (T/F)

2. A demand schedule shows people's willingness to buy specific quantities of a good at different prices. (T/F)

3. The market demand for a good is the sum of individual demands for the good. (T/F)

4. In the time period known as the market day, producers can sell more goods as their prices rise. (T/F)

5. An increase in the number of suppliers in a market will cause the supply curve to shift to the left. (T/F)

6. The short run is a period in which producers can devote larger quantities of some resources to production as prices increase. (T/F)

7. Long-run supply curves are steeper than short-run supply curves. (T/F)

8. The equilibrium price equates the quantity demanded to the quantity supplied. (T/F)

9. An increase in supply causes an excess demand at the original price, and competition between sellers leads to a lower equilibrium price. (T/F)

10. An increase in demand causes an excess demand at the original price, and competition between demanders leads to a higher equilibrium price. (T/F)

11. If the quantity demanded is greater than the quantity supplied, then the price must be above the equilibrium price. (T/F)

12. If the price of one good increases and the demand for another good increases as a result, then the goods must be substitutes. (T/F)

13. If income increases and the demand for a good increases, then it is a normal good. (T/F)

14. The long run is a time period sufficient to allow suppliers to make some, but not all, of the changes necessary to adjust the quantity supplied to price changes. (T/F)

15. A change in demand refers to a movement along a demand curve due to a price change, but a change in quantity demanded refers to a shift in the entire demand curve. (T/F)

Multiple-Choice Questions

1. If a market is in equilibrium, then
   a. demand curves and supply curves are the same
   b. at the equilibrium price, quantity demanded is equal to quantity supplied
   c. the short-run quantities of supply and demand equal the long-run quantities of supply and demand
   d. the short-run equilibrium price equals the long-run equilibrium price
   e. all demanders receive the goods they want, and all suppliers sell the goods they want

2. If excess demand exists in a market, then
   a. excess supply will emerge to absorb the excess demand
   b. the quantity supplied is less than the quantity demanded
   c. the quantity demanded is less than the quantity supplied
   d. the equilibrium price will fall
   e. the price will fall

3. The market demand for fish represents the
    a. sum of all individual demands for fish
    b. specific quantities consumers will buy, given the market-day supply
    c. relationship between price and quantity of fish demanded by a consumer on the fish market
    d. maximum quantity consumers will buy, given the limitations of their income
    e. changing tastes of consumers

4. An increase in demand causes
    a. an increase in supply as new firms enter the market
    b. an increase in price and an increase in supply
    c. an increase in price and an increase in the quantity supplied
    d. a decrease in demand in the future
    e. a decrease in price and an increase in the quantity supplied

5. The law of demand states that
    a. as price decreases, quantity demanded increases
    b. as income increases, demand increases
    c. as the number of consumers increases, demand increases
    d. as supply decreases, the quantity demanded decreases
    e. as price increases, quantity demanded increases

6. If, at a specific price, quantity demanded is greater than the quantity supplied, then price will
    a. increase until the excess supply is eliminated
    b. decrease until the excess supply is eliminated
    c. increase until the excess demand is eliminated
    d. remain unchanged, and quantity demanded will decrease
    e. decrease, and quantity supplied will increase

7. Suppose there is a widespread rumor that Japanese car manufacturers plan to increase the price of their cars by 50 percent next month.   You would expect that in the United States, the demand curve for Japanese cars would
    a. shift to the left next month
    b. shift to the right next month
    c. shift to the right before next month
    d. shift to the left before next month
    e. remain unchanged, but the price of U.S. cars would decrease next month

8. In the graph below, an increase in the price from 3 to 5 causes
   a. a market-day supply curve to shift to the right
   b. a short-run supply curve to shift
   c. suppliers to increase their use of all resources to produce 10 units
   d. the quantity supplied to increase from 5 to 10
   e. the supply to increase from 5 to 10

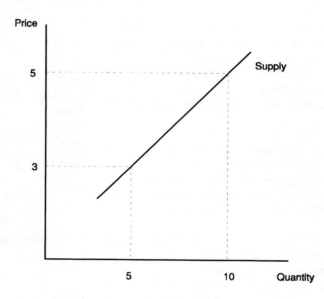

9. The long run refers to a time period long enough for producers to
   a. make partial adjustments in the resources used in production to price changes
   b. add more labor but not more capital to production
   c. add more capital but not more labor to production
   d. make complete adjustments in the resources used in production to price changes
   e. produce less in response to an increase in price

10. When economists refer to price as a rationing mechanism, they mean that
    a. the government can establish a rationing program by setting prices
    b. price weeds from the market those who want the good, but can't afford it
    c. most markets have chronic problems with excess demand so rationing is necessary
    d. suppliers ration goods by setting a price demanders can afford
    e. demanders ration their incomes by choosing only low-priced goods

11. In September, if consumers expect the price of snowboards to increase as the winter approaches
    a. the market-day supply of snowboards will shift to the left
    b. the demand for snowboards will decrease
    c. the quantity demanded of snowboards will increase
    d. the quantity demanded of snowboards will decrease
    e. the demand curve for snowboards will shift to the right

12. If the price of a good starts out above the equilibrium price, then
    a. consumers will compete to bid the price up
    b. suppliers will compete to bid the price up
    c. suppliers will compete to bid the price down
    d. consumers will compete to bid the price down
    e. producers will hire more labor to produce more of the good

13. The market-day supply is drawn as a vertical line at a particular level of production because
    a. output can easily be adjusted
    b. chronic excess supply is permanent
    c. output can completely adjust to price changes
    d. output can partially adjust to price changes
    e. output cannot be changed during the market-day

14. The demand and supply curves shown in the diagram below represent which of the following changes?
    a. an increase in demand and an increase in the equilibrium price
    b. a decrease in demand and a decrease in the equilibrium price
    c. a decrease in demand and a decrease in the quantity supplied
    d. an increase in the quantity demanded and an increase in supply
    e. an increase in the supply and an increase in the equilibrium price

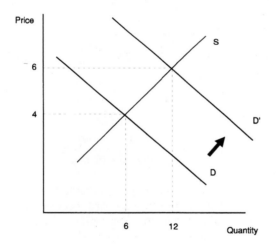

15. If consumers are presented with strong scientific evidence that a diet including moderate red wine consumption leads to lower rates of heart disease, which of the following changes is likely to occur?
    a. an increase in red wine prices
    b. an increase in white wine prices
    c. a decrease in brie cheese prices
    d. a decrease in grape prices
    e. an increase in beer prices

16. In general, as the time period considered moves from the short run to the long run, supply curves
    a. become steeper
    b. are perfectly vertical
    c. become flatter
    d. shift toward the left
    e. intersect with demand at a higher price

17. Which of the following will not cause a change in the supply of pencils?
    a. a change in pencil-making technology
    b. a change in resource prices associated with pencil making
    c. a change in the price of pens and other substitute goods
    d. a change in the price of pencils
    e. a change in the number of pencil suppliers

18. Suppose the demand and supply for strawberries decrease, but the decrease in demand is major while the decrease in supply is minor. Under these conditions
    a. price increases, and quantities demanded and supplied decrease
    b. price decreases, and quantities demanded and supplied increase
    c. price decreases, and quantities demanded and supplied decrease
    d. price increases, and quantities demanded and supplied increase
    e. price remains unchanged, but quantities demanded and supplied increase

19. Stan the news man on Channel 6 reports that the automobile prices were unchanged over the last year, yet automobile sales increased by 5 percent. In the same year, incomes rose by 2.5 percent. Based on this information, you could reasonably conclude that automobiles are
    a. substitute goods
    b. complementary goods
    c. normal goods
    d. priced below their equilibrium level
    e. priced above their equilibrium level

20. A change in quantity demanded of a good always results from a change in
    a. tastes
    b. the price of that good
    c. income
    d. the price of substitutes
    e. the price of complements

The following questions relate to the theoretical and applied perspectives in the text.

21. If the length of time from the market-day supply to the long-run supply is ordered from the shortest to the longest time span for the number of new Subway sandwich franchises, board-feet of walnut lumber, teenage workers at amusement parks in the summer, and pounds of tomatoes at a summertime farmers' market we would have
    a. pounds of tomatoes, teenage workers, Subway franchises, walnut lumber
    b. teenage workers, Subway franchises, walnut lumber, pounds of tomatoes
    c. Subway franchises. walnut lumber pounds of tomatoes
    d. teenage workers, pounds of tomatoes, Subway franchises, walnut lumber
    e. pounds of tomatoes, teenage workers, Subway franchises, walnut lumber

22. The best explanation for the surge in demand for bottled water is a change in
    a. income
    b. tastes
    c. expectations about future prices
    d. the prices of related goods
    e. population

Fill in the Blanks

1. From the shortest to the longest, the time periods in which we consider supply are _____,

   _____, and _____.

2. Pairs of goods for which a price increase in one causes an increase in the demand for the other are

   called _____.

3. When the _____ is equal to the _____, the price is an

   _____ price.

4. Price serves as a _____ mechanism by removing from the market those who are

   _____ to purchase the good.

5. The market demand for a good is calculated by _____ all of the _____

   demand curves of consumers in the market.

Discussion Questions

1. Richard III was willing to exchange his kingdom for a horse. What was the opportunity cost of his having a horse?

2. What is the difference between a change in quantity demanded and a change in demand?

3. Contrast market-day supply, short-run supply, and long-run supply. Why does the nature of supply depend so much on the length of the time period being considered?

4. Would the following events cause a change in demand or a change in quantity demanded in the market for automobiles? Explain.

a. A limit is placed on the number of cars that can be imported from Japan.

b. Malaysia becomes a major new exporter of cars to the United States.

c. Congress passes a big income tax increase in an attempt to deal with the deficit.

d. A report is issued suggesting that air travel has become much less safe in recent years.

e. The legal driving age is lowered to 15.

Problems

1. The following table shows the demand and supply schedules for an initial release of the first compact disc by the new female pop group from England, the Nice Girls.

Price ($/CD)	Quantity Demanded (1,000s)	Quantity Supplied (1,000s)
24	0	100
22	20	100
20	40	100
18	60	100
16	80	100
14	100	100
12	120	100
10	140	100

a. Sketch a demand and supply diagram to represent the data from the table in the space below.

b. What time frame is represented by the supply curve you have drawn? How do you know?

c. What is the equilibrium price, quantity demanded, and quantity supplied?

d. At each price listed in the table, note whether an excess demand or supply exists and its magnitude.

e. Suppose that record executives had initially issued 120,000 compact discs for the Nice Girls's first album? How would your answers to parts c and d change?

2. Draw the market-day, the short-run, and the long-run supply curves. Why do the slopes of these supply curves differ?

3. The graph below shows the market for British beef after the announcement that consumption of beef posed the risk of Mad Cow Disease. The demand curve shifts to the left, from D to D′. Explain in detail how the market adjusts from a price of $6 per pound to $4 per pound as a result of the shift in demand.

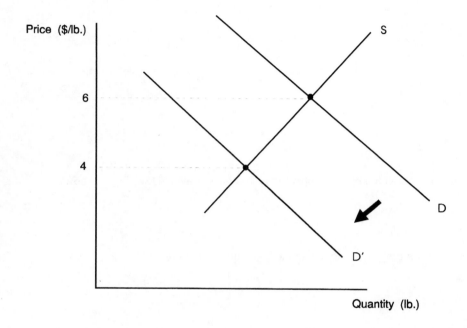

Everyday Applications

A fairly painless way to become better acquainted with the business world is to watch Nightly Business Report a few nights a week on your local PBS station. It's usually on in the early evening. Check your local listings. As you watch the show, keep in mind that a separate market exists for every stock and bond discussed. We'll present more detail on stocks and bonds in Chapter 7. For now, it's enough to know that the prices that you hear quoted on the show are set by the interaction of demand and supply, just as has been discussed in this chapter. Listen to the discussion of the "most active" stocks — those whose prices have changed most dramatically. Typically, something has happened in these markets to make the stock more or less attractive. Think about how various factors shift the demand and supply curves for stocks and bonds to change their prices.

Economics Online

The Christmas shopping season begins the day after Thanksgiving ("Black Friday" to some) and ends with the closing of shops and malls on Christmas Eve. This period produces huge revenues for suppliers and retailers. You can explore the numbers at

http://www.census.gov/PressRelease/www/releases/archives/factsforfeatures/001582.html, which details the effects of the holiday season on consumption of various goods. What do you suppose happens to demand between Thanksgiving and Christmas? What happens to supply? What impact do these changes have on price in your experience?

Answers to Questions

Key Terms Quiz

a. 4	**f.** 14	**k.** 7	**p.** 8
b. 5	**g.** 16	**l.** 3	**q.** 12
c. 9	**h.** 18	**m.** 6	**r.** 15
d. 11	**i.** 1	**n.** 17	
e. 13	**j.** 2	**o.** 10	

True-False Questions

1. False. The law of demand states that as price decreases, quantity demanded increases.
2. True
3. True
4. False. In the market-day period, quantity supplied is fixed no matter what happens to the price.
5. False. An increase in the number of suppliers in a market will cause the supply curve to shift to the right.
6. True
7. False. Long-run supply curves are flatter than short-run supply curves.
8. True
9. False. An increase in supply will cause an excess supply at the original price, then competition between sellers leads to a lower equilibrium price.
10. True
11. False. If quantity demanded is greater than quantity supplied, the price is less than the equilibrium price.
12. True
13. True
14. False. The long run is a time period long enough to allow producers to make any changes necessary to adjust the quantity supplied to price changes.
15. False. A change in demand is a shift in the entire demand curve due to a change in income, tastes, prices of other goods, expectations of price changes, and/or a change in the number of consumers. A change in quantity demanded is a movement along a demand curve due to a change in price.

Multiple-Choice Questions

1. b	**6.** c	**11.** e	**16.** c	**21.** d
2. b	**7.** c	**12.** c	**17.** d	**22.** b
3. a	**8.** d	**13.** e	**18.** c	
4. c	**9.** d	**14.** a	**19.** c	
5. a	**10.** b	**15.** a	**20.** b	

Fill in the Blanks

1. the market day; the short run; the long run
2. substitutes
3. quantity demanded; quantity supplied; equilibrium
4. rationing; less willing
5. summing; individual

Discussion Questions

1. If Richard III was willing to give up his kingdom for a horse, then the opportunity cost of his having a horse was his kingdom. Remember that opportunity cost represents what we are willing to sacrifice in order to have something or do something. Prices and opportunity costs are linked in this way. The price that Richard III was willing to pay for a horse was his kingdom.

2. A change in quantity demanded is always the result of a change in the price of the good. When the price changes, there is a movement along a specific demand curve between the two prices. On the other hand, when demand changes, it is due to a change in income, tastes, prices of other goods, expectations about future prices, and/or the number of consumers in the market. A change in demand results in a shift in the demand curve.

3. The market-day supply corresponds to the shortest time period a supplier faces. In fact, it is so short that production cannot be adjusted at all in response to price changes. The short-run supply allows the supplier to change the quantities of some (but not all) resources used in production. The long-run supply is a time period long enough to allow for changes in the quantities of all resources used in production. The market-day supply curve is drawn as a vertical line at the quantity that is put on the market and can't be changed. The short-run and the long-run supply curves are drawn as upward sloping so that as price increases, the quantity supplied increases. However, the long-run supply curve is flatter than the short-run supply curve because in the long run a producer can make greater adjustments to the resources used in production; hence, for any price change, the change in output will be greater in the long run than in the short run.

4. a. A limit on the number of cars imported from Japan will cause the supply curve for automobiles to shift to the left; therefore, the quantity demanded of cars will decrease.

   b. If Malaysia becomes a major new exporter of cars to the United States, then the supply of cars will increase, and the quantity demanded of cars will increase as the price falls.

   c. A big tax increase will decrease consumers' after-tax incomes; therefore, the demand for cars will decrease.

   d. If air travel is reported to have become much less safe, then tastes for automobiles will change and the demand for cars will increase.

   e. If the legal driving age is lowered to 15, then the number of consumers of cars will increase and the demand for cars will increase.

Problems

1. a. See the diagram shown on the following page. Note that the units on the quantity axis are 1,000s of CDs.

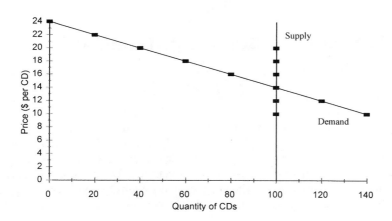

b. The supply curve shown above is a market-day supply because it is drawn vertically at the level of output equal to 100,000 compact discs. This output cannot be changed on the market day no matter what happens to price.

c. At a price equal to $14 per CD, the quantity demanded equals the quantity supplied at 100,000 compact discs.

d. When the price is $24 per disc, the excess supply is 100,000.
   When the price is $22 per disc, the excess supply is 80,000.
   When the price is $20 per disc, the excess supply is 60,000.
   When the price is $18 per disc, the excess supply is 40,000.
   When the price is $16 per disc, the excess supply is 20,000.
   When the price is $12 per disc, the excess demand is 20,000.
   When the price is $10 per disc, the excess demand is 40,000.

e. If 120,000 compact discs had been issued initially, the market-day supply would shift to the right by 20,000. The new equilibrium price would be equal to $12 per disc. Excess supply at each price would increase by 20,000 until a price of $10 per disc was reached where the excess demand would be 20,000 discs.

2. The market-day supply curve is drawn as a vertical line at the output level that is given. The short-run supply curve has a positive slope, as does the long-run supply curve, but the short-run supply curve is steeper. The slopes of these curves differ because they reflect the different abilities of producers to alter resources devoted to production in response to price changes in different time periods. In the market day, the amount of resources devoted to production cannot be changed, no matter what the price change is. In the short run, some resources devoted to production can be changed, but not all of them. In the long run, the producer can change the level of all the resources devoted to production in response to price changes.

3. The announcement that consumption of British beef might lead to a risk of contracting Mad Cow Disease caused a decrease in demand for British beef due to a change in tastes. The demand curve shifted to the left, and, at the original price of $6 per pound, an excess supply of beef existed. Beef producers competed with one another to lower the price in order to eliminate the excess supply. As price fell, quantity demanded increased along D′ and quantity supplied decreased along the supply curve until the new equilibrium price of $4 was reached. At $4 per pound, the quantity of beef demanded along D′ equals the quantity of beef supplied.

APPENDIX

APPLICATIONS OF SUPPLY AND DEMAND

Appendix in a Nutshell

These applications of supply and demand analysis move from an examination of one child's desire for a puppy whose price is beyond the child's means — a sad situation for the child, but hardly a tragedy — to consideration of some unique markets where the pure market outcome would be ethically intolerable to many people. For example, consider the market for Seeing Eye dogs. Although the market price for Seeing Eye dogs is $25,000, a price too high for all but a handful of the blind people who need them, donations to suppliers of Seeing Eye dogs permit them to supply 1,000s of dogs at the more affordable $100 per dog price.

Supply and demand analysis can be used to examine the market for organ transplants as well. Although the market price for, say, a human kidney is extremely high, perhaps $140,000, the National Transplant Organ Act of 1984 prohibited the private sale of organs. All transplant organs must come from voluntary donors so that, in effect, hospitals become the suppliers of organs and they charge what it costs to harvest the organ from a donor. The problem that has arisen with this system is a chronic excess demand for transplant organs. Price cannot play its rationing function in this market, so other rationing mechanisms take its place such as age, urgency, or geography.

Scalper's market is the only key term presented in this appendix. In a scalper's market, a good is resold at a price higher than the original or official published price. Scalper's markets are common sights at many prominent sporting events and at sold-out concerts. These markets operate according to the same principles of supply and demand as any other markets. On the supply side of the market are those who are willing to sell their tickets to a scalper rather than attend the event and on the demand side are individuals who are willing to pay for the tickets in the scalper's market. But beware! Though scalper's markets seem like ordinary free markets, they are illegal in most cities. Cincinnati is one of the few cities in the United States that permits tickets for various events to be resold for a profit.

Discussion Questions

1. How does normative economic analysis enter into our examination of the market for Seeing Eye dogs and transplant organs? In your answer, be careful to distinguish between positive analysis in these markets that focuses on questions about what is and normative analysis that focuses on what ought to be.

2. Should people be allowed to offer their organs for sale in a free market? Refer to panel *c* in Exhibit A3 as you think about how to answer this question.

Problems

1. a. Tina Turner recently played to a sold-out audience at the Wright State University Nutter Center Arena on
       what is being billed as her farewell tour. Would it be in Tina's interest to call the tour a farewell tour
       even though she might change her mind in a few years and tour again?   What impact would the news
       have on prices in the scalper's market? How would sellers in the scalper's market respond?

   b. Suppose the official price for tickets is $60. The table below depicts the scalper's market for tickets to
       the Tina Turner show. The willingness to sell their $60 tickets is shown in the quantity supplied column
       in the table. The willingness of fans to buy those tickets is shown in the quantity demanded column.
       How much will scalpers be paid for their $60 tickets? How many tickets are "scalped" (sold) at this
       price?

Price	Quantity Supplied	Quantity Demanded
$100	300	900
$120	400	700
$140	500	500
$160	600	300
$180	700	100

   c. Suppose that two days before the show, there is a report that Tina Turner has a bad cold and sore throat.
       She's performing, but not at her peak. As a result, more people are willing to part with their $60 tickets
       so that at each price level, 200 more tickets are offered. Fill in this quantity supplied below. On the
       demand side of the market, 100 fewer tickets are being purchased at each price level on the news
       of Tina's cold. Fill in the new figures for quantity demanded in the table. What price are scalpers
       getting for their tickets now and how many are sold?

Price	Quantity Supplied	Quantity Demanded
$100		
$120		
$140		
$160		
$180		

Answers to Questions for the Appendix

Discussion Questions

1. In the case of the Seeing Eye dog, positive economic analysis shows us that the price of a dog is extremely high — $25,000. The $25,000 price is a reflection of the high opportunity cost associated with producing these extraordinary dogs. Enormous amounts of training and care go into producing the dogs. Normative economic analysis applied to this problem suggests that the $25,000 price, which would put the dogs beyond the financial reach of many blind people who need them, is ethically inappropriate. The market outcome needn't be the end of the story. Suppliers of seeing eye dogs and others with an interest in the well-being of blind persons solicit donations and supply the dogs for the nominal $100 price.

   The case of transplant organs is quite different. Although positive analysis shows that the market for human kidneys might generate a price as high as $140,000 for a potential donor, the government has made the normative decision that the private sale of organs should be prohibited. Therefore, hospitals become suppliers of transplant organs on a not-for-profit basis. The cost of transplant organs then becomes the cost of harvesting them from donors. The price of the transplant organs is thus reduced, however, chronic excess demand at the lower price may be a problem.

2. Exhibit A3, panel *c* in the text depicts organ-for-a-price supply curves. If the supply curve for kidneys sold in the market looks like line *abc*, then the organ-for-a-price plan might seem like a good idea. A small increase in the price leads to a relatively large increase in the quantity supplied. However, if the supply curve appears like the steeper line *abd*, then fewer kidneys will be donated at a much higher price of $60,000. The worst case scenario in this example is line aa'e. In this situation, non-paid donors reduce the number of kidneys that they supply by 5,000 and the price goes up to $70,000. The total quantity of kidneys supplied at this price drops to 24,000. The organ-for-a-price program looks less appealing in the cases of the steep supply curves.

Problems

1. a. The demand for tickets will increase because this is the farewell tour. Should she decide to make a comeback, the fans will forgive her for tricking them the time before. The price of tickets in the scalper's market will increase due to the increase in the demand for tickets to a sold-out show. As a result of the increase in demand and increase in price, the quantity of tickets supplied in the scalper's market will increase.

   b. The price of the tickets is $140 and 500 tickets are traded at this price.

c. The completed table is shown below.

Price	Quantity Supplied	Quantity Demanded
$100	500	800
$120	600	600
$140	700	400
$160	800	200
$180	900	0

The equilibrium price decreases to $120 and the number of tickets traded in 600.

Homework Questions

True-False Questions — If a statement is false, explain why.

1. If the quantity supplied of a good is greater than the quantity demanded, then the price must be above the equilibrium price. (T/F)

2. Short-run supply curves are vertical. (T/F)

3. An increase in the price of a good will cause the supply curve to shift to the right. (T/F)

4. If two goods are complements, then one can replace the other in consumption. (T/F)

5. The expectation that the price of a good will increase can cause the demand for that good to increase. (T/F)

Multiple-Choice Questions

1. If supply increases and demand does not change, then price
   a. as well as quantities demanded and supplied will increase
   b. will decrease, and quantity demanded and supplied will increase
   c. will decrease, and quantity demanded and supplied will decrease
   d. and quantity demanded remain unchanged
   e. remains unchanged, but both quantities demanded and supplied will decrease

2. Suppose that the price of computer chips increases by 20 percent during the early stages of an economic recovery. Intel, a chip manufacturer, increases its payroll by 1,000 workers. Intel's hiring of new workers is best described as a
   a. long-run adjustment to the price change
   b. complete adjustment to the price change
   c. market-day adjustment to the price change
   d. short-run adjustment to the price change
   e. shift to the left in Intel's supply curve for computer chips

3. When price is higher than its equilibrium level, we can expect that
   a. as the equilibrium price rises, the quantity supplied will increase
   b. as the equilibrium price rises, the quantity demanded will decrease
   c. the quantity supplied and demanded will both fall as the equilibrium price adjusts
   d. the quantity supplied and demanded will both rise as the equilibrium price adjusts
   e. as the price falls to its equilibrium level, the quantity demanded will increase

4. A decrease in the prices of resources used in the production of automobiles will cause
   a. an increase in price since the quantity demanded increases
   b. a decrease in price since the quantity supplied increases
   c. a decrease in supply
   d. an increase in supply
   e. an increase in demand

5. A movement along a supply curve results from a _____ while a shift in the supply curve results from a _____.
    a. change in price; change in technology
    b. change in the prices of resources; change in price
    c. change in the number of suppliers; change in tastes
    d. change in the prices of other goods; change in income
    e. change in price; change in demand

Discussion Questions/Problems

1. Use graphs and words to explain the market day supply, short-run supply, and long-run supply.

2. a. Think of your favorite good. What was the price of this good the last time you purchased it? Sketch a graph to show the supply and demand for this good with the price the last time you purchased it shown as the equilibrium price.

    b. On your graph, show what happens when the demand for the good increases. How will the price change? How will the quantity produced change? What might cause an increase in demand for your favorite good?

PART I — THE BASICS OF ECONOMIC ANALYSIS

COMPREHENSIVE SAMPLE TEST

Give yourself 50 minutes to complete this exam and see how you do. The answers follow. Don't look until you are finished!

True-False Questions — If a statement is false, explain why. Each question is worth 2 points.

1. Positive economics addresses questions about what is in the economy. (T/F)

2. The *ceteris paribus* assumption allows economists to examine many variables that are all changing at the same time. (T/F)

3. A forest is an example of a renewable resource that can be depleted if timber is cut faster than trees can mature. (T/F)

4. A capital good is a good used only to produce more capital goods. (T/F)

5. An innovation is an applied technology that permits a larger output to be produced with a given amount of resources. (T/F)

6. If a country has a comparative advantage over another country in the production of shirts, then it can produce shirts in less time than the other country. (T/F)

7. The market-day supply curve is vertical because the market day is a period of time too short for a producer to alter production levels in response to price changes. (T/F)

8. Given a short-run supply curve, an increase in demand will cause an increase in the equilibrium price and a decrease in the quantity demanded and supplied. (T/F)

9. An increase in income will cause an increase in the quantity demanded for a good. (T/F)

10. A production possibilities curve that is bowed-out from the origin exhibits the law of demand. (T/F)

Multiple-Choice Questions — Each question is worth 2 points.

1. The circular flow model depicts the flows of resources, goods and services, and money in an economy in order to
   a. perfectly represent the economy
   b. shift attention away from the roles of banks and government in the economy
   c. allow us to focus on the main elements of an economy
   d. give some attention to all the elements in an economy
   e. accurately measure the importance of imports and exports to an economy

2. _____ analysis is used to examine the behavior of the economy as a whole while _____ is used to study the behavior of individual economic units like households and firms
   a. Microeconomic; macroeconomic
   b. Macroeconomic; microeconomic
   c. Positive; normative
   d. Normative; positive
   e. Econometric; modeling

3. Suppose that demand and supply increase simultaneously in a market and that supply increases by proportionately more than does demand. In this case the equilibrium price will
   a. rise
   b. remain the same
   c. fall then rise
   d. fall
   e. rise then fall

4. Given an economy with the choice to produce either capital goods or consumption goods, a shift of resources from the production of consumption goods to the production of capital goods could cause all of the following **except**
   a. an immediate decline in living standards
   b. an increase in living standards in the long run
   c. a slowdown in economic growth
   d. an increase in the production of consumption goods in the long run
   e. an increase in the production of capital goods

5. An economy whose resources are fully employed will produce combinations of goods that correspond to points
   a. inside the production possibilities curve
   b. outside the production possibilities curve
   c. on the market-day supply curve
   d. on the long-run supply curve
   e. on the production possibilities curve

6. A change in any of the following will cause a change in demand for a good **except**
   a. the price of that good
   b. income
   c. tastes
   d. population
   e. the prices of related goods

7. Most of the income earned by an entrepreneur comes from
   a. loans
   b. wages
   c. salaries
   d. interest
   e. profit

8. The opportunity cost of putting an unemployed worker back on the job is
   a. $54,000
   b. the value of her unemployment insurance
   c. zero
   d. greater than her income
   e. equal to the wages she earns at the new job

9. We analyze supply in the context of three time periods — the market day, the short run, and the long run — in order to show that
   a. supply is always changing
   b. producers are able to respond more flexibly to changes in the market given more time
   c. producers are unwilling to change their output in the short run
   d. producers use econometrics to arrive at their equilibrium output levels
   e. markets adjust slowly to supply changes

10. A producer who is able to make partial adjustments in output in response to price changes by hiring or laying off workers is
    a. operating in the short run
    b. operating in the long run
    c. still in the market-day period
    d. anticipating a price increase
    e. anticipating a price decrease

11. If the price in a market starts out above the equilibrium price, then it is clear that
    a. the excess demand will cause the price to rise higher
    b. the demand curve will shift to the right in order to adjust to an equilibrium
    c. the excess supply will result in a decrease in price and an adjustment to equilibrium
    d. the economy is operating inside its production possibilities curve
    e. consumers are trying to purchase more goods than are available

12. When economists argue that prices set in markets serve as a rationing mechanism for goods and services, they mean that
    a. goods and services are provided to those people who have the strongest taste for them and can afford them
    b. markets are always in equilibrium
    c. the market will never provide a large enough supply to satisfy all those with the ability to pay
    d. everyone with a willingness to pay gets some of the product
    e. rationing by other means is ineffective

13. An increase in the price of Pepsi will likely lead to an increase in the demand for Coke because the two goods
    a. are complements because they are consumed together
    b. are normal goods
    c. are substitutes because they can replace each other in consumption
    d. people's tastes for the two drinks change as a result of a price change in one of them
    e. the incomes for Coke drinkers will increase

14. To say that Brazil has a comparative advantage in sugar production over Florida means that
    a. Brazil can produce a given amount of sugar in less time than can Florida
    b. Brazil can produce more sugar in a given amount of time than can Florida
    c. sugar is cheaper in Brazil
    d. the opportunity cost of producing sugar is lower in Brazil
    e. Brazil has an advantage over Florida because it is a nation and Florida is a state

15. Demand for a good will always rise when
    a. the price of a complementary good falls
    b. the price of a substitute good falls
    c. tastes change
    d. income decreases
    e. the price of the good falls

16. The weather patterns caused by El Niño wreaked havoc on South American countries in the 1990s, especially Ecuador, destroying much of the country's infrastructure (roads, telephone systems, homes, and factories). An economist using the production possibilities model to describe the effect of El Niño on Ecuador would show
    a. an inward shift in the country's production possibilities curve
    b. an outward shift in the country's production possibilities curve
    c. a movement along the production possibilities curve from consumption goods to capital goods
    d. a movement along the production possibilities curve from capital goods to consumption goods
    e. a movement from a point on the curve to a point inside the curve

17. Suppose the Ecuadoran government announces a program to rebuild the country's infrastructure financed by higher taxes on the Ecuadoran people. The immediate effect noted in the production possibilities model is
    a. an inward shift in the country's production possibilities curve
    b. an outward shift in the country's production possibilities curve
    c. a movement along the production possibilities curve from consumption goods to capital goods
    d. a movement along the production possibilities curve from capital goods to consumption goods
    e. a movement to a point beyond the curve in the impossibilities region

18. At $2 per gallon, John buys 50 gallons of gasoline per week, Mary buys 20 gallons per week, and Tom buys 30 gallons per week. Which of the following is a point on their combined market demand curve for gasoline?
    a. Q = 120 gallons per week, P = $2
    b. Q = 100 gallons per week, P = $3
    c. Q = 100 gallons per week, P = $2
    d. Q = 120 gallons per week, P = $6
    e. Q = 70 gallons per week, P = $2

19. In Adam Smith's famous pin factory example, one man draws out the wire, another straightens it, and a third cuts it. Other people are employed, some pointing the pins, others whitening them, and still others packaging pins. The total output from this factory is much higher than if each person employed performed all the operations necessary for making a pin individually. Smith's example illustrates
   a. comparative advantage
   b. absolute advantage
   c. the law of increasing costs
   d. economic efficiency
   e. labor specialization

20. Economists classify resources as factors of production. The four factors of production are
   a. rent, wages, interest, and profits
   b. land, labor, capital, and entrepreneurship
   c. plant and equipment, labor, management, inventories
   d. human capital, physical capital, money, rent
   e. entrepreneurship, technology, innovation, land

Discussion Questions/Problems — Each question is worth 10 points.

1. In the space provided below, draw a production possibilities curve to show an economy that can produce either consumption goods or capital goods or both. On the curve, label two points A and B to show positions that emphasize consumption goods production and capital goods production, respectively. Why is a move from point A to point B much harder for a poor country to make than for a rich country?

2. The table below shows the world demand for U.S. corn and the quantities U.S. farmers will supply at different prices.

Price ($/bushel)	Quantity Demanded (millions of bushels per year)	Quantity Supplied (millions of bushels per year)
5	1	5
4	2	4
3	3	3
2	4	2
1	5	1

   a. On the axes provided below, draw the demand and supply curves that correspond to the data shown in the table. Carefully label your graph.

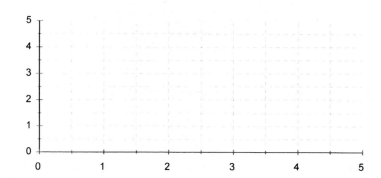

b. What is the equilibrium price and what is the quantity demanded and supplied at that price?

c. Suppose that because of a financial crisis in Asia, the world demand for U.S. corn is cut in half; that is, at each price, only 50 percent of the previous quantity is now demanded. What are the new quantities demanded at each price shown in the table above? Plot these values in the graph you drew above and label the new demand curve D′.

d. What is the new equilibrium price and what is the quantity demanded and supplied at that price?

e. Explain in detail how the market adjusts from the original equilibrium price to the new one.

3. The following table shows the amounts of sugar or oranges that can be produced in one month in Florida and Brazil.

	Sugar (tons)	Oranges (tons)
Florida	300	300
Brazil	400	300

a. Which producer has an absolute advantage in sugar production? Orange production? Explain.

b. Which producer has a comparative advantage in sugar production? Orange production? Explain.

c. Could Florida and Brazil benefit from specialization? Explain.

4. Use a production possibilities curve diagram to show the impact of losing a war on a country's economy. How does one explain the observation that countries recover remarkably quickly after wars are lost?

Answers to the Sample Test on Part I

True-False Questions

1. True
2. False. The *ceteris paribus* assumption holds all but one variable constant so that one-on-one cause-and-effect relationships can be identified.
3. True
4. False. A capital good is a good used to produce other goods. The other goods may be either capital or consumption goods.
5. True
6. False. If the country has a comparative advantage in shirt production, then it can produce shirts at a lower

opportunity cost.
7. True
8. False. An increase in demand will cause an increase in the equilibrium price and an increase in the quantity demanded and supplied in the short run.
9. False. An increase in income will cause an increase in the demand for a normal good.
10. False. A production possibilities curve that is bowed-out from the origin exhibits the law of increasing costs.

Multiple-Choice Questions

1. c	6. a	11. c	16. a
2. b	7. e	12. a	17. c
3. d	8. c	13. c	18. c
4. c	9. b	14. d	19. e
5. e	10. a	15. a	20. b

Discussion Questions/Problems

1. The graph below shows the production possibilities curve for this problem.

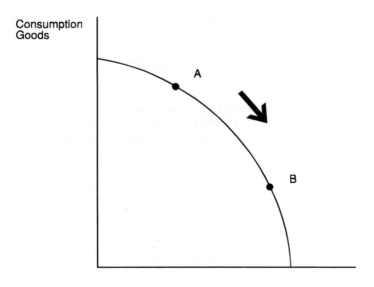

Point A shows that mostly consumption goods are being produced while point B shows that resources have been shifted to the production of more capital goods. The move from point A to point B is harder for a poor country because a large portion of a poor country's resources must be devoted to consumption goods production just to provide for subsistence. Moreover, as a poor country shifts resources from producing consumption goods to producing capital goods, it will give up larger and larger amounts of consumption goods just to increase capital goods production by equal amounts because of the law of increasing costs.

2. a. The graph that corresponds to the answers to part a and part c is shown on the next page.

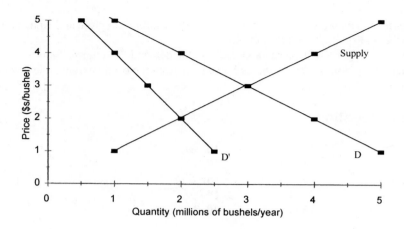

b. The equilibrium price is $3, and the quantity demanded equals the quantity supplied at 3 million bushels per year.

c. At each price, the quantity demanded is half what it was on the original demand curve. D' shows these points.

d. The new equilibrium price is $2, and quantity demanded now equals quantity supplied at 2 million bushels per year.

e. Once demand decreases to D', there is an excess supply at the original price of $3. In this case, the excess supply is 1.5 million bushels of corn. Producers compete with one another to lower price. As the price decreases, quantity demanded increases along D', and quantity supplied decreases along the supply curve until the new equilibrium is reached at a price of $2 per bushel.

3. a. Brazil has an absolute advantage in sugar production because it can produce more sugar in one month than Florida— 400 tons versus 300 tons. Neither Brazil nor Florida has an absolute advantage in orange production — they both produce 300 tons.

   b. Brazil has a comparative advantage in sugar production. The opportunity cost of one ton of sugar in Florida is one ton of oranges. The opportunity cost of one ton of sugar in Brazil is 3/4 ton of oranges. Brazil gives up fewer oranges to produce sugar than does Florida. Florida has a comparative advantage in orange production. The opportunity cost of one ton of orange in Florida is one ton of sugar, while the opportunity cost of one ton of oranges in Brazil is 4/3 tons of sugar.

   c. Florida should specialize in oranges and Brazil should specialize in sugar. At the end of a month, there would be 300 tons of oranges and 400 tons of sugar between them. This is more than could be had if each producer split resources evenly between the production of the two goods.

4. If we suppose that the country's output is split between consumption goods and capital goods, the impact of losing a war is shown graphically below. The curve shifts inward toward the origin. The bigger the losses, the bigger the shift. Countries are able to recover faster than one might expect after losing a war because, in spite of the losses of human resources and physical resources (capital destroyed and land unsuitable to cultivation or habitation), the ideas on which production had been based cannot be destroyed. The knowledge that guided the applied technology in the country prior to the war still exists after the war. Once

the technology is applied again, perhaps even in improved form, the production possibilities curve will shift back to its original position or beyond.

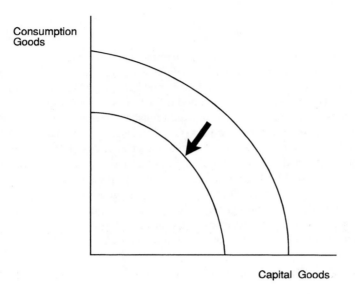

CHAPTER 4

AGGREGATE DEMAND AND AGGREGATE SUPPLY

Chapter in a Nutshell

You learned in Chapter 1 that economics is divided into two main branches — microeconomics and macroeconomics. We begin our detailed analysis of macroeconomics with this chapter. Macroeconomics focuses on the economy as a whole, rather than on individual economic behavior. Macroeconomists typically address such questions as why there are periods of **recession** and **inflation**, what causes **prosperity**, and what causes economic growth. Some of the concepts used by macroeconomists to measure changes in the economy will be introduced. For example, the **gross domestic product (GDP)** measures the dollar value of all final goods and services produced in the economy in a year. The **consumer price index (CPI)** is a measure comparing the prices of goods and services that a household typically purchases to the prices of those goods and services purchased in a base year. The **GDP deflator** is a measure comparing the prices of all goods and services produced in the economy during a given year to the prices of those goods and services purchased in a base year. The concepts of **aggregate demand** and **aggregate supply** are used to show how the level of **real GDP** (GDP excluding price changes) and the **price level** are determined in the economy. These are a few of the new concepts presented in this chapter that will enable you to explore macroeconomic topics.

After you study this chapter, you should be able to:

- Describe the phases of the **business cycle**.
- Explain how **gross domestic product** is used to measure output in a country.
- Transform **nominal GDP** to **real GDP** using the **GDP deflator**.
- Graph **aggregate demand** and **aggregate supply**.
- Account for the shapes of the **aggregate demand** and **aggregate supply** curves.
- Explain how the economy moves toward **macroequilibrium**.
- Show how an economy can be in equilibrium with either **unemployment**, or **inflation**, or both.
- Distinguish among **demand-pull inflation**, **cost-push inflation**, and **stagflation**.

Concept Check — See how you do on these multiple choice questions.

The business cycle is characterized by different economic phenomena in different phases. Which phase of the business cycle is characterized by inflation? Which by high unemployment?

1. The **business cycle** alternates between periods of _____, marked by **inflation**, and periods of _____, marked by relatively high unemployment.
   a. depression; recession
   b. recovery; recession
   c. prosperity; recession
   d. recession; depression
   e. unemployment; inflation

For this question, think about which type of GDP includes price changes and which doesn't.

2. The difference between **nominal GDP** and **real GDP** is that real GDP
    a. is larger than nominal GDP
    b. measures the level of output including price changes, while nominal GDP holds prices constant
    c. measures the level of output and nominal GDP measures the price level
    d. measures the price level and nominal GDP measures the level of output
    e. measures the level of output in constant prices, while nominal GDP includes price changes

How does the shape of the aggregate supply curve change as GDP increases?

3. If the **macroequilibrium** is at less than full employment, then
    a. the aggregate supply curve is relatively flat
    b. the aggregate supply curve is vertical
    c. the aggregate supply curve has a steep positive slope
    d. demand-pull inflation will be a problem
    e. cost-push inflation will be a problem

Learn the forumula for the GDP deflator.

4. The **GDP deflator** is used to calculate real GDP by
    a. multiplying the GDP deflator by nominal GDP
    b. dividing nominal GDP by the GDP deflator and multiplying by 100
    c. dividing nominal GDP by the GDP deflator and dividing by 100
    d. dividing nominal GDP by the GDP deflator
    e. dividing the GDP deflator by nominal GDP

What are the two types of inflation and what causes each one?

5. **Demand-pull inflation** is caused by _____, and **cost-push inflation** is caused by
_____.
    a. an increase in aggregate demand; a decrease in aggregate supply
    b. a decrease in aggregate supply; an increase in aggregate demand
    c. a decrease in aggregate demand; an increase in aggregate supply
    d. leveraged buyouts; government spending
    e. oil embargoes; leveraged buyouts

Am I on the Right Track?

Your answers to the questions above should be **c**, **e**, **a**, **b**, and **a**. This chapter describes how the economy moves toward a macroequilibrium. Macroequilibrium occurs when the price level is such that the aggregate quantity demanded and aggregate quantity supplied are equal. This may occur when the economy's resources are fully employed or when there are unemployed resources in the economy. Critical to your understanding of macroequilibrium is the aggregate demand and aggregate supply model. The graphing tutorial below describes the shapes of the aggregate demand and aggregate supply curves and the determination of macroequilibrium. Before doing that, there are many new key terms to learn.

Key Terms Quiz — Match the terms on the left with the definitions in the column on the right.

1. recession

_____ a. a severe recession

2. real GDP

_____ b. the reference year with which prices in other years are compared in a price index

3. depression

_____ c. a phase in the business cycle, following a recession, in which real GDP increases and unemployment declines

4. consumer price index

_____ d. a phase in the business cycle in which the decline in real GDP lasts for at least six months with high unemployment

5. prosperity

_____ e. the total quantity of goods and services demanded by households, firms, foreigners, and government at varying price levels

6. base year

_____ f. the bottom of a business cycle

7. inflation

_____ g. alternating periods of growth and decline in an economy's GDP

8. price level

_____ h. a period of stagnating real GDP, high inflation, and relatively high levels of unemployment

9. business cycle

_____ i. a phase in the business cycle in which real GDP declines, inflation moderates, and unemployment emerges

10. GDP deflator

_____ j. the total quantity of goods and services that firms in the economy are willing to supply at varying price levels

11. trough

_____ k. a phase in the business cycle marked by a relatively high level of real GDP, full employment, and inflation

12. aggregate supply

_____ l. GDP measured in terms of current market prices, unadjusted for inflation

13. recovery

_____ m. GDP adjusted for changes in the price level

14. aggregate demand

_____ n. inflation caused primarily by an increase in aggregate demand

15. peak

_____ o. total value of all final goods and services, measured in current market prices, produced in the economy during a year

16. macroequilibrium

_____ p. a measure comparing the prices of all goods and services produced in the economy during a given year to the prices of those goods and services purchased in a base year

17. downturn

_____ q. an increase in the price level

18. demand-pull inflation

_____ r. a primarily debt-financed purchase of all the stock or assets of a company

19. gross domestic product

_____ s. inflation caused primarily by a decrease in aggregate supply

20. stagflation

_____ t. the top of the business cycle

21. cost-push inflation

_____ u. a measure that compares the prices of consumer goods that a household purchases to the prices of those goods and services purchased in a base year

22. nominal GDP

_____ v. the level of real GDP and the price level that equate the aggregate quantity demanded and the aggregate quantity supplied

23. leveraged buyout

_____ w. a measure of prices in one year expressed in relation to prices in a base year

Graphing Tutorial

This chapter introduces you to the aggregate demand and aggregate supply curves that we use to derive the macroequilibrium for an economy. Aggregate demand and aggregate supply curves must not be confused with demand and supply curves that we use to represent markets in microeconomics. Aggregate demand and aggregate supply measure the quantities of all goods and services demanded and supplied in the economy at varying price levels. Demand and supply measure the quantities of particular goods and services demanded and supplied in particular markets at different prices. The axes measure different variables for aggregate demand and aggregate supply than we found for demand and supply graphs. For example, the horizontal axis in an aggregate demand and aggregate supply graph measures real GDP in dollars (trillions of dollars for the U.S. economy). The vertical axis in an aggregate demand and aggregate supply graph measures the price level. Recall that the axes for demand and supply graphs in microeconomics have quantity measured in physical units per unit of time on the horizontal axis and price measured in dollars per unit on the vertical axis. Presented below is a representative aggregate demand and aggregate supply graph.

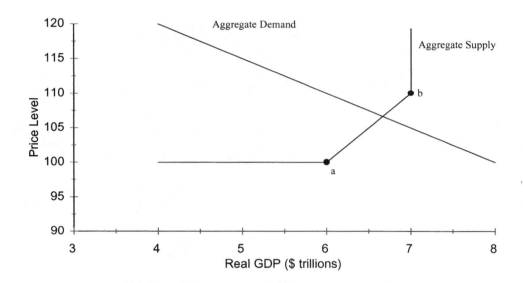

Note that the aggregate supply curve is drawn with three distinct segments. The horizontal segment shows that aggregate supply can increase up to point a without affecting the price level. In this range of GDP, there are readily available supplies of unemployed resources that can be used to increase aggregate supply with no increase in the price level. From point a to point b, the quantity of goods and services increases, but only with increases in the price level. Between points a and b, unused resources become less available, and firms may be willing to offer higher prices to employ them. The higher prices paid for these resources raises the prices of goods produced with them. Another way of explaining the upward-sloping segment is to suppose that the price level increases from 100 to 110. As the price level increases, so does the spread between prices and costs. Producers earn higher profits as a result. Higher profits stimulate greater production from existing firms and attract new firms into production. The vertical segment of the aggregate supply curve, above point b, shows the full-employment level of real GDP. Since all resources are fully employed, aggregate supply and real GDP cannot increase beyond the $7 trillion limit.

Aggregate demand represents the purchases of goods and services by households, firms, government, and foreigners. As the price level decreases, the total quantities demanded by these groups increase. Thus, the aggregate demand curve is downward sloping — as the price level decreases, the total quantities demanded of goods and services increases. This downward slope can be explained by three effects. First, the real wealth effect states that as the price level decreases, people's wealth (assets held such as cash, savings accounts, stocks, and government bonds) increases, so they can purchase more goods and services. Second, the interest rate effect states that a decrease in the price level means that people need to borrow less to make desired purchases. The decreased demand for borrowed money causes the interest rate (the cost of borrowed money) to fall. However, a decrease in the interest rate will make borrowing to purchase goods and services more attractive to households and firms. Thus, people will demand more goods and services as interest rates decrease due to a decrease in the price level. Finally, the international trade effect of a price level decrease will cause the total quantities demanded of goods and services to increase. If the price level in the United States decreases while price levels in the rest of the world stay the same, then U.S. goods are relatively less expensive to domestic consumers and foreigners. As a result, people will demand more goods and services as the U.S. price level declines.

Shifts in the aggregate demand and aggregate supply curves are fairly easy to explain. The aggregate demand curve shifts to the right (increases) as a result of increases in government spending or decreases in taxes; increases in spending by consumers, businesses and foreigners; and rising expectations about the future. As a result of decreases in government spending or increases in taxes, decreases in spending by consumers, businesses, and foreigners, and falling expectations about the future, the aggregate demand curve shifts to the left (decreases). Aggregate supply increases when it shifts to the right. Aggregate supply is shifted to the right by the increased availability of resources — more workers, more capital, more land, and more entrepreneurial energies. A decrease in resource prices also shifts the aggregate supply to the right. On the other hand, if resources become less available, or if their prices increase, the aggregate supply curve shifts to the left — a decrease in aggregate supply.

Macroequilibrium occurs at the price level and real GDP combination that equates aggregate demand and aggregate supply. In our diagram, this happens at the intersection of aggregate demand and aggregate supply — a price level of about 106 and a real GDP level of approximately $6.7 trillion. At price levels above 106, aggregate quantity demanded is less than the aggregate quantity supplied, so the price level begins to fall due to competition among suppliers. Conversely, for price levels below 106, aggregate quantity demanded is greater than aggregate quantity supplied, so the price level begins to rise due to competition among demanders. In each case, the macroequilibrium is restored.

Graphing Pitfalls

Graphs that represent demand and supply in particular markets in microeconomics are labeled with price, measured in dollars per unit on the vertical axis, and quantity, measured in physical units on the horizontal axis. The axes are different in the aggregate demand and aggregate supply diagrams that we use in macroeconomics. The price level, not price, is measured on the vertical axis. The price level is the average of all prices in the economy measured with an index number like the GDP deflator. The dollar value of real GDP is measured on the horizontal axis. All goods and service produced are included rather than the good or service produced in just one market. So the demand and supply diagram you learned in Chapter 3 and the aggregate demand aggregate supply diagram you are learning now are completely different. Don't mislabel the axes as shown in the graph on the following page.

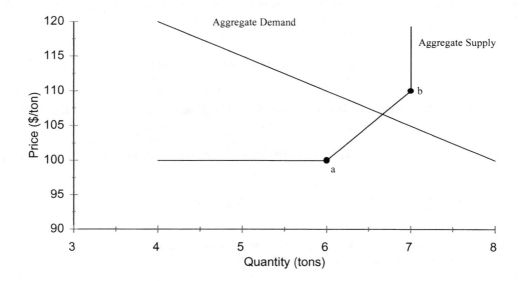

Don't make the mistake of mislabeling the axes on a graph of aggregate demand and aggregate supply in the same way you would for a demand and supply diagram in microeconomics. The price level is measured on the vertical axis, not price; and real GDP is measured on the horizontal axis, not quantity measured in some kind of physical units as shown above.

True-False Questions — If a statement is false, explain why.

1. Aggregate demand is basically the same concept as demand for a good or service, such as a banana or health services, that is the subject of analysis in microeconomics. (T/F)

2. One reason the aggregate demand curve is downward sloping is that as the price level decreases, real wealth increases so that people consume more. (T/F)

3. The horizontal segment of the aggregate supply curve suggests that ample resources are available to increase real GDP without causing inflation. (T/F)

4. The most inclusive measure of inflation is the consumer price index. (T/F)

5. Real GDP is equal to nominal GDP multiplied by 100, divided by the GDP deflator. (T/F)

6. If an increase in the price level creates higher profits and, as a result, causes real GDP to increase, then the aggregate supply curve must be vertical. (T/F)

7. The depression of the 1930s was a period in American economic history marked by significant cost-push inflation. (T/F)

8. Real GDP remains constant if increases in the price level alone cause nominal GDP to increase. (T/F)

9. In order for a recession to exist, a decline in the nation's real GDP must persist for at least half a year. (T/F)

10. Stagflation is a period of rapidly growing real GDP, inflation, and relatively high unemployment. (T/F)

11. During a recovery, real GDP increases and unemployment declines. (T/F)

12. The upward-sloping portion of the aggregate supply curve suggests that an increase in the price level will be associated with an increase in real GDP. (T/F)

13. A cut in government spending will cause the aggregate demand curve to shift to the right. (T/F)

14. Demand-pull inflation occurs when increases in aggregate demand shift the aggregate demand curve to the right while the aggregate supply curve remains unchanged at full-employment real GDP. (T/F)

15. The price level increase associated with increased aggregate demand during World War II was exacerbated by a decrease in aggregate supply caused by a labor force shift to the military. (T/F)

Multiple-Choice Questions

1. The upward slope of the trend line through a business cycle indicates that
    a. the economy is in a recovery phase
    b. the economy is in a period of stagflation
    c. there is a positive relationship between real GDP and the price level
    d. the economy's output increases in the long run
    e. the quantity supplied of a certain good increases as the price decreases

2. One characteristic of the recovery phase of the business cycle is that
    a. upward pressure on the economy's price level begins to build
    b. output reaches its maximum level
    c. a recession will soon follow
    d. inflation is moderating
    e. unemployment is increasing

3. One way that the government can increase aggregate demand is by
   a. reducing government spending
   b. reducing income taxes
   c. increasing taxes
   d. creating stagflation
   e. reducing the economy's supply of labor

4. The measure that compares the prices of all goods and services produced in the economy in any year to the prices of those goods and services produced in a base year is known as the
   a. GDP deflator
   b. real GDP
   c. nominal GDP
   d. CPI
   e. full employment GDP

5. All of the following conditions are consistent with general prosperity in the economy **except**
   a. unemployment is relatively low
   b. wage rates are relatively high
   c. real GDP is relatively high
   d. morale among workers and management is relatively high
   e. the price level decreases

6. It is important to control for price increases when comparing GDP between two years because
   a. nominal GDP can rise due to either an increase in output or an increase in the price level
   b. economists are only interested in price changes
   c. price increases are usually larger in relative terms than quantity increases
   d. price increases can reduce nominal GDP
   e. price increases can increase real GDP

7. If nominal GDP is $6 trillion in 1996 and the GDP deflator is 120, then real GDP is
   a. $5 trillion
   b. $50 trillion
   c. $7.2 trillion
   d. $72 trillion
   e. $12 trillion

8. The upward-sloping segment of the aggregate supply curve can be explained by
   a. tight resource markets, which, in turn, cause increases in the price of goods produced
   b. increases in the price level that raise profits, inducing firms to produce more
   c. the full employment of resources
   d. all of the above
   e. a and b

9. The aggregate supply curve shifts to the right when
   a. supplies of resources increase
   b. wage rates increase
   c. consumption decreases
   d. investment increases
   e. population decreases

10. Demand-pull inflation is the result of
    a. a leftward shift in the aggregate supply curve
    b. a rightward shift in the aggregate supply curve
    c. an increase in taxes
    d. a leftward shift in the aggregate demand curve
    e. a rightward shift in the aggregate demand curve

11. The difference between nominal and real GDP is that
    a. nominal GDP includes price changes while real GDP doesn't
    b. nominal GDP measures aggregate supply while real GDP measures aggregate demand
    c. real GDP is always equal to or higher than nominal GDP, depending on the phase of the business cycle
    d. real GDP includes price changes while nominal GDP doesn't
    e. real GDP is derived from the CPI while nominal GDP is derived from the GDP deflator

12. In the aggregate demand and aggregate supply model, the intersection of the AD and AS curves determines
    a. the price level and real GDP
    b. the equilibrium price and quantity combination
    c. the difference between real and nominal GDP
    d. the price level and the rate of inflation
    e. the rate of economic growth

13. The sequence of phases in a business cycle is
    a. recovery, recession, prosperity, downturn
    b. prosperity, recovery, downturn, recession
    c. prosperity, downturn, recovery, recession
    d. recession, recovery, prosperity, downturn
    e. recession, recovery, downturn, prosperity

14. The aggregate supply curve shifts to the right when
    a. consumers, with no change in nominal GDP, save less and consume more
    b. consumers, with no change in nominal GDP, save more and consume less
    c. people, with no change in the price level, decrease their supply of labor
    d. people, with no change in the price level, increase their supply of labor
    e. as a result of war, people shift from civilian to military production

15. If real GDP is $1,600 billion and the GDP deflator is 125, then nominal GDP is
    a. $2,000 billion
    b. $2,500 billion
    c. $1,800 billion
    d. $2,400 billion
    e. $1,000 billion

16. If the price level in the United States is constant while price levels in other countries increase, then
    a. aggregate supply in the United States shifts to the right
    b. aggregate demand in other economies shifts to the left
    c. real GDP in the United States increases more rapidly than in other economies
    d. U.S. exports increase, shifting U.S. aggregate demand to the right
    e. U.S. exports decrease, shifting U.S. aggregate demand to the left

17. The aggregate demand curve shifts to the left when
    a. consumers, with no change in the price level, save less and consume more
    b. consumers, with no change in the price level, save more and consume less
    c. people, with no change in the price level, decrease their supply of labor
    d. people, with no change in the price level, increase their supply of labor
    e. as a result of war, people shift from civilian to military production

18. If more capital is made available in an economy, one consequence will be
    a. a decrease in aggregate demand
    b. an increase in aggregate demand
    c. greater unemployment
    d. a shift to the right in the aggregate supply curve
    e. an increase in the slope of the upward-sloping portion of the aggregate supply curve

19. Cost-push inflation refers to an increase in the price level due to
    a. an increase in aggregate expenditures
    b. rising government spending due to national emergencies like war or depression
    c. a shift to the right in the aggregate supply curve
    d. rising costs of critical inputs such as energy, labor, and capital
    e. excessive government spending

20. One of the main reasons for the recession and economic stagnation of the early 1990s was
    a. an OPEC-designed increase in oil prices that caused stagflation
    b. an increase in defense spending due to the war in the Persian Gulf
    c. a decrease in consumer spending in response to high levels of debt
    d. unsuccessful leveraged buyouts
    e. a commercial real estate boom

The following questions relate to the interdisciplinary, applied, and global perspectives in the text.

21. Which of the following is not a phase of the business cycle?
    a. unemployment
    b. prosperity
    c. recession
    d. downturn
    e. recovery

22. The three groups of goods and services that are given the largest percentage weights in the calculation of the consumer price index are
    a. housing, transportation, food and beverages
    b. housing, medical care, education and communication
    c. housing, education and communication, food and beverages
    d. housing, transportation, medical care
    e. housing, transportation, apparel

23. Suppose that you are the Minister of Economics for Inflationland. Your president is challenged when it comes to understanding economic theory. You want to present the most impressive numbers possible regarding economic growth during his first three years in office. You should choose a base year
    a. that is fairly recent and report real GDP statistics
    b. that is fairly recent and report nominal GDP statistics
    c. that is fairly recent and report the CPI levels
    d. from long ago and report nominal GDP statistics
    e. from long ago and report real GDP statistics

Fill in the Blanks

1. The business cycle consists of alternating periods of _____ and _____ in an economy's GDP.

2. The _____ is the reference year with which prices in other years are compared using a _____.

3. The aggregate demand curve is downward sloping due to the _____ effect, the _____ effect, and the _____ effect.

4. If workers' _____ decrease while the price level remains constant, then the aggregate supply curve will shift to the _____.

5. During World War II, aggregate demand shifted to the _____ while the aggregate supply curve shifted to the _____, causing the price level to _____.

Discussion Questions

1. Define gross domestic product. How can GDP increase over time?

2. How is the consumer price index constructed?

3. Why do we say that the GDP deflator is a more inclusive measure of inflation than the consumer price index?

4. What's the difference between nominal GDP and real GDP?

5. Why does the aggregate supply curve have three distinct segments?

6. Why is the aggregate demand curve downward sloping?

7. Distinguish between demand-pull inflation and cost-push inflation.

Problems

1. Suppose the GDP deflator is 140 for 1996. The base year is 1992. If nominal GDP in 1996 is $3.6 trillion, calculate real GDP in 1992 dollars. Show your work.

2. Suppose that the cost of the market basket of goods and services that represents the CPI is $3,000 in the base year, 1992. Suppose also that the cost of the same market basket of goods in 1994 was $3,300. What was the value of the CPI index for 1994? Explain what the 1994 CPI means.

3. Suppose the value of the market basket from question 3 was $4,000 in 1996. What was the average annual rate of inflation between 1994 and 1996? Show your work.

4. Use an aggregate demand/aggregate supply diagram to show what happened to the economy as a result of the OPEC-designed oil price increases of the 1970s. Explain your graph in words and make sure it is labeled carefully.

Everyday Applications

As you read the newspaper and watch the economic news on television, think about whether the U.S. economy is currently in macroequilibrium. What economic data would you use to answer this question? Is the aggregate demand/aggregate supply model relevant today?

Economics Online

Stat-USA is an Internet site that provides current and historical economic and financial data. The site is a service of the U.S. Department of Commerce. Find out changes in real GDP, the price level, and other key economic variables by visiting the site (*http://www.stat-usa.gov/*).

Answers to Questions

Key Terms Quiz

a. 3	**f.** 11	**k.** 5	**p.** 10	**u.** 4
b. 6	**g.** 9	**l.** 22	**q.** 7	**v.** 16
c. 13	**h.** 20	**m.** 2	**r.** 23	**w.** 8
d. 1	**i.** 17	**n.** 18	**s.** 21	
e. 14	**j.** 12	**o.** 19	**t.** 15	

True-False Questions

1. False. Aggregate demand refers to all goods and services purchased in the economy while demand refers to a particular good or service purchased in one market.
2. True
3. True
4. False. The most inclusive measure of inflation is the GDP deflator. The CPI measures the prices of goods and services typically bought by households, while the GDP deflator measures the prices of all goods and services produced in the economy.
5. True
6. False. Aggregate supply must be upward sloping for output to increase as the price level increases.
7. False. The depression of the 1930s was characterized by high unemployment and falling price levels caused by a dramatic decline in aggregate demand.
8. True
9. True
10. False. Stagflation is a period of stagnating or falling real GDP, inflation, and relatively high unemployment.
11. True
12. True
13. False. A cut in government spending will cause the aggregate demand curve to shift to the left.
14. True
15. True

Multiple-Choice Questions

1. d	**6.** a	**11.** a	**16.** d	**21.** a
2. a	**7.** a	**12.** a	**17.** b	**22.** a
3. b	**8.** e	**13.** d	**18.** d	**23.** d
4. a	**9.** a	**14.** d	**19.** d	
5. e	**10.** e	**15.** a	**20.** c	

Fill in the Blanks

1. growth; decline
2. base year; price index
3. real wealth; interest rate; international trade
4. wages; right
5. right; left; rise

Discussion Questions

1. Gross domestic product is the total value of all final goods and services produced in a country during a calendar year. GDP can increase if the quantity of goods and services produced increases or if the price of these goods and services increases.

2. The consumer price index is constructed by dividing the cost of a fixed market basket of goods and services purchased in a particular year by the cost of the same market basket of goods and services in a base year and multiplying by 100. The market basket represents purchases made by the typical American household.

3. The GDP deflator includes the prices of all final goods and services produced in a year, while the CPI includes only consumer goods and services that a household typically purchases. For instance, the GDP deflator includes airline ticket prices and the CPI does not.

4. Nominal GDP, measured in current market prices, includes the effect of price changes. Real GDP is adjusted for changes in the price level. Real GDP is equal to nominal GDP multiplied by 100 and divided by the GDP deflator.

5. Each segment of the aggregate supply curve reflects a different set of macroeconomic circumstances. For example, the horizontal segment reflects an economy operating well below full employment, so real GDP can be increased without any upward pressure on the price level. The upward-sloping segment shows that resources are becoming more scarce as the economy approaches full employment. Employers bid for resources, driving up their prices, which causes costs of production and the price level to rise. Price level increases raise employers' profits so they increase output. In the vertical segment, full employment exists and resources are unavailable to increase real GDP. Only the price level can rise.

6. The aggregate demand curve is downward sloping because of the real wealth effect, the interest rate effect, and the international trade effect. As the price level decreases, the purchasing power of wealth increases, and consumption spending increases as a result. As the price level decreases, consumers and businesses don't have to borrow as much to finance their spending. Therefore, the demand for borrowed funds decreases and interest rates decrease. As a result of lower interest rates, spending by consumers and businesses increases. If the price level in the United States decreases while the price level in other countries stays the same, spending on U.S. exports by foreigners increases, and people in the United States buy fewer imports. As the price level decreases, foreign demand for exports increases and domestic demand for imports decreases.

7. Demand-pull inflation is caused by a shift to the right in the aggregate demand curve. Demand-pull inflation can result from an increase in aggregate demand beyond that necessary to achieve full employment. Spending by households, businesses, government, or foreigners or some combination of these can trigger demand-pull inflation. An example of demand-pull inflation is the inflation of the 1960s during the Vietnam War.

   Cost-push inflation is caused by a shift to the left in the aggregate supply curve. Cost-push inflation can result from decreasing availability of resources including labor, capital, land (natural resources), and entrepreneurial energies or from an increase in the prices of these resources. A good example of cost-push inflation is that caused by OPEC's increases in oil prices from 1973 through 1982. Because oil is an essential resource for many types of production and is used as a primary source of energy for heating and power generation, the prices of virtually all goods and services were affected by the increased price of oil.

Problems

1. Real GDP is equal to nominal GDP multiplied by 100 and divided by the GDP deflator. In this case, real GDP is equal to $3.6 trillion x 100/140 = $2.57 trillion.

2. The value of the CPI for 1994 is 3,300/3,000 multiplied by 100, which is 110. The 1994 CPI equal to 110 means that prices rose between 1992 and 1994 by 10 percent.

3. The value of the CPI for 1996 is 4,000/3,000 x 100 = 133. The average annual rate of inflation between 1994 and 1996 is (133 − 110)/110 multiplied by 100 then divided by 2, or 10.45 percent. You must divide by 2 because there are two years covered by the change in the CPI — 1994 -1996.

4. Your graph should look like the one shown on the following page. The OPEC-designed price increases caused the aggregate supply curve to shift to the left. These events are shown by a shift in the aggregate supply curve from AS to AS′, a decrease in the equilibrium level of GDP to GDP′, and an increase in the equilibrium price level to P′.

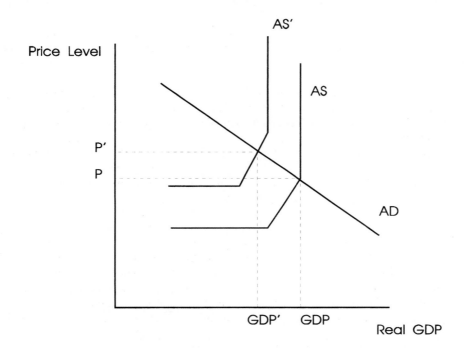

Homework Questions

True-False Questions — If a statement is false, explain why.

1. The vertical segment of the aggregate supply curve corresponds to a level of real GDP that represents full employment. (T/F)

2. The aggregate demand curve is downward sloping because as the price level increases, real wealth increases, so people purchase more. (T/F)

3. Demand-pull inflation occurs when the price of a critical resource like oil increases dramatically. (T/F)

4. The depression of the 1930s was a period when the economy was in equilibrium on the upward-sloping segment of the aggregate supply curve. (T/F)

5. An economy that is experiencing inflation will have a nominal GDP that is greater than the real GDP. (T/F)

Multiple-Choice Questions

1. If nominal GDP is $12 trillion in 2003 and the GDP deflator is 120, then real GDP is
   a. $120 trillion
   b. $10 trillion
   c. $1.2 trillion
   d. $9.6 trillion
   e. $10.8 trillion

2. Which of the following is not a reason for the downward slope of the aggregate demand curve?
   a. as price decreases, quantity demanded increases
   b. as the price level decreases, interest rates decrease, so consumption increases
   c. as the price level decreases, American goods are more attractive than imports, so net exports increase
   d. as the price level decreases, interest rates decrease, so investment increases
   e. as the price level decreases, real wealth increases, so aggregate demand increases

3. The upward-sloping segment of the aggregate supply curve reflects
   a. the presence of large amounts of unemployed resources so that GDP can increase without an increase in the price level
   b. tightness in resource markets so that GDP can increase, but only with increases in the price level
   c. full employment of resources
   d. the absence of inflation
   e. an economy that is operating on its production possibilities curve

4. Demand-pull inflation results when
    a. aggregate demand shifts to the right
    b. aggregate supply shifts to the left
    c. aggregate demand shifts to the left
    d. aggregate supply shifts to the right
    e. stagflation exists

5. Cost-push inflation can be represented on a graph of aggregate demand and aggregate supply by
    a. a shift to the right of the aggregate demand curve
    b. a movement to the left along the aggregate supply curve
    c. a movement to the right along the aggregate supply curve
    d. a shift to the right of the aggregate supply curve
    e. a shift to the left of the aggregate supply curve

Discussion Questions/Problems

1. Discuss the difference between demand-pull inflation and cost-push inflation. Sketch a graph to depict each type of inflation.

2. Suppose that 2003 is chosen as the base year and a typical household's market basket of goods and services costs $800. In 2004, the same market basket of goods costs $1,000. What is the value of the consumer price index in 2003? In 2004? Show your work.

CHAPTER 5

GROSS DOMESTIC PRODUCT ACCOUNTING

Chapter in a Nutshell

Gross domestic product was introduced in the previous chapter as a basic measure of macroeconomic performance. This chapter identifies the component parts of GDP and describes their significance — personal consumption expenditures, gross private domestic investment, government purchases, and net exports. The **circular flow of goods, services, and resources** and the **circular flow of money** are used to show how gross domestic product can be viewed as either flows of expenditure on newly produced **final goods and services** or as equivalent flows of money income to people who provide the resources used to produce goods and services. These two views of GDP are represented by the **expenditure approach** and the **income approach to measuring GDP**.

The expenditure approach focuses on four categories of expenditures. **Personal consumption expenditures** are made up of spending by households for **durable goods, nondurable goods**, and services. **Gross private domestic investment** consists of spending for new plant and equipment, residential housing, and **inventory investment**. Government spending is comprised of federal, state, and local governmental purchases of goods and services. **Net exports** are the difference between a country's exports and imports. The 2003 GDP in the United States was over $10.8 trillion.

Although GDP is a comprehensive measure, certain types of goods and services are excluded from the calculations, including the value of housework, the value of leisure, and the **underground economy**. Also, changes in the quality of goods and services and the costs of environmental damage associated with production may not be accurately measured in the GDP accounts.

The income approach looks at the payments made to households that supply resources to the firms producing final goods and services. National income is the sum of all payments made to resource owners and includes the categories of employee's compensation, rental income, corporate profit, net interest, and proprietors' income. National income in 2003 was approximately $8.62 trillion, with about 70.7 percent representing payments to workers. When adjustments are made for **capital depreciation** and indirect business taxes, GDP and national income match, thus demonstrating the equivalence of the circular flows.

After studying this chapter, you should be able to:

- Explain the equivalence between the **circular flow of money** and the **circular flow of goods, services, and resources**.
- List the categories of spending on final goods and services used in the **expenditure approach** to measuring **GDP**.
- Distinguish between **durable and nondurable consumer goods**.
- Compare the relative magnitudes of the different components used in the **expenditure approach** to measuring GDP.
- Explain how economists bring GDP and **national income** into accord.
- Derive **personal income** and **disposable personal income** from **national income**.
- Explain why GDP is an imperfect measure of overall economic activity in a country.

Concept Check — See how you do on these multiple-choice questions.

Between which two groups are the flows occurring in the circular flow model?

1. The **circular flow of goods, services, and resources** shows how
    a. households and firms are independent from each other
    b. households supply their resources to firms in resource markets and demand goods and services in product markets
    c. the circular flow of money inaccurately measures real GDP
    d. households demand resources and firms demand goods and services
    e. too much spending on consumer goods can cause an economy to collapse

As you consider the answers to this question, think about why businesses keep inventories.

2. Changes in business inventories that are counted as **inventory investment** represent
    a. changes in the stocks of finished final goods, as well as stocks of resources used to produce those goods
    b. intended buildups of inventories
    c. the largest part of gross private domestic investment
    d. opportunities for firms to run inventory clearance sales
    e. accumulations of consumer durables

Which measure, GDP or GNP, emphasizes ownership and which emphasizes location?

3. The difference between **GDP** and **GNP** is that
    a. GDP measures what is produced and earned by a nation's people and property and GNP measures what is produced and earned in the domestic economy
    b. GDP emphasizes ownership and GNP emphasizes location
    c. GDP measures what is produced and earned in the domestic economy and GNP measures what is produced and earned by a nation's people and property
    d. GDP includes depreciation and GNP does not
    e. GDP is always larger than GNP

Are transfer payments an addition to GDP?

4. All of the following are examples of **transfer payments except**
    a. government retirement benefits
    b. unemployment insurance benefits
    c. Social Security benefits
    d. rental income
    e. subsidies to farmers

How would GDP change if activities in the underground economy were reported and included?

5. Because most economic activity in the **underground economy** goes unreported, GDP is
    a. overstated
    b. unaffected
    c. understated
    d. understated, but this is offset by the inclusion of the value of housework
    e. overstated, but this is offset by the exclusion of the value of housework

Am I on the Right Track?

Your answers to the questions above should be **b**, **a**, **c**, **d**, and **c**. There are two keys to your success in understanding the material in this chapter. First, make sure that you understand the circular flow of goods, services, and resources and the circular flow of money. These two circular flows are connected. Households supply flows of resources to firms in return for money payments — wages, interest, rent, and profit. Then the money payments to households for resources come back to firms as the expenditures on the final goods and services they have produced. The expenditure approach and the income approach to measuring GDP are embedded in these circular flow models. The second key to success with this chapter is to learn the key terms. As was true in the previous chapter, there are many new terms.

Key Terms Quiz — Match the terms on the left with the definitions in the column on the right.

1. circular flow of goods, services, and resources _____ a. the movement of income in the form of resource payments from firms to households, and of income in the form of revenue from households to firms

2. services _____ b. a method of calculating GDP by adding all the incomes earned in the production of final goods and services

3. circular flow of money _____ c. personal income minus personal taxes

4. inventory investment _____ d. the difference between the value of a good that a firm produces and the value of the goods the firm uses to produce it

5. final goods _____ e. the value of existing capital stock used up in the process of producing goods and services

6. income approach _____ f. the sum of all payments made to resource owners for the use of their resources

7. intermediate goods _____ g. all goods and services bought by households

8. national income _____ h. the movement of goods and services from firms to households, and of resources from households to firms

9. value added _____ i. the purchase by firms of plant, equipment, and inventory goods

10. gross national product (GNP) _____ j. all goods and services bought by government

11. personal consumption expenditures _____ k. GDP minus capital depreciation

12. capital depreciation _____ l. an economy's exports to other economies, minus its imports from other economies

13. gross private domestic investment _____ m. stocks of finished goods and raw materials that firms keep in reserve to facilitate production and sales

14. net domestic product (NDP) _____ n. goods used to produce other goods

15. expenditure approach _____ o. goods expected to last less than one year

16. personal income _____ p. the market value of all final goods and services in an economy produced by resources owned by people of that economy, regardless of where the resources are located

17. government purchases _____ q. the unreported or illegal production of goods and services in the economy that is not counted in GDP

18. transfer payments _____ r. national income, plus income received but not earned, minus income earned but not received

19. net exports

        _____ s. productive activities that are instantaneously consumed

20. disposable personal income

        _____ t. goods expected to last at least a year

21. durable goods

        _____ u. income received but not earned

22. underground economy

        _____ v. a method of calculating GDP that adds all expenditures made for final goods and services by households, firms, and government

23. nondurable goods

        _____ w. goods purchased for final use, not for resale

True-False Questions — If a statement is false, explain why.

1. The circular flow of goods, services, and resources and the circular flow of money show equivalent streams measured in dollars. (T/F)

2. Personal consumption expenditures comprise about 20 percent of GDP. (T/F)

3. A final good or service is produced for resale. (T/F)

4. Sales of previously owned automobiles are included in GDP. (T/F)

5. Gross private domestic investment includes government spending on the National Guard but excludes other military spending. (T/F)

6. An increase in net exports causes GDP to decrease. (T/F)

7. An estimate of the value of production in the underground economy is included in official GDP statistics that are compiled by the government. (T/F)

8. Disposable personal income is equal to personal income minus personal taxes. (T/F)

9. Durable goods are expected to last for at least one year. (T/F)

10. Transportation facilities are among the goods and services that the government purchases. (T/F)

11. The sum of the values of intermediate goods will be equal to GDP. (T/F)

12. National income measures the sum of all payments made to resource owners for the use of their resources. (T/F)

13. People who provide firms with capital receive interest income. (T/F)

14. Stockholders in corporations receive proprietors' income. (T/F)

15. GDP and GNP are precisely equal to each other. (T/F)

Multiple-Choice Questions

1. If all American firms operating overseas decided to relocate within the United States, then
   a. GNP would increase
   b. GNP would be unchanged but GDP would increase
   c. both GNP and GDP would decrease
   d. GNP and GDP would be unchanged
   e. GNP would decrease and GDP would increase

2. The circular flow of goods, services, and resources shows the interdependence of
   a. the supplies of goods and the supplies of services
   b. firms and investment
   c. intermediate goods and final goods
   d. net imports and net exports
   e. households and firms

3. The largest component of GDP measured by the expenditures approach is
   a. consumption
   b. investment
   c. government spending
   d. net exports
   e. compensation of employees

4. The expenditure approach to measuring GDP is the sum of expenditures in all of the following categories **except**
   a. gross private domestic investment
   b. personal consumption expenditures
   c. government spending on goods and services
   d. transfer payments by the government
   e. the difference between exports and imports

5. If C = $500, I = $200, G = $150, and X - M = -5, what is GDP?
   a. $850
   b. $855
   c. $845
   d. $755
   e. $745

6. If a large number of Egypt's citizens work overseas, then perhaps the best measure of the Egyptian people's economic well-being is
   a. the GDP deflator
   b. real GNP
   c. real GDP
   d. nominal GNP
   e. nominal GDP

7. The income approach calculates GDP with all of the following **except**
   a. interest
   b. wages
   c. rent
   d. investment
   e. profits

8. A decline in inventories shows up as
   a. a decrease in gross private domestic investment
   b. increases in production
   c. an increase in gross private domestic investment
   d. a decrease in production
   e. decreases in services

9. In order to calculate disposable personal income
   a. direct taxes are subtracted from national income
   b. transfer payments are added to national income
   c. transfer payments are subtracted from personal income
   d. direct taxes are subtracted from personal income
   e. direct taxes are added to personal income

10. In the circular flow model of goods, services, and resources, _____ flow(s) from firms to households.
    a. labor
    b. capital
    c. land
    d. profits
    e. goods

11. GDP understates the total value of all final goods and services produced for all the following reasons **except**
    a. the costs of environmental problems are not included
    b. quality improvements in products are not included
    c. the value of leisure is not included
    d. the value of housework is not included
    e. the value of the underground economy is not included

12. All of the following are considered to be components of investment in calculating GDP **except**
    a. new residential construction
    b. net increases in inventory
    c. new factories
    d. purchases of new equipment by firms
    e. financial investment

13. If depreciation is zero,
    a. GDP is the same as NDP
    b. GDP will shrink over time
    c. gross investment exceeds depreciation
    d. inventory investment is positive
    e. the capital stock grows

14. It is necessary to subtract _____ from net domestic product in order to compute national income.
    a. indirect business taxes
    b. capital depreciation
    c. transfer payments
    d. net exports
    e. factor payments to the rest of the world

15. The largest share of national income is accounted for by
    a. corporate profit
    b. proprietors' income
    c. compensation of employees
    d. consumption of nondurable goods
    e. income taxes

16. Net domestic product (NDP) is GDP minus
    a. depreciation
    b. indirect business taxes
    c. GNP
    d. transfer payments
    e. personal taxes

17. All of the following are examples of transfer payments **except**
    a. Social Security benefits
    b. unemployment benefits
    c. the wages of government employees
    d. veterans' benefits
    e. Aid to Families with Dependent Children

18. The largest component of consumption expenditures is
    a. compensation to employees
    b. profits
    c. rents and royalties
    d. services
    e. proprietors' income

19. The value-added approach to GDP computation involves
    a. problems with double counting
    b. subtracting income from expenditures
    c. summing the addition to value at each stage in production
    d. summing the price times quantity for all intermediate goods
    e. improving technology so that value is added at each stage

20. Because most economic activity in the underground economy goes unreported, GDP is
    a. overstated
    b. unaffected
    c. understated
    d. understated, but this is offset by the inclusion of the value of housework
    e. overstated, but this is offset by the exclusion of the value of housework

The following questions relate to the historical, theoretical, global, and applied perspectives in the text.

21. One difference between Adam Smith's conception of GDP and the modern conception of GDP is that
    a. modern economists only count goods in GDP and not services
    b. modern economists count both intermediate and final goods and services in order to inflate GDP statistics while Smith only counted final goods and services
    c. Smith excluded services from his calculation of GDP while modern economists include services
    d. Smith counted only agricultural production in GDP while modern economists include all types of production
    e. Smith included the value of activities in the underground economy in GDP while modern economists do not

22. In the expanded version of the circular flow model, corresponding to the flows of goods, services, and resources, there is a
    a. percentage deduction from GDP because finite natural resources are consumed in production
    b. percentage deduction from GDP because some of these goods and services are exported
    c. percentage deduction from GDP because some of these goods and services are imported
    d. percentage increase added to GDP because some of these goods and services are exported
    e. counterbalancing money flow

23. Examination of the composition of GDP in the United States as well as for other industrialized market economies shows that _____ is the largest category of expenditures.
    a. consumption
    b. investment
    c. government spending
    d. net exports
    e. compensation to employees

24. Among those who underreport their income on federal tax returns, the biggest offenders are
    a. drug dealers
    b. prostitutes
    c. corporations
    d. informal suppliers
    e. sole proprietorships

Fill in the Blanks

1. The expenditure approach to measuring GDP consists of the sum of _____,

   _____, _____, and

   _____.

2. GDP has limitations as a measure of economic well-being because it excludes _____,

    _____, _____, _____, and

    _____.

3. National income is the sum of _____, _____,

    _____, _____, and

    _____.

4. One of the driving forces behind the underground economy is _____.

5. Gross national product is GDP _____ receipts of factor income from the rest of the world,

    _____ payments of factor income to the rest of the world.

Discussion Questions

1. How do the expenditure approach and the income approach to measuring GDP relate to the circular flow model?

2. Approximately what percentage of GDP is represented in each of the four categories of expenditure?

3. Why are inventories counted as part of investment?

4. Approximately what percentage of national income is represented in each of its categories?

5. Why would an economist, interested in a country's rate of growth, look at its NDP rather than GDP?

6. If you were studying living standards in a country, which measure would you find more informative, national income or personal income? Why?

Problems

1. Use the following data to calculate GDP, GNP, NDP, national income, personal income, and disposable personal income.

Personal Consumption Expenditures	1,000
Interest	80
Corporate Profit	200
Government Purchases	400
Depreciation	100
Rent	300
Gross Private Domestic Investment	400
Compensation of Employees	750
Exports	100
Imports	180
Indirect Business Taxes	70
Proprietors' Income	220
Income Tax	200
Income Earned but not Received	110
Income Received but not Earned	200
Receipt of Factor Incomes from the Rest of the World	80
Payment of Factor Incomes to the Rest of the World	70

2. Suppose that in the following year, economic activity for Problem 1 undergoes the changes that are listed in the table below. How does GDP change?

Corporate Profits	-100
Depreciation	50
Exports	+80
Income Earned but not Received	+10

Everyday Applications

Think of some specific examples of the underground economy. Do you know anyone who has worked in the underground economy? How would a lowering of tax rates affect the underground economy and measured GDP? What would be the impact of legalizing marijuana?

Economics Online

One of the earliest groups that devoted itself to the collection of economic data like that included in the GDP accounts is the National Bureau of Economic Research (NBER). The NBER was founded in 1920 and continues to promote a better understanding of the economy through the research it supports. Visit the NBER Web site (*http://www.nber.org/*).

Answers to Questions

Key Terms Quiz

a. 3	**f.** 8	**k.** 14	**p.** 10	**u.** 18
b. 6	**g.** 11	**l.** 19	**q.** 22	**v.** 15
c. 20	**h.** 1	**m.** 4	**r.** 16	**w.** 5
d. 9	**i.** 13	**n.** 7	**s.** 2	
e. 12	**j.** 17	**o.** 23	**t.** 21	

True-False Questions

1. True
2. False. Personal consumption expenditures account for approximately two-thirds of GDP.
3. False. A final good is produced for final use.
4. False. A used car has already been counted as part of a previous year's GDP.
5. False. Expenditures on the National Guard and other military expenditures are part of government purchases.
6. False. An increase in net exports causes GDP to increase.
7. False. The underground economy is left out of GDP calculations.
8. True
9. True
10. True
11. False. The sum of the value added for intermediate goods will equal GDP.
12. True
13. True
14. False. Stockholders receive corporate profit in the form of dividend income.
15. False. GNP is equal to GDP plus factor income to Americans producing overseas minus factor income to foreigners producing in the United States.

Multiple-Choice Questions

1. b	**6.** b	**11.** a	**16.** a	**21.** c
2. e	**7.** d	**12.** e	**17.** c	**22.** e
3. a	**8.** a	**13.** a	**18.** d	**23.** a
4. d	**9.** d	**14.** a	**19.** c	**24.** e
5. c	**10.** e	**15.** c	**20.** c	

Fill in the Blanks

1. personal consumption expenditures; gross private domestic investment; government purchases; net exports
2. the value of housework; the underground economy; leisure; improvement in the quality of goods and services; the cost of environmental damage
3. compensation of employees; rental income; corporate profits; net interest; proprietors' income
4. tax avoidance
5. plus; minus

Discussion Questions

1. The expenditure approach corresponds to the money flow from households, businesses, government, and the international sector purchasing final goods and services. The income approach corresponds to the money flow from buyers of resources to the households that supply those resources for use in production. The two money flows are equivalent.

2. Consumption is by far the largest category of expenditure. Consumption accounted for some 68 percent of GDP in 1996. Government spending accounted for approximately 18 percent of 1996 GDP, investment accounted for another 15 percent, and net exports were negative. As a percentage of GDP, the difference between exports and imports was about 1 percent.

3. Inventories are unsold output. Firms keep stocks of finished final goods, as well as stocks of resources used to produce those goods, in reserve in order to promote efficiency in production and sales. A firm can't expect to sell or to produce if it doesn't have a stock of goods to sell or raw materials to use in production.

4. Compensation of employees dwarfs all the other categories with about 71 percent of the total in 1996. Rental income was only 2.3 percent of the total in 1996. Corporate profit, net interest, and proprietors' income were 12 percent, 6.8 percent, and 8.3 percent of national income, respectively, in 1996.

5. NDP is a better measure of a country's rate of growth because it excludes investment expenditures made to replace used-up capital. NDP focuses on investment over and above depreciation. An economy must have positive net investment in order to grow over time.

6. Personal income is probably more useful. This is because personal income shows the income that households actually receive, including transfer payments. Also, certain taxes that are withheld from income, like Social Security taxes, are accounted for by personal income. Personal income minus direct taxes gives disposable personal income.

Problems

1. GDP = Consumption + Investment + Government Purchases + Exports − Imports
   = 1,000 + 400 + 400 + 100 − 180 = $1,720

   GNP = GDP + Factor Incomes from the Rest of the World − Factor Incomes to the Rest of the World
   = 1,720 + 80 − 70 = $1,730

   NDP = GDP − Depreciation = 1,720 − 100 = $1,620

   National Income = NDP − Indirect Business Taxes = 1,620 − 70 = $1,550

   Personal Income = National Income − Income Earned but not Received + Income Received but not Earned
   = 1,550 − 110 + 200 = $1,640

   Personal Income − Direct Taxes = 1,640 − 200 = $1,440

2. GDP will decrease by $20 to $1,700 because the $100 drop in corporate profits is partly offset by an $80 increase in exports. Changes in depreciation and income earned but not received have no effect on GDP.

Homework Questions

True-False Questions — If a statement is false, explain why.

1. The United States GNP measures the dollar value of all final output by United States citizens while the GDP measures the dollar value of all final output produced in the United States. (T/F)

2. The circular flow of goods, services, resources, and money shows that for every dollar's worth of output produced, there is a dollar's worth of income generated. (T/F)

3. A trade deficit (imports greater than exports) causes GDP to increase. (T/F)

4. If inventories accumulate over a year for a firm, they are regarded as depreciation since storing them is expensive. (T/F)

5. Transfer payments do not add to GDP. (T/F)

Multiple-Choice Questions

1. One difference between GDP and GNP is that
   a. factor incomes to foreign-owned firms in the United States are included in GNP
   b. depreciation is excluded from GNP
   c. the corporate profits tax is excluded from GDP
   d. indirect business taxes are counted twice in GDP
   e. factor incomes to foreign-owned firms in the United States are included in GDP

2. One of the reasons for not including such items as leisure in the calculation of GDP is that
   a. including these items is conceptually difficult
   b. these are not government-sanctioned items
   c. it is difficult to accurately measure the value of these items on a consistent basis
   d. to include these items would cause GDP to decrease
   e. these items add nothing to productivity

3. The smallest portion of personal consumption expenditures is accounted for by
   a. inventory investment
   b. productivity
   c. purchases of services
   d. purchases of nondurable goods
   e. purchases of durable goods

4. Adam Smith maintained that only the production of goods that promote economic growth should be included in GDP because
   a. services are less valuable than goods
   b. services are hard to measure
   c. goods sustain the physical well-being of people and contribute to the wealth of nations
   d. services are generated by people who lack a work ethic
   e. goods can be reproduced but services cannot

5. Disposable personal income is
   a. taxes and transfer payments
   b. households' consumption expenditures
   c. households' savings
   d. expenditures on luxury items by households
   e. the sum of personal consumption expenditures and saving

Discussion Questions/Problems

1. If capital depreciation is greater than gross private domestic investment, what will be the effect on GDP? Explain.

2. Describe three ways that the calculation of GDP might be improved.

CHAPTER 6

CONSUMPTION AND INVESTMENT

Chapter in a Nutshell

Producers and consumers make their production and consumption decisions simultaneously and independently of each other. This simple observation may help to explain why the economy can, at times, slide into recession and at other times bound into prosperity. For example, if production exceeds consumption, then inventories accumulate and firms will likely cut back production, causing an increase in unemployment. On the other hand, if consumption exceeds production, then firms will increase production, hire more workers, and cause unemployment to decrease. So it is critical to understand how households make consumption decisions.

Economists posit that a relationship exists between people's consumption and their disposable income. The **consumption function** is written as C = f(Y), that is to say, consumption is a function of income. John Maynard Keynes developed the **absolute income hypothesis,** which states that as national income increases, consumption increases, but by diminishing amounts. Keynes believed that the **marginal propensity to consume (MPC)** decreased as the absolute level of income increased. However, Simon Kuznets's research showed that the MPC tends to remain fairly constant regardless of the absolute level of national income. New hypotheses about consumption were developed as a result of Kuznets's work. These included Duesenberry's **relative income hypothesis**, Friedman's **permanent income hypothesis**, and Modigliani's **life-cycle hypothesis**. As a result of the work done by these and other economists on the nature of consumption spending, we now represent consumption as a straight-line curve that increases as national income increases. Some consumption, called **autonomous consumption**, would occur at zero national income. The consumption curve shifts as a result of changes in real asset and money holdings, expectations of price changes, changes in credit and interest rates, and changes in taxation. Based on the fact that the part of national income not spent on consumption is **saving**, a saving curve can be derived from the consumption curve. The **marginal propensity to save (MPS)**, which is the slope of the saving curve, is analogous to the MPC.

Another spending decision in the economy is that made by producers on investment. Economists use the concept **autonomous investment** to reflect the fact that investment is independent of the level of national income. Determinants of investment include the level of technology, the interest rate, expectations of future economic growth, and the rate of capacity utilization. Compared to consumption, investment is quite volatile, meaning that it can change quite dramatically over short periods of time. Together, consumption and investment form the two major building blocks of the Keynesian model.

After you study this chapter, you should be able to:

- Discuss Keynes's **absolute income hypothesis**.
- Define the **marginal propensity to consume**.
- Describe Duesenberry's **relative income hypothesis**.
- Explain Friedman's **permanent income hypothesis**.
- Present examples to illustrate the **life-cycle hypothesis** of consumption.
- List factors that cause shifts in the consumption curve.
- Derive the saving curve from the consumption curve.
- Write an equation for the consumption function.
- Discuss the determinants of **autonomous investment**.
- Explain the volatile nature of investment.

Concept Check — See how you do on these multiple choice questions.

What was Keynes's hypothesis about change in the marginal propensity to consume as income increased?

1. Keynes's **absolute income hypothesis** states that as a person's
   a. income increases, his/her MPC decreases
   b. income increases, his/her MPC increases
   c. income increases, his/her MPC is constant
   d. income is more transitory, his/her MPC is lower
   e. age increases, his/her MPC decreases

How does a person's social class status influence consumption behavior in Duesenberry's theory?

2. Duesenberry's **relative income hypothesis** states that the marginal propensity to consume is
   a. the same across different social classes
   b. lower for people with high incomes than for people with low incomes
   c. decreasing as income is increasing
   d. a function of disposable income
   e. a function of transitory income

What does autonomous mean?

3. **Autonomous consumption** is
   a. a function of disposable income
   b. a function of national income
   c. a function of GDP
   d. a function of saving
   e. independent of the level of income

If the marginal propensity to consume is the change in consumption that results from a change in income, then what would be the definition of the marginal propensity to save?

4. When the consumption curve is a straight line, the **marginal propensity to save**
   a. is equal to one plus the MPC
   b. increases as income increases
   c. is equal to one minus the MPC
   d. decreases as income increases
   e. is that part of national income not spent on consumption

How do changes in the current level of income influence autonomous investment?

5. **Autonomous investment** is determined by all of the following **except**
   a. income
   b. the level of technology
   c. the interest rate
   d. expectations of future economic growth
   e. the rate of capacity utilization

Am I on the Right Track?

Your answers to the questions above should be **a**, **b**, **e**, **c**, and **a**. You need to take four distinct steps to get on the right track in this chapter. First, you must understand the various hypotheses about consumption that have been advanced by different economists. Second, you need to be comfortable graphing the consumption curve and working with the consumption equation. That done, graphing the saving curve should be no problem because saving is the part of national income not spent on consumption. The last step is to understand the determinants of investment spending by firms and why economists use the concept of autonomous investment.

Key Terms Quiz — Match the terms on the left with the definitions in the column on the right.

1. consumption function
2. transitory income
3. absolute income hypothesis
4. autonomous consumption
5. marginal propensity to consume (MPC)
6. saving
7. relative income hypothesis
8. marginal propensity to save (MPS)
9. permanent income hypothesis
10. 45-degree line
11. life-cycle hypothesis
12. intended investment
13. permanent income
14. autonomous investment

_____ a. consumption spending that is independent of the level of income

_____ b. as national income increases, consumption spending increases at a constant rate

_____ c. investment spending that producers intend to undertake

_____ d. the unexpected gain or loss of income that a person experiences

_____ e. a line drawn at a 45-degree angle showing all points at which the distance to the horizontal axis equals the distance to the vertical axis; same as income line

_____ f. the ratio of the change in consumption spending to a given change income

_____ g. the change in saving induced by a change in income

_____ h. the relationship between consumption and income

_____ i. investment that is independent of the level of income

_____ j. the regular income a person expects to earn annually

_____ k. that part of national income not spent on consumption

_____ l. a person's consumption spending is related to his or her permanent income

_____ m. as national income increases, consumption spending increases, but by diminishing amounts

_____ n. typically, a person's MPC is high during young adulthood, decreases during the middle-age years, and increases when the person retires

Graphing Tutorial

It would be surprising to find any students who have not graphed linear equations in their high school algebra classes. Drawing these graphs wasn't terribly difficult then, and it isn't now. The consumption curve, saving curve and investment curve are all variants of graphs of equations for straight lines. Suppose that we have a consumption function in the form $C = a + bY$, where C is consumption spending, a is autonomous consumption, b is the MPC, and Y is the level of national income. Let $a = 100$ and $b = .75$. Now the equation reads $C = 100 + .75Y$. Graphing this equation is fairly easy because we know the value for autonomous consumption and the MPC. In algebraic terms, autonomous consumption is the vertical intercept for the graph of the consumption equation, and the MPC is the slope. We know that when $Y = 0$, $C = 100$ and that for every $100 increase in national income there is a $75 increase in consumption. That's all we need to know in order to graph the consumption curve. The consumption curve that corresponds to this consumption equation is shown on the following page along with the income line.

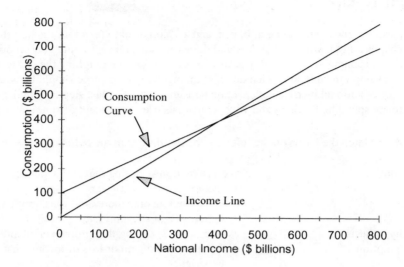

Note that the intercept on the consumption axis for the consumption curve is $100 billion. This is autonomous consumption — the value for a in the consumption equation. Also, for each $100 billion increase in national income, there is a $75 billion increase in consumption spending, which gives us a slope of .75 — the value for b in the consumption equation. The income line (also known as the 45-degree line) shows all of the points where the distance along the horizontal axis is equal to the distance along the vertical axis.

Now let's derive the saving function and graph the saving curve. We know that saving is the amount of national income that isn't spent on consumption. Therefore, national income minus consumption is equal to saving. Algebraically, we have $Y - C = S$, where S is saving. Substituting our expression $a - bY$ for C in the equation we have $S = Y - (a + bY)$. Factoring and rearranging terms, the saving equation can be written as $S = -a + (1 - b)Y$. In this equation, the vertical intercept is equal to $-a$ and the slope is equal to $1 - b$. Staying with the values for a and b used above for the consumption function, when income is equal to zero, saving is $-$100 billion and the slope of the saving function (the marginal propensity to save) is equal to $1 - .75$, or .25. For every $100 increase in national income, there is a $25 increase in saving. The saving equation is $S = -100 + .25Y$. The saving curve that corresponds to this saving equation is shown below.

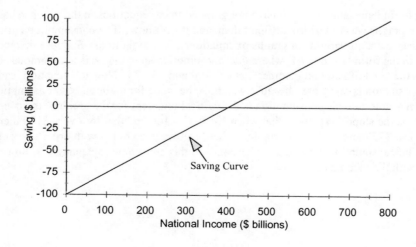

Compare

the consumption curve to the saving curve. Suppose that national income is $800 billion. In the graph of the consumption curve, when national income is $800 billion, consumption is $700 billion. Therefore, national income minus consumption *(Y – C)* is $100 billion. This is the value of saving at the $800 billion level of national income. The saving curve shows that saving is indeed $100 billion when national income is $800 billion.

Now find the point in the graph of the saving curve where saving is zero. This point corresponds to a national income of $400 billion. In the graph of the consumption curve, at an income level of $400 billion, the consumption curve intersects the income line. National income minus consumption, which is equal to saving, is zero at the $400 billion income level. You can see the correspondence between the points on the consumption curve and the points on the saving curve at different levels of national income.

Finally, we turn to graphing the investment curve. Investment is considered autonomous, that is, independent of the level of national income. Therefore, the investment curve can be graphed as a horizontal line at the level of autonomous investment. Suppose that the level of autonomous investment is $75 billion. A graph of this investment curve is shown below.

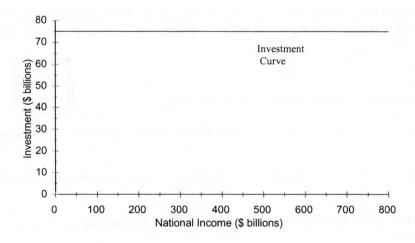

Graphing Pitfalls

The consumption curve, saving curve, and investment curve are all plotted on axes that measure national income on the horizontal axis and consumption, saving, and investment, respectively, on the vertical axis. Therefore, each of these curves will start from an intercept on the vertical axis. You will never find one of these curves starting from the national income axis. For example, the consumption curve drawn below, starting from the national income axis, makes no sense. What is autonomous consumption in this case? Why aren't there values for consumption when national income is below $100 billion? The consumption function always originates from an intercept on the vertical axis.

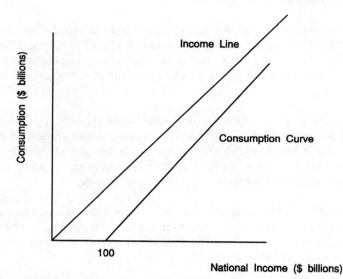

Never draw a consumption curve with the intercept on the national income axis.
The intercept for the consumption curve is always on the consumption axis!

True-False Questions — If a statement is false, explain why.

1. Consumption spending decisions are carefully coordinated with production decisions in our economy. (T/F)

2. The most important factor determining people's consumption behavior is the level of their income. (T/F)

3. Keynes's absolute income hypothesis asserts that as national income increases, consumption increases, but at an increasing rate. (T/F)

4. Keynes believed that the marginal propensity to consume is constant. (T/F)

5. Simon Kuznets's data supported the idea that the marginal propensity to consume is constant. (T/F)

6. Duesenberry's relative income hypothesis suggests that the rich have relatively high MPCs and the poor have relatively low MPCs. (T/F)

7. If all people's incomes increase at the same rate, then their relative incomes increase as well. (T/F)

8. Modigliani's life-cycle hypothesis suggests that consumption fluctuates less than income over a person's lifetime. (T/F)

9. The expectation that the price level will increase induces consumers to save less and consume more now, which causes the consumption function to shift upward. (T/F)

10. If autonomous consumption increases, then the consumption curve shifts up and the saving function shifts down. (T/F)

11. An increase in interest rates shifts the consumption curve upward. (T/F)

12. We can determine consumption spending for any income level if we know the level of autonomous consumption and the marginal propensity to consume. (T/F)

13. The saving curve crosses the national income axis at the level of income where the consumption curve crosses the income line. (T/F)

14. Intended investment will increase when new technology is introduced. (T/F)

15. Because intended investment is related to the level of national income, it is called autonomous investment. (T/F)

Multiple-Choice Questions

1. All of the following are characteristics of intended investment **except** that
   a. its level is influenced by the rate of capacity utilization
   b. as the interest rate falls, the quantity of intended investment increases
   c. its size is dependent on the level of national income
   d. it is by nature volatile
   e. its level is influenced by the introduction of new technologies

2. Milton Friedman proposed the
   a. permanent income hypothesis
   b. life-cycle hypothesis
   c. absolute income hypothesis
   d. relative income hypothesis
   e. saving equals investment hypothesis

3. At a specific level of national income, saving can be measured by
   a. the MPS multiplied by the level of national income
   b. 1+ MPC multiplied by the level of national income
   c. the vertical distance between the income line and the consumption function
   d. the vertical distance between the consumption function and the saving function
   e. 1 – MPC multiplied by the level of national income

4. The theory of consumption which argues that consumption is based on a household's long-run estimate of their income is called the
   a. relative income hypothesis
   b. Duesenberry theory
   c. permanent income hypothesis
   d. Modigliani life-cycle hypothesis
   e. Keynes absolute income hypothesis

5. All of the following are examples of Friedman's concept of transitory income concept **except**
   a. a jockey winning the Triple Crown — the Kentucky Derby, the Preakness, and Belmont — in one year
   b. a $10 million winner of the Texas lottery
   c. a farmer whose crops are wiped out by a drought
   d. a physician experiencing a 20-fold increase in her patient load during a one-year epidemic
   e. David Letterman's $14 million salary at CBS

6. The marginal propensity to save (MPS)
   a. plus the MPC = national income
   b. plus the MPC = one
   c. plus intended investment = one
   d. minus national income = consumption
   e. represents the economy's level of savings

7. One conclusion to be drawn from the Modigliani life-cycle hypothesis is that consumption is
   a. a decreasing function of income for the entire economy
   b. a smaller fraction of income during a person's peak income years
   c. determined by one's class status
   d. very responsive to changes in transitory income
   e. virtually impossible to model because of its volatile nature

8. Because intended investment is independent of the level of national income, we graph the investment curve as
   a. downward sloping
   b. upward sloping
   c. horizontal
   d. vertical
   e. diagonal

9. The change in consumption divided by the change in income is
   a. Keynes's relative income hypothesis
   b. the marginal propensity to consume
   c. equal to $a + bY$
   d. equal to $1 + MPS$
   e. equal to autonomous consumption

10. Keynes's absolute income hypothesis cannot be correct because studies have shown that
   a. as disposable income increases, consumption increases at a diminishing rate
   b. the marginal propensity to consume is constant
   c. rich households save a larger fraction of additional income than poor households
   d. income is never absolute and thus a hypothesis can't be formed
   e. autonomous consumption is zero

11. Autonomous consumption refers to
    a. MPCs that are less than one
    b. MPCs that are greater than one
    c. consumption that is independent of the level of income
    d. permanent consumption associated with Friedman's permanent income hypothesis
    e. transitory consumption associated with Friedman's permanent income hypothesis

12. Shifts in the consumption curve are caused by all of the following **except** changes in
    a. asset holdings
    b. income
    c. price level expectations
    d. credit availability
    e. interest rates

13. If the consumption curve is drawn through the origin,
    a. consumption and income are the same
    b. the marginal propensity to consume is zero
    c. autonomous saving is very high
    d. autonomous consumption is zero
    e. the marginal propensity to consume will decrease as income increases

14. If the government increases income taxes, the
    a. intended investment curve shifts upward
    b. consumption curve shifts upward
    c. consumption curve shifts downward
    d. national income decreases because people's after-tax income has fallen
    e. actual investment curve shifts downward

15. When the MPS = 0.30 and autonomous consumption is $30 billion, then
    a. the MPC = 0.30
    b. consumption spending = $10 billion
    c. the MPC = 0.70
    d. consumption spending = $900 billion
    e. the MPC = 1.00

16. When the MPS = 0.30 and autonomous consumption is $30 billion, then the consumption equation is
    a. $C = 90 + .3Y$
    b. $C = 10 + 30Y$
    c. $C = 0.3 + 30Y$
    d. $C = 30 + 0.3Y$
    e. $C = 30 + 0.7Y$

17. The demand curve for investment is downward sloping. When it is graphed, it shows _____ on the horizontal axis and _____ on the vertical axis.
    a. income; investment
    b. investment; income
    c. investment; the interest rate
    d. the interest rate; investment
    e. income; the interest rate

18. Which of the following is not a determinant of autonomous investment?
    a. income
    b. the level of technology
    c. the interest rate
    d. expectations of future economic growth
    e. the rate of capacity utilization

19. If producers expect economic growth to be more rapid in the future, then it is likely that
    a. saving will decrease
    b. interest rates will decrease
    c. the investment curve will shift up
    d. the marginal propensity to consume will decrease
    e. autonomous consumption will decrease

20. If stock market prices increase dramatically so that those who own stock perceive that their wealth has increased, then, *ceteris paribus*
    a. the consumption function shifts downward because saving increases
    b. intended investment increases because it is now more profitable
    c. the saving curve shifts upward
    d. the saving curve is unchanged because only consumption is affected
    e. the consumption function shifts upward

The following questions relate to the historical and theoretical perspectives in the text.

21. Keynes's approach to dealing with the Great Depression of the 1930s differed from the conventional wisdom of classical economics in that
    a. he argued the depression was temporary and the economy would recover on its own
    b. he advanced long-run economic policies to end the depression whereas classical economics focused on the short run
    c. he pushed for harsher reparations from Germany to provide financial resources for the British economic recovery
    d. he believed the economy would not recover on its own and that policies should focus on the short run
    e. he advanced a theory of probability that could be applied to economics

22. Research suggests that the short-run consumption curve _____ while the long-run consumption curve _____.
    a. is quite steep; is very flat
    b. intersects the vertical axis above the origin; runs through the origin
    c. has a large average propensity to consume; has a large marginal propensity to consume
    d. has a large marginal propensity to consume; has a small marginal propensity to consume
    e. has a large marginal propensity to consume; has a large average propensity to consume

23. Which of the following is not a reason for saving according to either Alfred Marshall or Christopher Carroll?
    a. family affection
    b. to increase the wealth of the family for future generations
    c. to acquire power
    d. to increase the level of consumption achieved during retirement
    e. to acquire social status

Fill in the Blanks

1. The consumption function is a _____ relationship stating that a(n) _____ in

   income _____ consumption.

2. Friedman developed the permanent income hypothesis that distinguishes between _____

   income and _____ income and states that consumption is dependent on

   _____ income.

3. Empirical research done by Simon Kuznets showed that contrary to Keynes's

   _____, the nation's _____ is constant.

4. The consumption function shifts due to changes in _____,

   _____, _____, and _____.

5. Because changes in investment tend to be unrelated to the level of _____,

   investment is regarded as _____.

Discussion Questions

1. Suppose that Keynes's absolute income hypothesis had been shown to be correct. What would happen to consumption spending as national income increased in a country? How would producers respond to this change in consumption spending and what would be the likely impact on GDP growth over time?

2. Suppose that your boss gives you a year-end bonus and you count it as transitory income. Suppose that this happens three years in a row. Would you continue to count this income as transitory? Why or why not?

3. Why does Duesenberry's relative income hypothesis predict that the MPC will be constant as national income increases?

4. What is the difference between a shift in the consumption curve and a movement along the consumption curve?

Problems

1. a. Suppose that autonomous consumption is $600 and the marginal propensity to consume is 0.60. Write an algebraic expression for the consumption equation.

   b. Sketch a graph of this consumption curve that corresponds to the consumption equation above. Include the income line in your drawing and label autonomous consumption.

   c. Calculate the level of income at which income is equal to consumption, that is, where the consumption curve intersects the income line.

2. a. Using the consumption equation from problem 1, what is the MPS for the corresponding saving curve?

   b. At what level of income will saving be zero? (Hint: What is the level of income where consumption is equal to income?) Use this point and the MPS to sketch the saving curve.

Everyday Applications

Duesenberry, Friedman, and Modigliani each presented very different hypotheses to explain consumption spending behavior. Apply each theory to your own family's experience. How well do these economists' ideas describe your family's consumption behavior? Does one theory seem to fit better than the others?

Economics Online

Most of you are entering young adulthood — the stage of the life cycle where people typically accumulate substantial debt. You may be incurring debt with your college education. Buying a home and a new car with borrowed funds are other ways that young adults add to their debt levels. You can generate considerable information about these key life-cycle consumption spending decisions from the Web. Intellichoice (*http://www.intellichoice.com*) is a site that provides dealer prices and ownership costs on many car makes and models. FinancCenter/Smartcalc (*http://www.financenter.com*) will calculate your car and mortgage payments and show you how much you need to save in order to retire. It's never too soon to start planning.

Answers to Questions

Key Terms Quiz

a. 4	**f.** 5	**k.** 6
b. 7	**g.** 8	**l.** 9
c. 12	**h.** 1	**m.** 3
d. 2	**i.** 14	**n.** 11
e. 10	**j.** 13	

True-False Questions

1. False. Consumption spending and consumption-production decisions are made independently of each other.
2. True
3. False. The absolute income hypothesis states that as national income increases, consumption increases at a decreasing rate.
4. False. Keynes believed that the marginal propensity to consume decreases as income increases.
5. True
6. False. Duesenberry's relative income hypothesis suggests that the poor have high MPCs and the rich have relatively low MPCs. The economy's MPC is constant, however.
7. False. If all incomes go up at the same rate, relative income is unchanged.
8. True
9. True
10. True
11. False. Consumer purchases of costly durable goods, which are typically financed, will fall, and the consumption curve shifts down.
12. True
13. True
14. True
15. False. Investment is called autonomous because it is unrelated to the level of income.

Multiple-Choice Questions

1. c	6. b	11. c	16. e	21. d
2. a	7. b	12. b	17. c	22. b
3. c	8. c	13. d	18. a	23. d
4. c	9. b	14. c	19. c	
5. e	10. b	15. c	20. e	

Fill in the Blanks

1. causal; increase; increases
2. permanent; transitory; permanent
3. absolute income hypothesis; MPC
4. real asset and money holdings; expectations of changes in the price level; credit and interest rates; taxes
5. national income; autonomous

Discussion Questions

1. Because Keynes's absolute income hypothesis for consumption spending states that the MPC decreases as national income increases, consumption spending would tend to rise at a rate slower than national income. Producers would probably note unsold goods piling up in their warehouses and would respond by slowing production. GDP growth would likely slow down over time as a result.

2. Probably not. Once income that is initially perceived to be transitory is received in consecutive years, it becomes part of permanent income. Is three years enough? Would you expect to earn a bonus every year? If so, this year-end bonus becomes a part of permanent income.

3. The relative income hypothesis states that the MPC differs between social classes with the poor and middle classes having a higher MPC than upper-class households. However, as national income increases, if everyone's income rises at roughly the same rate, the poor are still poor in relative terms. Therefore they will still have a higher MPC than those who earn higher incomes. On average, for the entire spectrum of social classes, the MPC remains unchanged.

4. A shift in the consumption curve is caused by a change in one or more of the determinants of consumption — real asset and money holdings, expectations of changes in the price level, credit and interest rates, and taxes. Movements along the consumption function are caused by changes in national income. If national income increases, then consumption increases at a rate determined by the marginal propensity to consume — the slope of the consumption function.

Problems

1. a. The consumption equation is $C = 600 + .6Y$.

   b. The graph of this equation is shown on the following page..

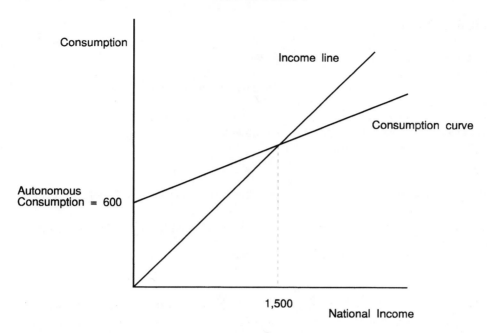

c. The consumption curve intersects the income curve at the $1,500 level of national income. This can be
   calculated by setting consumption equal to national income and solving for Y. We can write
   $C = 600 + .6Y = Y$. Then, $600 = .4Y$ and $Y = 1,500$.

2. a. Because we know that the MPC + MPS = 1, the MPS must be .4 if the MPC = .6.

   b. Saving will be zero at the $1,500 level of national income. This is because saving is that part of national
      income not spent on consumption. If consumption is equal to national income, then saving must be zero.
      The saving curve must run through the point $1,500 on the national income axis. In order to draw the
      saving curve, we need one more point. We can use the fact that the slope is .4 to find another point.
      Suppose there is a change in national income equal to $-1,500$. Then, $.4$ = change in saving/$-1,500$. The
      change in saving is equal to $.4 \times -1,500 = -600$. When income is zero, saving is -600. A sketch of the
      saving curve is shown below.

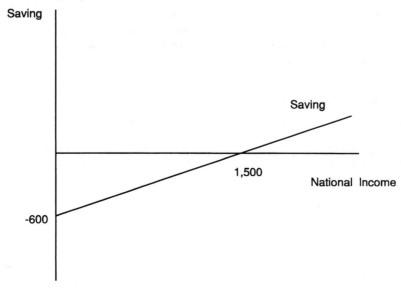

Homework Questions

True-False Questions — If a statement is false, explain why.

1. In the Keynesian aggregate expenditures model, investment is independent of the level of income. (T/F)

2. Duesenberry's relative income hypothesis holds that poorer households have higher marginal propensities to consume than do middle class and wealthy households. (T/F)

3. Keynes's idea that as income increases, consumption increases, but at a slower rate was shown to be correct in subsequent research. (T/F)

4. A decrease in autonomous consumption will cause the saving curve to shift upward. (T/F)

5. Dramatic advances in technology associated with production of goods and services will cause the investment curve to shift upward. (T/F)

Multiple-Choice Questions

1. Research regarding the relationship between consumption and the level of national income shows that the marginal propensity to consume
   a. increases as income increases
   b. decreases as income increases just as Keynes predicted
   c. is constant as income increases
   d. is higher for workers in their peak income earning years than for retirees
   e. is lower for young people who have just finished college

2. All of the following are determinants of autonomous investment **except**
   a. interest rates
   b. credit availability
   c. the level of income
   d. changes in the level of income
   e. the pace of technological change

3. The life-cycle hypothesis on consumption behavior suggests that people at various stages of the life cycle,
   a. spend everything they earn so saving ends up at zero
   b. increase their marginal propensity to consume as income increases
   c. decrease their marginal propensity to consume as income increases
   d. have differing MPCs, which is still consistent with a constant MPC for the economy
   e. consume according to class status

4. When the marginal propensity to save is equal to 0.2 and autonomous consumption is $200 billion, then the consumption equation is
   a. C = 200 + .3Y
   b. C = 100 + 30Y
   c. C = .2 + 300Y
   d. C = 200 + .8Y
   e. C = 20 + .3Y

5. One difference between the short-run consumption curve and the long-run consumption curve is that the short-run consumption curve
   a. has its intercept above the origin and the long-run consumption curve runs through the origin
   b. runs through the origin and the long-run consumption curve has its intercept above the origin
   c. runs through the origin and the long-run consumption is the income line
   d. has its intercept above the origin and the long-run consumption curve has its intercept on the national income axis to the right of the origin
   e. has its intercept above the origin and the long-run consumption curve has its intercept below the origin

Discussion Questions/Problems

1. Why do people save?

2. Suppose the consumption equation is given by $C = 100 + .75Y$.

   a. Write an equation for saving that corresponds to this consumption equation.

   b. Sketch a graph for the saving curve. Calculate and label on your graph the level of national income where saving is equal to zero.

CHAPTER 7

EQUILIBRIUM NATIONAL INCOME

Chapter in a Nutshell

Two very different groups of people are always at work making decisions concerning spending, saving, and investment that affect each other. The income households earn is spent and saved: $Y = C + S$. Producers produce an equivalent value of goods and services in the form of consumption and investment: $Y = C + I$. By definition, $C + I = C + S$. But the I (investment) in this last equation is **actual investment**. It's what producers end up investing, not necessarily what they intended to invest, I_i. Sometimes they end up with more actual investment than they intended (creating **unwanted inventories**) and so cut output. At other times, their actual investment is less than what they intended to produce, and as a result, they increase output. How they respond to their actual investments and why they do it is what this chapter's about.

The total of what people spend on consumption, businesses spend on investment, government spends on its purchases, and foreigners spend on net exports is described as **aggregate expenditures**. Are these expenditures greater than, less than, or equal to the total income earned in the economy? The answer determines whether national income increases, decreases, or is in equilibrium. In any case, if the economy is not in equilibrium, it is always on its way there. Why is this so?

Suppose that consumers spend on consumption an amount less than what producers produced for consumption. Some consumer goods remain unsold as **unwanted inventories**. Actual investment is greater than intended investment. Producers lay off workers, employment declines, and national income declines until it reaches the **equilibrium level of national income** where aggregate expenditures equal national income at a lower level.

Now suppose that consumers spend on consumption an amount greater than what producers produced for consumption. Wanted inventories (investment goods) are converted into consumption goods. Actual investment is less than intended investment. Producers hire more workers to restore their inventories, causing both national income and employment increase. Aggregate expenditures and national income rise toward a higher equilibrium level of national income. Only when producers produce for consumption an amount equal to what consumers purchase for consumption will producers' intended investment be equal to saving by consumers. When producers' intended investment is equal to consumers' saving, the economy is in equilibrium.

Changes in intended investment cause the equilibrium level of national income to change. The relationship between these two changes is explained by the **income multiplier**. An increase in intended investment leads to an increase in income, a fraction of which is consumed (the marginal propensity to consume multiplied by the initial increase in investment) and becomes income for other people. Repeated rounds of income increases and consumption increases occur, with each round being smaller than the previous one. The multiplier, equal to $1/(1 - MPC)$, gives the factor by which the initial round of investment is multiplied into new income. Just as an increase in investment causes a multiple expansion in national income, a decrease in investment will cause a multiple decrease in national income.

The consumers' and producers' behavior that leads the economy to equilibrium also produces a rather surprising consequence known as the **paradox of thrift**. It says: The more people try to save, the more national income will fall, leaving them with no more, and perhaps less, saving in the end. Why? An increase in saving is really the same as a decrease in consumption, which is a decrease in aggregate expenditures. It sets in motion a fall in national income to a new and lower level of equilibrium. There, saving is the same or less than it was at the original level of income.

After you study this chapter, you should be able to:

- Explain why consumption spending and **intended investment** spending decisions are independent.
- Define **aggregate expenditure** and graph the **aggregate expenditure curve**.
- Show how changes in inventories move the economy toward an **equilibrium level of national income**.
- Explain the relationship between **saving** and **investment**.
- Create an example to show the logic of the **income multiplier**.
- Illustrate the **paradox of thrift** with a numerical example.

Concept Check — See how you do on these multiple-choice questions.

This question asks you to think about what aggregate expenditures includes.

1. **Aggregate expenditure** is equal to
   a. spending by consumers on consumption goods
   b. spending by businesses on investment goods
   c. spending by government
   d. spending by foreigners on net exports
   e. the sum of a, b, c, and d

What determines the size of the income multiplier?

2. The **income multiplier** is larger when
   a. the marginal propensity to consume is larger
   b. the marginal propensity to save is larger
   c. spending by government is larger
   d. the change in income is smaller
   e. the marginal propensity to consume is smaller

What is the impact of an increase in saving on aggregate expenditures and the equilibrium level of national income?

3. An example of the **paradox of thrift** is
   a. consumers who attempt to save more but find they cannot go without basic consumption goods
   b. an increase in saving that leads to a lower equilibrium level of national income and the same or lower saving
   c. a high marginal propensity to save that is matched by a high marginal propensity to consume
   d. an increase in saving that leads to more investment, higher income, and higher consumption
   e. an increase in interest rates that leads to lower investment and lower saving

The economy moves automatically toward equilibrium. Will national income rise or fall in order to move toward equilibrium in the case described in this example? How does it happen?

4. If the level of national income is above the **equilibrium level of national income**, then
   a. autonomous consumption will fall and the economy will move toward equilibrium
   b. inventories will accumulate and production will fall, moving the economy toward equilibrium
   c. intended investment is equal to saving
   d. consumption spending is greater than the value of consumption goods produced
   e. the marginal propensity to save is too low to achieve equilibrium

When do unwanted inventories become part of actual investment? When does the decrease in wanted inventories decrease actual investment?

5. When **actual investment** is equal to intended investment,
    a. saving is zero
    b. unwanted inventories are increasing
    c. unwanted inventories are decreasing
    d. unwanted inventories are zero
    e. the economy is below the equilibrium level of national income

Am I on the Right Track?

Your answers to the questions above should be **e**, **a**, **b**, **b**, and **d**. The consumption spending decisions by consumers and the production decisions by producers will match each other only by accident. Therefore, the level of national income that is produced is unlikely to be the equilibrium level of national income. If consumption spending is less than the production of consumption goods, unwanted inventories accumulate, production decreases, and national income declines toward its equilibrium level. If consumption spending is greater than the production of consumption goods, wanted inventories are converted to consumption goods, production increases, and national income rises toward its equilibrium level. The mechanics of these adjustments toward equilibrium will be explored in the graphing tutorial.

Key Terms Quiz — Match the terms on the left with the definitions in the column on the right.

1. aggregate expenditure   _____ a. goods produced for consumption that remain unsold
2. aggregate expenditure (AE) curve   _____ b. the more people try to save, the more income falls, leaving them with no more, and perhaps with even less, saving
3. equilibrium level of national income   _____ c. the multiple by which income changes as a result of a change in aggregate expenditure
4. income multiplier   _____ d. spending by consumers on consumption goods, by businesses on investment goods, by government, and by foreigners on net exports
5. unwanted inventories   _____ e. a curve that shows the quantity of aggregate expenditures at different levels of national income or GDP
6. paradox of thrift   _____ f. investment spending that producers actually make — that is, intended investment plus or minus unintended changes in inventories
7. actual investment   _____ g. the level of national income where saving is equal to intended investment

Graphing Tutorial

This chapter presents a new graph that combines the consumption curve and the investment curve to show the equilibrium level of national income. Let's continue with the example presented in the graphing tutorial for Chapter 21 of the study guide to examine how the consumption curve and the investment curve are used to generate the aggregate expenditure curve in order to graph the equilibrium level of national income.

The consumption equation from the previous graphing tutorial is $C = 100 + .75Y$. and autonomous investment is $I_i = 75$. Autonomous investment is intended investment. These two equations are presented as curves along with the income line (45-degree line) in the graph below.

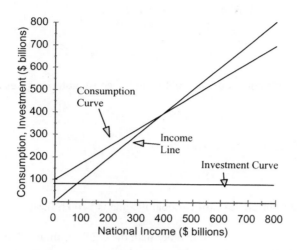

The aggregate expenditure curve can be drawn by adding the investment curve to the consumption curve. This will shift the consumption curve up by a constant $75 billion in the graph. The graph below shows the consumption curve and the aggregate expenditure curve that lies above and parallel to the consumption curve.

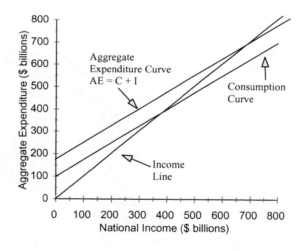

How do we locate the equilibrium level of national income in this diagram? We have defined the equilibrium level of national income as the level where $I_i = S$. In the graph, $C + I_i$ is the aggregate expenditure curve and $C + S$ is the income curve. Aggregate expenditure is equal to income where the two curves intersect at the $700 billion level of national income, so this is the equilibrium level of national income. At $700 billion, $I_i = S$.

Let's check our graph by calculating the equilibrium level of national income algebraically.

$$\text{In equilibrium} \quad Y = C + I_i$$
$$\text{and} \quad C = 100 + .75Y$$
$$\text{and} \quad I_i = 75$$
$$\text{then} \quad Y = (100 + .75Y) + 75.$$

Subtracting $.75Y$ from both sides of the equation and combining the constant terms gives us

$$.25Y = 175.$$

Finally, dividing both sides by .25 reduces the equation to

$$Y = 700.$$

This confirms our graph — the equilibrium level of national income is $700 billion.

What if we start at a level of national income other than the equilibrium level of national income? After all, it would be a chance event for the economy to automatically start out in equilibrium. How can we show the adjustment toward the equilibrium level of national income on the aggregate expenditure, national income graph? Consider the graph below, which shows just the aggregate expenditure curve and the income line.

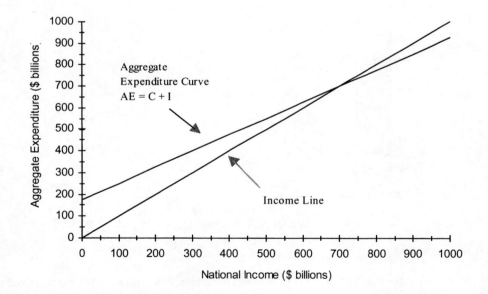

Suppose we start at a level of national income below the equilibrium, say, at $500 billion. The aggregate expenditure curve is above the income curve at $500 billion. Aggregate expenditure is greater than income so inventories decline. Wanted inventories are converted to consumer goods. Let's check our interpretation of the graph algebraically. Aggregate expenditure equals $C + I_i = 175 + .75Y = 175 + .75(500) = $ $550 billion. Aggregate expenditure exceeds national income by $50 billion. Therefore, producers increase output to restore their inventories, so employment and national income both increase as the economy moves toward the $700 billion level.

Suppose we start at a level of national income above the equilibrium, say, at $900 billion. The aggregate expenditure curve is below the income curve at $900 billion. Aggregate expenditure is less than national income so unwanted inventories accumulate. Checking our interpretation of the graph algebraically, we have $AE = 175 + .75Y = 175 + .75(900) = 850$. Now aggregate expenditure falls short of national income by $50 billion. Therefore, producers reduce output to rid themselves of unwanted inventories, so both employment and national income decrease as the economy moves toward the $700 billion level.

Graphing Pitfalls

When you add the investment curve to the consumption curve in order to draw the aggregate expenditure curve, make sure the aggregate expenditure curve is parallel to the consumption curve. Otherwise, you'll end up with the wrong equilibrium level of national income. It is tempting, perhaps, to draw the aggregate expenditure curve through the intersection of the consumption curve and the income curve, as depicted in the graph below. Don't make this mistake. Check to make sure that the consumption curve and the aggregate expenditure curve are parallel with the vertical distance between them equal to the amount of autonomous investment.

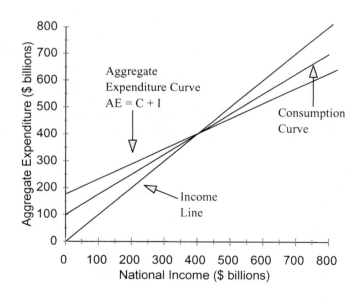

The aggregate expenditure curve should be parallel to and above the consumption curve by a vertical distance equal to autonomous investment. The two curves should not intersect, as drawn above.

True-False Questions — If a statement is false, explain why.

1. The amount that people intend to save will automatically equal the amount that investors intend to invest. (T/F)

2. Actual investment exceeds intended investment when inventories accumulate. (T/F)

3. If inventories are less than intended (or wanted) inventories, then production, employment, and national income will increase. (T/F)

4. Assuming there is no government spending and no foreign trade, then aggregate expenditure is equal to consumption plus saving. (T/F)

5. Spending by consumers on consumption goods is equal to consumption goods production at the equilibrium level of national income. (T/F)

6. When autonomous investment increases by $100, national income will increase by $100. (T/F)

7. A decrease in autonomous investment will have a smaller effect on national income than an equal increase in autonomous investment. (T/F)

8. The paradox of thrift states that if everyone decided to save more, consumption spending would fall, which would decrease national income, and with less income, people would end up saving no more than they did before. (T/F)

9. If the marginal propensity to consume increases, the income multiplier decreases. (T/F)

10. A decrease in the price level along an aggregate demand curve is reflected by an upward shift in the aggregate expenditure curve. (T/F)

11. Intended investment equal to saving is a signal for firms to reduce their inventories. (T/F)

12. An upward shift in the aggregate expenditure curve, caused by an increase in autonomous investment, appears as a rightward shift in the aggregate demand curve. (T/F)

13. The multiplier effect of an increase in investment is a new round of spending equal to the new investment followed by successive rounds of increased income with each one larger than the preceding round. (T/F)

14. The multiplier is the reciprocal of the marginal propensity to consume. (T/F)

15. J. M. Keynes believed that aggregate supply was more important than aggregate demand in determining the equilibrium level of national income. (T/F)

Multiple-Choice Questions

1. If actual investment is greater than intended investment, then
   a. the economy is in equilibrium
   b. national income must rise
   c. inventory investment is negative
   d. consumers are purchasing fewer goods and services than are produced
   e. unemployment will decrease

2. In the aggregate expenditure model of equilibrium national income determination,
   a. aggregate supply is vertical
   b. aggregate demand increases as the price level decreases
   c. the price level is assumed to be constant
   d. investment is a function of income
   e. the economy may move away from the equilibrium level of national income

3. If you read in the paper that intended investment hasn't changed but inventories are accumulating, then it is likely that
   a. the economy is about to experience a period of rapid growth
   b. the price level will rise dramatically
   c. the economy will experience a drop in production, employment, and income
   d. the economy will experience a rise in productivity
   e. intended investment will change

4. The income multiplier means that changes in autonomous investment will lead to
   a. a quick end to recessions
   b. even larger changes in national income
   c. a larger marginal propensity to consume
   d. a larger marginal propensity to save
   e. lower autonomous consumption

5. Suppose that the consumption equation is $C = \$50 + 0.75Y$ and $I = \$200$. The equilibrium level of national income is
   a. $10,000
   b. $1,000
   c. $100
   d. $750
   e. $333.33

6. Using the information given in question 5, if the level of national income is actually $1,200, then
   a. inventories will accumulate and production and income will fall
   b. inventories will accumulate and production and income will rise
   c. inventories will decline and production and income will rise
   d. inventories will decline and production and income will fall
   e. the economy will adjust to a new equilibrium

7. The graph below shows that if national income equals $800,
   a. inventories will decline and national income will increase
   b. inventories will decline and national income will decrease
   c. inventories will increase and national income will decrease
   d. inventories will increase and national income will increase
   e. intended investment and savings are equal

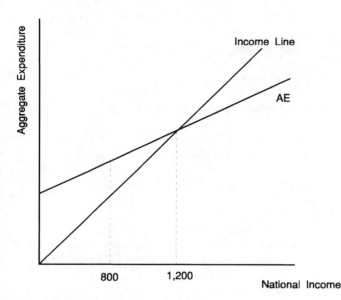

8. The income multiplier is the process whereby
   a. an increase in spending leads to exactly the same increase in equilibrium national income
   b. an increase in spending is multiplied into a larger increase in equilibrium national income
   c. an economy can automatically return to full employment during a recession
   d. the price level increases by multiples during periods of high inflation
   e. an economy can increase its GDP through increases in saving

9. Given a marginal propensity to consume of 0.90, an increase in investment spending equal to $100 will
   lead to a(n)
   a. decrease in national income of $1,000
   b. increase in national income of $1,000
   c. increase in national income of $100
   d. increase in national income of $900
   e. decrease in national income of $900

10. The basic idea behind the paradox of thrift is that
    a. by saving more people end up with higher incomes in the future
    b. it takes money to make money
    c. an increase in saving decreases national income so much that saving is, at best, unchanged
    d. it is impossible for savers to increase saving because somebody will always increase spending by
       an equivalent amount
    e. saving only benefits producers who invest, not the actual savers

11. When aggregate expenditures (consumption plus investment) are less than national income
    a. inventories will decline
    b. inventories will increase
    c. intended investment is greater than saving
    d. savings will decline
    e. real GDP will decrease

12. When consumption goods production is $2,400 billion and consumers purchase $2,000 billion of consumer goods, it is clear that
    a. not enough consumer goods are being produced
    b. to move toward equilibrium, national income must increae
    c. actual investment will be equal to intended investment
    d. the economy is in equilibrium
    e. actual investment will be higher than intended investment

13. The main reason why changes in the equilibrium level of national income should be expected is that
    a. consumption changes frequently
    b. saving changes frequently
    c. investment is fairly volatile
    d. the multiplier is quite large
    e. the rounds of spending in the multiplier keep increasing

14. If autonomous investment decreases by $200 billion and the marginal propensity to consume is 0.75, then national income will
    a. rise by $200 billion
    b. fall by $200 billion
    c. fall by $267 billion
    d. rise by $267 billion
    e. fall by $800 billion

15. An increase in the marginal propensity to save from 0.20 to 0.50 means that
    a. the marginal propensity to consume falls from 0.80 to 0.50
    b. less is saved at every level of national income
    c. more is consumed at every level of national income
    d. the marginal propensity to consume increases as well from 0.20 to 0.50
    e. intended investment increases by 30 percent

16. An increase in saving will generate a decrease in aggregate expenditures such that
    a. national income will increase
    b. consumption will increase
    c. saving is the same at a lower level of equilibrium national income
    d. investment increases as the level of national income increases
    e. the saving curve eventually decreases

17. The effect of an increase in the price level on the position of the aggregate expenditure curve is to
    a. shift the curve up parallel to the original curve
    b. shift the curve down parallel to the original curve
    c. increase the slope of the curve
    d. decrease the slope of the curve
    e. shift the curve down and decrease the slope of the curve

18. The equilibrium level of national income will not be reached automatically by pure chance because
    a. firms typically produce excessively so unwanted inventories accumulate
    b. firms typically produce less than is needed satisfy demand so wanted inventories are consumed
    c. the consumption goods production decisions by firms are unlikely to match the consumption spending decisions by households
    d. the price level cannot adjust to equate the quantity supplied and the quantity demanded
    e. autonomous investment is volatile

19. When the income multiplier works in reverse (is negative),
    a. the change in investment must have been negative
    b. the marginal propensity to consume must have fallen
    c. the marginal propensity to save must have fallen
    d. the consumption curve must have risen
    e. employment must increase

20. If the level of consumption equals the level of national income,
    a. the economy is in equilibrium
    b. autonomous consumption must be zero
    c. aggregate expenditure is equal to intended investment
    d. saving is zero
    e. saving equals consumption

The following questions relate to the applied, interdisciplinary, and global perspectives in the text.

21. According to Irving Gottheil, the author's brother who produces hats in Canada, his biggest problem from year to year in the hat business is
    a. determining price
    b. finding a retailer for his hats
    c. adopting new technology to lower per unit labor costs
    d. choosing new styles for hats
    e. determining how many hats consumers will want to purchase

22. When Keynes suggested that pyramid-building might serve to increase wealth, the modern lesson is that
    a. governments should focus spending on wondrous projects
    b. societies value monuments enormously
    c. the act of spending to construct the pyramids set in motion more spending that increased income
    d. Keynes was referring to the use of low-cost slave labor
    e. government spending creates wealth for a small elite in society

23. When investment spending shifts location as, for example, when firms in southern Italy moved to northern Italy, the effect of this change was to
    a. open up new opportunities for new firms in southern Italy
    b. benefit northern Italy without hurting southern Italy
    c. encourage workers in southern Italy to become entrepreneurs
    d. cause a multiplier increase in income in the north and a multiplier decrease in income in the south
    e. equalize incomes in Italy between the poorer south and the richer north

24. Upstream and downstream linkages associated with investment in a business enterprise refer to links between
    a. firms that are located along a waterway producing similar goods and services
    b. firms and their suppliers and the retailers who sell the finished goods to consumers
    c. workers for firms who earn income from the firm and the government which taxes income
    d. countries that produce goods for export overseas and the importing countries
    e. workers for firms, their managers, and the stockholders in the company

Fill in the Blanks

1. If consumers purchase just as much as producers produce for consumption, then the

   _____ that producers intend to make will equal the _____ consumers

   make.

2. If wanted inventories are converted into consumption goods, then producers will increase

   _____ and _____ to replenish their inventory stock.

3. J. M. Keynes believed that _____ was primarily responsible for determining the

   equilibrium level of national income.

4. Actual investment is equal to intended investment plus or minus _____ in

   inventories.

Discussion Questions

1. What is the difference between actual and intended investment?

2. Why doesn't an increase in aggregate expenditures cause the price level to increase in the aggregate expenditure model of equilibrium national income determination?

3. Explain the logic of the multiplier.

4. Do Keynesian economists think that saving is a bad thing?

Problems

1. a. Suppose that the consumption function is $C = 80 + .8Y$ and the income level is $1,400 billion. Calculate what consumers intend to consume and save at this income level.

   b. Continue with the information in part a. Now suppose that at an income level of $1,400 billion producers intend to produce $1,300 billion of consumption and intend to invest $100 billion. Is the economy in equilibrium? Explain, using a graph to aid discussion.

   c. If this economy is not in equilibrium, what would the equilibrium level of national income be, assuming that intended investment remains at $100 billion? How does the economy adjust to the new equilibrium?

2. Suppose an economy is described by the following equations: $C = \$100 + 0.75Y$ and $I = \$300$.

    a. Calculate the equilibrium level of income.

    b. Graph the aggregate expenditures curve and the 45-degree line.

    c. Suppose saving increases by \$50 at every level of national income. How would the aggregate expenditures curve you drew be affected? Explain. Calculate the new equilibrium level of national income.

    d. Calculate the level of saving at the original equilibrium and at the new equilibrium. Does this example demonstrate the paradox of thrift? Explain.

3. Illustrate the original equilibrium level of national income and the change in the equilibrium level of national income due to the increase in saving from problem 2 above using the saving and investment graph. Explain your graph carefully.

Everyday Applications

Have you worked in a business where inventory management was a key part of the job? Even if you have not, you can imagine the sequence of events once inventories build up to unwanted levels or fall to levels below those that are desired. When inventories begin to pile up, the inventory manager calls the producers telling them to stop sending so much. What else could happen but a cut in production? It's just the opposite when inventories are drawn down. The manager gets on the phone, says send us some more, and production, employment, and income all rise.

Economics Online

The Bureau of Economic Analysis, an agency of the U. S. Department of Commerce, is the nation's economic accountant. The agency prepares estimates of future levels of key economic variables. Visit its Web site (*http://www.bea.doc.gov/*) to learn more about how the agency makes estimates for key regional, national, and international economic variables.

Answers to Questions

Key Terms Quiz

a. 5   **e.** 2
b. 6   **f.** 7
c. 4   **g.** 3
d. 1

True-False Questions

1. False. Only by accident will intended investment be equal to saving because different groups make investment and saving decisions independent of each other.
2. True
3. True
4. False. Aggregate expenditure is equal to consumption plus intended investment.
5. True
6. False. An increase in autonomous investment causes national income to increase by a multiple of that amount.
7. False. Changes in autonomous investment that are equal in magnitude will have equal and opposite effects on the equilibrium level of national income.
8. True
9. False. As the marginal propensity to consume increases, so does the income multiplier.
10. True
11. False. If intended investment is equal to saving, then the economy is at the equilibrium level of national income, and there are no unwanted inventories.
12. True
13. False. The multiplier effect of an increase in investment is an initial increase in income equal to the increase in investment followed by successive increases in spending and income that diminish in each round.
14. False. The income multiplier is equal to $1/(1 - MPC)$.
15. False. Keynes believed that aggregate expenditure was more important than aggregate supply as a determinant of the equilibrium level of national income.

Multiple-Choice Questions

1. d	**6.** a	**11.** b	**16.** c	**21.** e
2. c	**7.** a	**12.** e	**17.** b	**22.** c
3. c	**8.** b	**13.** c	**18.** c	**23.** d
4. b	**9.** b	**14.** e	**19.** a	**24.** b
5. b	**10.** c	**15.** a	**20.** d	

Fill in the Blanks

1. investment; saving
2. production; employment
3. aggregate expenditure
4. unintended changes

Discussion Questions

1. Intended investment includes the purchases of new plant and equipment and inventories that businesses plan to make. Intended investment is the same as autonomous investment. Actual investment includes unintended changes in inventories. For example, if consumers don't purchase all of the consumption goods that producers produce, there will be unintended inventory investment. On the other hand, if consumers purchase more consumption goods than producers produce, wanted inventories will be turned into consumption goods. Investment in inventories will be less than was intended.

2. The price level is assumed to be constant in the aggregate expenditure model for national income determination. An increase in aggregate expenditure causes output to increase via the income multiplier. The model assumes implicitly that ample supplies of resources are available to use for increased production.

3. The logic behind the multiplier is that an increase in autonomous expenditure becomes income for people, who then spend a fraction of the increase as determined by the marginal propensity to consume. In turn, this increase in consumption becomes income for another group of consumers who spend a fraction of the increase. These rounds of spending go on and on, with each successive round becoming smaller. The multiplier process can also work in reverse, starting with a decrease in autonomous expenditure.

4. Keynesian economists don't believe that saving is a bad thing. Increased saving accompanied by increased investment is good and necessary because this is how society accumulates more capital to promote economic growth. The problems with saving arise when an increase in saving is not coupled with an increase in intended investment. Under such circumstances, the paradox of thrift is observed, national income declines, and at the new equilibrium, saving may be no more or even less than it was originally.

Problems

1. a. Consumers intend to consume $1,200 billion and save $200 billion.

   b. This economy is not in equilibrium because $100 billion of unwanted inventories will accumulate. As shown in the graph below, at an income level of $1,400 billion, aggregate expenditure falls short of national income. Consumer spending is $1,200 billion and investment spending is $100 billion. Unwanted inventories accumulate in the amount of $100 billion.

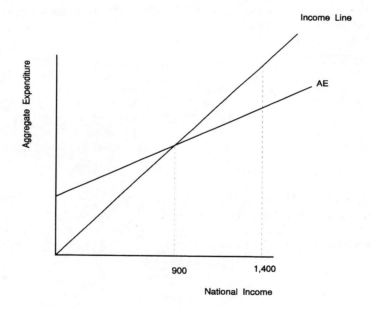

c. The equilibrium is $900 billion. Aggregate expenditure is equal to $C + I_i = (80 + .8Y) + 100$. Solving for the equilibrium level of national income, we have $Y = 180 + .8Y$, which gives $Y = 900$. The economy adjusts to $Y = 900$ because inventories increase at the $1,400 level, causing firms to cut production and employment so that income falls to the $900 billion level.

2. a. The equilibrium level of income is calculated by setting $Y = (\$100 + 0.75Y) + \$300$ and solving for Y. The equation reduces to $Y = 400 + .75Y$. This becomes $.25Y = 400$, so $Y = \$1,600$.

b.

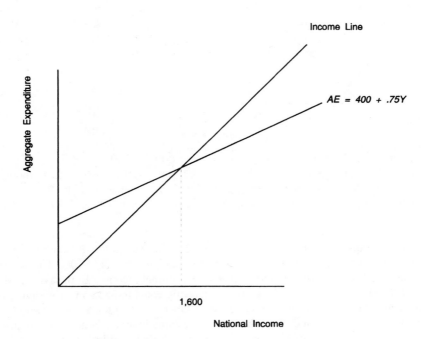

c. An increase in saving is represented by a downward shift in the aggregate expenditures curve by $50. The equilibrium level of income decreases to $1,400. These changes are shown in the graph. Aggregate expenditures falls from $AE = 400 + .75Y$ to $AE' = 350 + .75Y$, and the equilibrium level of income falls to $1,400 showing the multiplier effect. These changes appear in the graph on the following page..

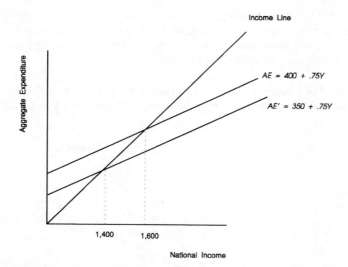

d. When $Y = 1,600$, $C = 100 + .75(1,600) = 1,300$. $S = Y - C = 1,600 - 1,300 = \$300$.
    When $Y = 1,400$, $C = 50 + .75(1,400) = 1,100$. $S = Y - C = 1,400 - 1,100 = \$300$. Even though saving increased at the $1,600 level, the income multiplier caused national income to fall by $200 to $1,400, and the level of saving at this income level was the same as at the $1,600 level. This shows the paradox of thrift.

3. The saving and investment graph that corresponds to problem 2 is shown below. Because autonomous consumption is $100, we know that the vertical intercept for the saving curve is $-\$100$. The saving curve, labeled S, intersects the investment curve at the $1,600 level of national income. Both saving and investment are equal to $300 in equilibrium. An increase in saving equal to $50 shifts the saving curve up by $50 parallel to the original curve. The new saving curve is labeled S'. At the $1,600 level of national income, saving is greater than investment on S'. Therefore, unwanted inventories accumulate, production decreases, employment decreases, and national income decreases along S' until the new equilibrium level of national income is achieved at $1,400. $S = I = \$300$ at the new equilibrium, illustrating the paradox of thrift.

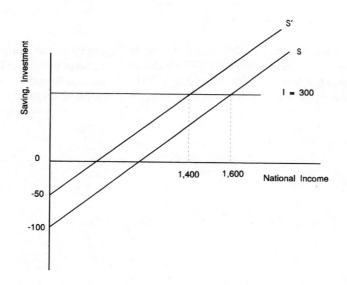

Homework Questions

True-False Questions — If a statement is false, explain why.

1. When actual investment is greater than intended investment, unwanted inventories accumulate and production decreases. (T/F)

2. An increase in autonomous investment causes national income to increase by more than the increase in investment. (T/F)

3. When the economy is in equilibrium, actual investment is less than intended investment. (T/F)

4. If saving increases, then aggregate expenditures decrease and national income will decrease. (T/F)

5. As the marginal propensity to consume decreases, the value of the income multiplier increases. (T/F)

Multiple-Choice Questions

1. Suppose that the consumption function is given by $C = 500 + .8Y$ and investment is $I = 500$. The equilibrium level of income is
   a. 2,500
   b. 1,000
   c. 5,000
   d. 4,000
   e. 7,500

2. An increase in autonomous investment will
   a. lead to an equal increase in national income
   b. lead to an even larger increase in national income
   c. cause the marginal propensity to save to fall
   d. cause saving to decrease due to the increase in borrowing in the economy
   e. lead to an equivalent decrease in aggregate expenditures

3. If unwanted inventories cause a decrease in prices instead of national income, then we can expect
   a. no increase in unemployment
   b. savings to rise faster than consumption
   c. a change in the equilibrium level of national income
   d. the income multiplier to cause an increase in national income
   e. intended investment to increase

4. The "paradox" in the paradox of thrift is that as people try to save more
   a. aggregate expenditures increase
   b. national income increases
   c. investment increases
   d. income decreases and saving doesn't increase
   e. income increases and saving doesn't increase

5. If the marginal propensity to save is 0.25, then the income multiplier is
   a. 0.75
   b. 4
   c. 2
   d. 1.25
   e. 1.75

Discussion Questions/Problems

1. Suppose that consumption is $C = 600 + .75Y$ and $I = 400$. Write an equation for aggregate expenditures, calculate the equilibrium level of national income, and sketch a graph of the aggregate expenditure curve to show the equilibrium level of national income.

2. Explain how the economy adjusts to the equilibrium level of national income when the actual level of national income is below and above the equilibrium level of national income? What assumption is made about prices in this analysis?

CHAPTER 8

FISCAL POLICY: COPING WITH INFLATION AND UNEMPLOYMENT

Chapter in a Nutshell

To say that an economy is in equilibrium tells us very little about the general state of the economy. The model showing the equilibrium level of national income presented in Chapter 22 allows for an economy to be in equilibrium at high levels of unemployment. Some of the unemployment is caused by insufficient aggregate expenditures. But unemployment can have other causes. Economists identify five types: **frictional unemployment**, **structural unemployment**, **cyclical unemployment**, **discouraged workers**, and the **underemployed**.

The Bureau of Labor Statistics (BLS), which establishes the official unemployment count and rate of unemployment for the economy, calculates the rate of unemployment by surveying households. Those who are either working or seeking employment are counted as being in the **labor force**. That excludes discouraged workers. The unemployment rate is the number of people who are not working but are seeking work, divided by the labor force. That excludes underemployed workers. The BLS defines this rate as the actual rate of unemployment.

Economists distinguish between the **actual rate of unemployment** and the **natural rate of unemployment**. The natural rate of unemployment consists of workers who are frictionally and structurally unemployed. It is "natural" and the result of positive dynamic forces in the economy — people looking for better jobs and technological change occurring — so the natural rate is not at all worrisome. What remains is cyclical unemployment. To economists, the economy is at **full employment** when the actual rate of unemployment is equal to the natural rate of unemployment. In other words, the economy is at full employment when cyclical unemployment is zero.

When inflation occurs, some groups of people are harmed while others benefit. Those who are hurt by inflation include people living on fixed incomes, such as landlords and savers. Those who gain from inflation include borrowers and, to some extent, the government. The government benefits from inflation when it borrows. Unions bargain for cost-of-living allowances in their wage contracts to protect themselves from the erosion of real wages.

What's the relationship between the full-employment level of national income and the equilibrium level? A **recessionary gap** exists when the equilibrium level of national income falls below the full-employment level. The amount by which spending must increase in order to achieve full employment defines the recessionary gap. An **inflationary gap** exists when the equilibrium level of national income is above the full-employment level. The inflationary gap defines the amount by which spending must decrease in order to achieve full employment without inflation.

Fiscal policy involves the government not only increasing or decreasing its spending, but also increasing or decreasing its tax take. Just as an increase in government spending creates a multiple increase in national income, an increase in taxes creates a multiple decrease in national income. The **tax multiplier** is $-MPC/(1 - MPC)$. When the government increases its spending and taxes by the same amount, both the income and tax multipliers are at work. The net effect is an increase in national income that equals the increase in spending and taxes. The **balanced budget multiplier** equals one. The government can create a **balanced budget** where $G = T$, a **surplus budget** where $T > G$, or a **deficit budget** where $G > T$.

After you study this chapter, you should be able to:

- Describe the different types of unemployment.
- Calculate the **unemployment rate**, given the appropriate data.
- Explain the meaning of the **natural rate of unemployment**.
- Identify winners and losers from inflation.
- Understand **recessionary gaps** and **inflationary gaps** in the aggregate expenditure model.
- Show how **recessionary** and **inflationary gaps** can be closed using **fiscal policy**.
- Derive the **tax multiplier** and the **balanced budget multiplier**.

Concept Check — See how you do on these multiple-choice questions.

As you consider the responses to this question, recall that when the cyclical rate of unemployment is zero, the economy is at full employment.

1. **Cyclical unemployment** refers to workers who are unemployed because
   a. they have left one job to look for a better one
   b. of technological changes in production
   c. they are close to the retirement phase of the life cycle and no one will hire them
   d. new goods have been substituted for the goods they were trained to produce
   e. the economy is in a recession phase

Which types of unemployment are the natural result of dynamic forces in the economy?

2. The **natural rate of unemployment** is equal to
   a. discouraged workers plus underemployed workers
   b. frictional plus structural unemployment
   c. cyclical plus structural unemployment
   d. cyclical plus frictional unemployment
   e. structural unemployment plus underemployed workers

If a recession results from insufficient aggregate expenditure in the economy, then what is the recessionary gap?

3. A **recessionary gap** exists when
   a. structural unemployment is excessive
   b. frictional unemployment is excessive
   c. aggregate expenditure falls short of that needed to generate full employment
   d. aggregate supply falls short of that needed to generate full employment
   e. supply creates its own demand

Should fiscal policy increase or decrease aggregate expenditure to close a recessionary gap?

4. An appropriate **fiscal policy** to close a **recessionary gap** is to
   a. increase government spending
   b. decrease taxes
   c. decrease government spending
   d. increase taxes
   e. a and b are both appropriate policies

Suppose that taxes are decreased. Do households spend the full amount of the tax cut? How does this impact the size of the tax multiplier compared to the income multiplier?

5. Compared to the income multiplier, the **tax multiplier**
   a. causes a weaker income magnification
   b. is better for closing a recessionary gap
   c. is better for closing an inflationary gap
   d. causes a stronger income magnification
   e. causes an equal income magnification.

Am I on the Right Track?

Your answers to the questions above should be **e**, **b**, **c**, **e**, and **a**. Along with learning about the different types of unemployment and the impact of inflation on different groups in the economy, you need to be able to use a graph to distinguish between recessionary and inflationary gaps. A recessionary gap occurs when aggregate expenditure is insufficient to generate a full-employment level of GDP. An inflationary gap results when aggregate expenditure is more than is needed to generate a full-employment level of GDP. A variety of fiscal policy options exists to close both gaps.

Key Terms Quiz — Match the terms on the left with the definitions in the column on the right.

1. frictional unemployment

2. recessionary gap

3. structural unemployment

4. inflationary gap

5. cyclical unemployment

6. fiscal policy

7. discouraged workers

8. balanced budget

9. underemployed workers

10. tax multiplier

11. labor force

12. balanced budget multiplier

13. natural rate of unemployment

_____ a. workers employed in jobs that do not utilize their productive talents or experience

_____ b. an employment level at which the actual rate of unemployment is equal to the economy's natural rate of unemployment

_____ c. unemployment that results from technological changes in production, or from the substitution of new goods for customary ones

_____ d. government spending equals tax revenues

_____ e. people who are gainfully employed or actively seeking employment

_____ f. brief periods of unemployment caused by people who quit work to seek more attractive employment

_____ g. government spending and taxation policy to achieve macroeconomic goals of full employment without inflation

_____ h. the effect on the equilibrium level of national income of an equal change in government spending and taxes

_____ i. the amount by which aggregate expenditure exceeds the aggregate expenditure level needed to generate equilibrium national income at full employment without inflation

_____ j. unemployment associated with the downturn and recession phases of the business cycle

_____ k. the multiple by which the equilibrium level of national income changes when a dollar change in taxes occurs

_____ l. the rate of unemployment caused by frictional plus structural unemployment

_____ m. the amount by which aggregate expenditure falls short of the level needed to generate equilibrium national income at full employment without inflation

14. budget deficit   _____ n. tax revenues exceed government spending
15. full employment   _____ o. unemployed people who give up looking for work after
                                                       repeated failures trying to find work
16. budget surplus   _____ p. government spending exceeds tax revenues

Graphing Tutorial

This chapter uses the model of equilibrium national income presented in Chapter 22 to show recessionary gaps and inflationary gaps and the ways they can be closed with fiscal policy. Suppose we have an economy that is in equilibrium at a national income equal to $1,600 billion and the full-employment level of national income is $2,000 billion. The graph below represents this situation.

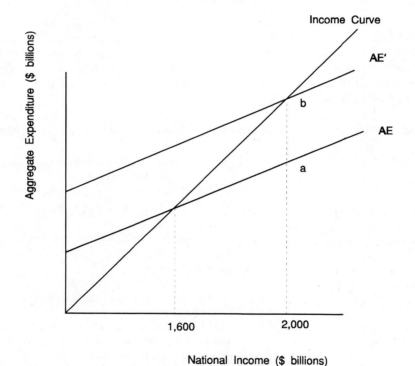

The vertical distance between the aggregate expenditure curves *AE* and *AE'* labeled *ab* defines the recessionary gap. It can be closed with a variety of fiscal policy options. Suppose that we choose to close the gap with an increase in government spending. Assuming the marginal propensity to consume is .75, the income multiplier is $1/(1 - MPC) = 1/(1 - .75) = 4$. We know that $\Delta Y = 4\Delta G$. National income must increase by $400 billion. So, $400 = 4\Delta G$, and $\Delta G = \$100$ billion. An increase in government spending equal to $100 billion will close the recessionary gap.

To illustrate an inflationary gap, suppose that the equilibrium level of national income is $2,400 billion and the full-employment level of national income is $2,000 billion. This situation is shown in the graph on the following page.

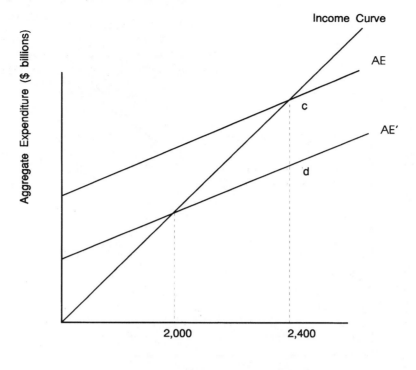

National Income ($ billions)

In this case, aggregate expenditure exceeds the amount necessary to achieve a full-employment level of national income. The vertical distance between *AE* and *AE'* labeled *cd* defines the inflationary gap — the amount by which aggregate expenditure must decrease to achieve the full employment level of national income. Suppose that we choose to close the inflationary gap with a tax increase and the $MPC = .75$. We know that the tax multiplier is $-MPC/(1 - MPC) = -.75/(1 - MPC) = -3$. Therefore, $\Delta Y = -3\Delta T$, and national income must decrease by $400 billion. So, $-\$400 = -3\Delta T$ and $\Delta T = \$133.33$ billion. A tax increase equal to $133.33 billion will shift the aggregate expenditure curve downward to achieve the full-employment level of national income.

Graphing Pitfalls

Closing a recessionary gap with an increase in government spending, a decrease in taxes, or some combination of the two results in an upward shift of the aggregate expenditure curve parallel to the original curve so that it intersects the income curve at the full-employment level of national income. Both the increase in government spending and the increase in consumption spending due to a tax cut compensate for a shortfall in autonomous investment that prevented the economy from reaching the full-employment level. You may think of the increase in government spending as public investment. In the context of our model, the impact of increased government spending is the same as an increase in autonomous investment — an upward shift of the aggregate expenditure curve parallel to the old curve. So don't make the mistake of rotating the aggregate expenditure curve upward so that its slope becomes steeper as shown in the graph on the following page. Remember, the marginal propensity to consume is the slope of the aggregate expenditure curve, and an increase in government spending (or a decrease in taxes of the kind discussed in your text) does not change the *MPC*.

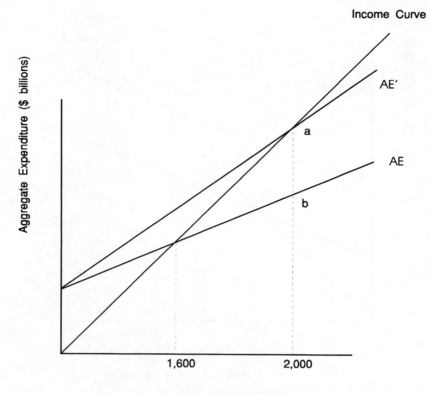

When a recessionary gap is closed with an increase in government spending, a cut in taxes, or some combination of the two, the aggregate expenditure curve shifts upward parallel to the original curve. It doesn't rotate upward as shown in this graph.

True-False Questions — If a statement is false, explain why.

1. Keynesians believe that the economy naturally moves toward equilibrium at full employment. (T/F)

2. The reason the economy may be at an equilibrium below full employment is that wages and prices are inflexible. (T/F)

3. The upward-sloping segment of the aggregate supply curve shows that increases in real GDP can only occur with increases in the price level. (T/F)

4. An inflationary gap can be closed by cutting taxes. (T/F)

5. The actual rate of unemployment is equal to the natural rate of unemployment when the rate of cyclical unemployment is zero. (T/F)

6. According to Keynesians, reducing the budget deficit closes a recessionary gap, while increasing the budget deficit closes an inflationary gap. (T/F)

7. Structural unemployment is included in the natural rate of unemployment. (T/F)

8. Discouraged workers are not counted in the natural rate of unemployment but are included in the actual rate of unemployment. (T/F)

9. Banks that provide loans to businesses and individuals are losers during periods of high inflation. (T/F)

10. People living on a fixed income, such as retirees, are harmed by inflation. (T/F)

11. The tax multiplier is larger than the income multiplier. (T/F)

12. According to Keynesians, an increase in government spending generates an increase in national income equal to that created by an increase in private investment of the same magnitude. (T/F)

13. Closing a recessionary gap using deficit financing requires less government spending than financing the closing with a balanced budget. (T/F)

14. A deficit budget results when tax revenues are greater than the government's spending. (T/F)

15. One drawback to using budget deficits created by increased government spending to close recessionary gaps is that once government spending is introduced, it is hard to reduce. (T/F)

Multiple-Choice Questions

1. The economy is considered to be at full employment when the rate of _____ is zero.
   a. cyclical unemployment
   b. seasonal unemployment
   c. frictional unemployment
   d. structural unemployment
   e. discouraged workers

2. When a balanced budget increases by $120 billion, national income increases by
   a. $60 billion
   b. $120 billion
   c. $240 billion
   d. $600 billion
   e. national income does not increase

3. Frictional unemployment can be the result of
   a. a change in the technology of production
   b. a recession
   c. people quitting one job to look for a better one
   d. a decrease in government spending
   e. friction in the workplace between workers and their employers

4. The type of unemployment associated with technological displacement of labor is
   a. cyclical
   b. structural
   c. frictional
   d. discouraged workers
   e. underemployed workers

5. When the economy is in equilibrium at a point on the vertical segment of the aggregate supply curve, an increase in government spending will
   a. cause a dramatic increase in national income
   b. cause the price level to increase with no change in national income
   c. close a recessionary gap
   d. decrease the budget deficit
   e. be followed by an increase in taxes

6. All of the following groups tend to be harmed by inflation **except**
   a. retirees
   b. minimum wage workers
   c. landlords
   d. lenders
   e. renters

7. The economy is considered to be at full employment when the rate of _____ is zero.
   a. frictional unemployment
   b. seasonal unemployment
   c. cyclical unemployment
   d. structural unemployment
   e. discouraged workers

8. According to the Bureau of Labor Statistics (BLS), all of the following make up the labor force **except**
   a. discouraged workers
   b. underemployed workers
   c. frictionally unemployed workers
   d. cyclically unemployed workers
   e. structurally unemployed workers

9. The government budget is balanced when
   a. taxes are increased
   b. government spending is decreased
   c. taxes are decreased
   d. government spending is increased
   e. government spending equals tax revenues

10. Assuming that the government starts with a balanced budget, a subsequent $100 billion deficit results from a(n)
    a. increase in G by $140 billion and an increase in T by $40 billion
    b. increase in G by $140 billion and an increase in T by $140 billion
    c. decrease in G by $140 billion and an increase in T by $40 billion
    d. decrease in G by $140 billion and a decrease in T by $140 billion
    e. decrease in G by $40 billion and an increase in T by $100 billion

11. Suppose national income is $2,000 billion and the full-employment level is $2,400 billion. Given a marginal propensity to consume equal to 0.80, the amount by which taxes must change in order to reach full employment is
    a. $80 billion
    b. -$80 billion
    c. -$400 billion
    d. $100 billion
    e. -$100 billion

12. Given the same information as in question 11, full employment can be reached by which of the following changes in government spending and taxes?
    a. increase G by $240 billion and decrease T by $200 billion
    b. decrease G by $240 billion and increase T by $200 billion
    c. decrease G by $240 billion and decrease T by $ 200 billion
    d. increase G by $240 billion and increase T by $200 billion
    e. increase G by $200 billion and increase T by $160 billion

13. One problem with increased government spending to eliminate recessionary gaps is that
    a. the government usually wastes the money it spends
    b. there is no need for the government to purchase more goods and services
    c. once government spending is started, it is very hard to cut it back
    d. government spending is usually inflationary
    e. the government cannot go into debt

14. The tax multiplier is
    a. 1/MPS
    b. -MPC/(1 - MPC)
    c. -1/(1 - MPC)
    d. MPS/(1 - MPS)
    e. T - G/(1+T)

15. Inflation can be the politician's friend when it causes tax revenues to
    a. increase without an increase in tax rates
    b. rise due to increases in people's real incomes
    c. fall due to tax cuts that are introduced to close inflationary gaps
    d. increase while people are distracted by increases in other prices
    e. increase at a time that tax increases are popular among voters

16. If the income multiplier is 4, government spending can increase by _____ and taxes by _____ to generate a $300 increase in national income.
    a. $250; $200
    b. $150; $100
    c. $200; $200
    d. $200; $250
    e. $300; $250

17. A frictionally unemployed person is one who
    a. lost a job due to a downturn or recession phase in the economy
    b. has retired from a job
    c. lost a job due to a technological change in the production process
    d. quit a job in order to find a better one
    e. takes a job that requires considerably less talent than that person has to offer

18. A budget surplus arises when
    a. the balanced budget multiplier generates a level of national income greater than the full-employment level
    b. the tax multiplier is greater than the income multiplier
    c. tax revenues exceed government spending
    d. the income multiplier is greater than the tax multiplier
    e. the tax increase necessary to balance the budget is more than the increase in government spending

19. If a $100 billion cut in government spending causes national income to fall by $500 billion, then the marginal propensity to consume is
    a. .75
    b. .8
    c. .9
    d. .25
    e. .2

20. Given a $10 billion recessionary gap and an $MPC = 0.75$, we know that the equilibrium level of national income is
    a. at the full-employment level of national income
    b. $30 billion below the full-employment level of national income
    c. $50 billion above the full-employment level of national income
    d. $30 billion above the full-employment level of national income
    e. $40 billion below the full-employment level of national income

The following questions relate to the interdisciplinary, historical, and applied perspectives in the text.

21. A discouraged workers is one who
    a. cannot find a job and has quit searching for work
    b. is suicidal as a result of lack of success on the job market
    c. takes a job that is below his or her skill level
    d. is laid-off due to an unexpected downturn in the business cycle
    e. is stuck in a low-paying low-skill job with no prospects for improvement

22. Which of the following is not a characteristic of hyperinflation?
    a. an inflation rate in excess of 50 percent per month
    b. a storeowner's willingness to accept a promise to pay a bill in cash in one month's time
    c. workers demanding to be paid twice a day
    d. people spending cash as soon as they get it
    e. an inability to save for the future

23. The validity of Say's Law, which states that supply creates its own demand, depends on the assumption that
    a. firms will cut output when there is a decline in demand
    b. most workers are unionized
    c. firms do not compete with one another over price
    d. prices, wages, and interest rates are flexible
    e. the economy produces mostly goods rather than services

24. Keynes argued that budget deficits were appropriate
    a. most of the time since a deficit does not harm the economy
    b. when the economy is at full employment in order to further stimulate growth
    c. during a cyclical downturn in the economy
    d. to help combat inflation
    e. as a political tool used to curb government spending

Fill in the Blanks

1. The natural rate of unemployment consists of workers who are _____ and

   _____ unemployed.

2. A _____ exists when the equilibrium level of national income is below the full-

   employment level.

3. Some groups of people hurt by inflation include _____, _____,

   and _____.

4. Unions bargain for _____ in their wage contracts in order to protect

   themselves from the _____ of real wages due to inflation.

Discussion Questions

1. Suppose that the economy is below full employment. Is it necessary to use fiscal policy in order to eliminate
   the recessionary gap? Explain.

2. Define the unemployment rate. Does the definition include all the people of working age who don't have jobs? Explain.

3. Why do bankers lose because of inflation?

4. Which is the most difficult type of unemployment to eliminate and why?

5. Why is the balanced budget multiplier equal to 1?

Problems

1. Graph a recessionary gap and an inflationary gap using the aggregate expenditure model of equilibrium national income determination.

2. Suppose that the full-employment level of national income is $3,000 billion, the equilibrium level of national income is $2,500 billion, and the marginal propensity to consume is 0.8. By how much will government spending have to increase in order to reach full employment?

3. Suppose that the full-employment level of national income is $2,000 billion and the equilibrium level of national income is $2,500 billion. Given a marginal propensity to consume equal to 0.80, how much will taxes have to change in order to reach full employment?

4. Suppose that the government wants to close the inflationary gap in problem 3, but wants to limit the tax increase to $50 billion. By how much will government spending have to change to accomplish this goal? What is the size of the surplus or deficit budget that results?

Everyday Applications

During the winter and spring of 1998, a massive spending bill to finance highway repairs and new highway construction made its way through the U.S. Congress at a time when the economy was operating with the lowest levels of unemployment since 1970. Viewed from the perspective of fiscal policy, was this bill appropriate? Why or why not? Can large amounts of new spending on America's highways be justified on grounds other than fiscal policy? Explain.

Economics Online

The Joint Economic Committee of Congress was created when Congress passed the Employment Act of 1946 that committed the government to designing fiscal policy that would promote full employment with low inflation. You can visit the home page for the JEC to find out more about the formulation of fiscal policy (*http://www.house.gov/jec/welcome.htm*).

Answers to Questions

Key Terms Quiz

a. 9	**f.** 1	**k.** 10	**p.** 14
b. 15	**g.** 6	**l.** 13	
c. 3	**h.** 12	**m.** 2	
d. 8	**i.** 4	**n.** 16	
e. 11	**j.** 5	**o.** 7	

True-False Questions

1. False. Keynesians believe that the economy can be in equilibrium either below or above a full-employment
   level of national income.
2. True
3. True
4. False. A recessionary gap can be closed by cutting taxes; an inflationary gap can be closed by increasing taxes.
5. True
6. False. Closing a recessionary gap requires an increase in the budget deficit while closing an inflationary gap requires a budget surplus.

7. True
8. False. Discouraged workers are not counted as unemployed because they are not considered to be in the labor force.
9. True
10. True
11. False. The income multiplier is $1/(1 - MPC)$ which generates a larger income magnification than the tax multiplier, equal to $-MPC/(1 - MPC)$.
12. True
13. True
14. False. A deficit budget results when government spending is greater than tax revenues..
15. True

Multiple-Choice Questions

1. a	6. e	11. e	16. b	21. a
2. b	7. c	12. d	17. d	22. b
3. c	8. a	13. c	18. c	23. d
4. b	9. e	14. b	19. b	24. c
5. b	10. a	15. a	20. e	

Fill in the Blanks

1. frictionally; structurally
2. recessionary gap
3. savers; landlords; people on fixed incomes
4. cost-of-living allowances; erosion

Discussion Questions

1. Keynesians believe that it is usually necessary to use fiscal policy to eliminate a recessionary gap. They argue that the equilibrium level of national income is determined primarily by aggregate expenditure. The equilibrium level of national income can be at less than the full-employment level. Since this is an equilibrium level, there is no reason for income to change by itself. Therefore, fiscal policy will be necessary to eliminate the recessionary gap — either an increase in government spending, a decrease in taxes, or some combination.

    Other economists believe it may not be necessary to use fiscal policy because the economy will eventually adjust back to full employment automatically. For example, there may be a change in technology that prompts many entrepreneurs to invest in new capital equipment, causing an increase in aggregate expenditure. Or, old capital may just wear out and have to be replaced, causing an increase in investment. The drawback to such automatic adjustment is that it may take a very long time.

2. The unemployment rate is the percentage of the labor force that is looking for work. This definition does not include all people of working age who don't have jobs. Some people of working age are not in the labor force so they can't be unemployed. For example, discouraged workers are not included in the calculation of the unemployment rate.

3. Bankers lend money and are repaid the principal plus interest at a future date. If they lend $100 in 1995 and receive the full loan of $100 back in 2000 while but in the five intervening years, inflation totaled 50 percent, the quantity of goods and services that $100 buys for the bankers is only 50 percent of what they could have bought with the $100 in 1995. Bankers and other who lend money may try to anticipate the impact of inflation on the purchasing power of the money they lend. The interest rate that bankers charge

typically includes a premium that is equal to their best estimate of the future rate of inflation. In this way, bankers can protect themselves to a degree from the impact of inflation on the purchasing power of the money they lend.

4. Structural unemployment is probably the most difficult type of unemployment to eliminate. Structural unemployment is the result of changes in tastes for goods that cause the demand for them to fall and/or changes in production technology that decrease the demand for certain skills. Either way, the workers affected may have difficulty finding other jobs because their skills are not immediately suited to the types of employment that are available. To ameliorate the problem of structural unemployment, retraining and education may be necessary to equip workers with skills that are in greater demand by employers. The problem of structural unemployment is compounded by the extent to which the affected workers are late in their careers.

5. The balanced budget multiplier is the sum of the income multiplier, $1/(1 - MPC)$, and the tax multiplier, $-MPC/(1 - MPC)$. $1/(1 - MPC) + -MPC/(1 - MPC) = (1 - MPC)/(1 - MPC) = 1$.

Problems

1. Graphs of a recessionary gap and an inflationary gap are presented in the graphing tutorial.

2. The change in national income required in this case is $500 billion. The multiplier is equal to $1/(1 - MPC) = 1/(1 - .8) = 5$. Therefore, $500 = 5\Delta G$, so $\Delta G = \$100$ billion.

3. The change in national income required is -$500 billion. The tax multiplier is equal to $-MPC/(1 - MPC) = -.8/(1 - .8) = -4$. Therefore, $-500 = -4\Delta T$, so $\Delta T = \$125$ billion.

4. The change in national income required is -$500 and the tax increase is limited to $50 billion. The tax multiplier is -4, so national income will decrease by $4(\$50) = \$200$ billion due to the tax increase. The level of national income must be reduced by another $300 billion with cuts in government spending. The income multiplier is 5; therefore a cut in government spending equal to $60 billion will decrease national income by $300 billion. The increase in taxes equal to $50 billion plus the cut in government spending equal to $60 billion combine to generate a $110 billion budget surplus, assuming the original budget was balanced.

Homework Questions

True-False Questions — If a statement is false, explain why.

1. Appropriate fiscal policies to use when the economy is experiencing high unemployment are tax increases and government spending decreases. (T/F)

2. The inflationary gap is the amount by which aggregate expenditures must increase in order to reach full employment. (T/F)

3. When the economy is at full employment, structural, cyclical, and frictional unemployment are all zero. (T/F)

4. Say's Law holds that the act of producing goods and services generates sufficient income for them to be purchased. (T/F)

5. The tax multiplier is greater than the income multiplier. (T/F)

Multiple-Choice Questions

1. Given a choice among the following fiscal policy options, the best one to combat demand-pull inflation would be
   a. a tax cut and a government spending decrease
   b. a tax increase and a government spending increase
   c. an increase in government spending matched by an equal increase in taxes
   d. a tax increase and a government spending decrease
   e. a tax cut and a government spending increase

2. The type of unemployment that fiscal policy is best suited to control is
   a. natural
   b. structural
   c. discouraged
   d. cyclical
   e. frictional

3. If government policy creates a deficit budget while the economy is already at full employment, then
   a. national income is falling
   b. fiscal policy is inflationary
   c. fiscal policy is recessionary
   d. the balanced budget multiplier must be less than 1
   e. the balanced budget multiplier must be greater than 1

4. Suppose national income is $3,000 billion and the full-employment level is $2,400 billion. Given a marginal propensity to consume equal to 0.75, the amount by which taxes must change in order to reach full employment is
   a. $60 billion
   b. -$60 billion
   c. $600 billion
   d. $100 billion
   e. $200 billion

5. People who are on fixed incomes are adversely affected by inflation because
   a. their incomes buy fewer goods and services
   b. while their income may increase with inflation, it increases at a lower rate than the rate of inflation
   c. they typically have large outstanding debts like a mortgage
   d. the minimum wage that they receive does not increase
   e. they are unable to pick cheaper goods and services to buy as they did before the inflation

Discussion Questions/Problems

1. Distinguish inflation and high inflation from hyperinflation. Give some examples of hyperinflations.

2. a. Suppose that $C = 100 + .75Y$, $I = 150$ and $G = 50$ (units are billions of dollars). Calculate the equilibrium level of national income.

   b. If the full employment level of national income is $1,800 billion, is there a recessionary gap or an inflationary gap? Explain.

   c. By how much would government spending have to change in order to reach full employment? By how much would taxes have to change in order to reach full employment? How do you account for the difference in you answers?

CHAPTER 9

ECONOMIC GROWTH, BUSINESS CYCLES,

AND COUNTERCYCLICAL FISCAL POLICY

Chapter in a Nutshell

Up to this point in our analysis of macroeconomics, our focus has been on understanding why the economy is either in or moving toward equilibrium. This chapter presents a very different approach to macroeconomic analysis. Instead of assuming that the economy moves incessantly toward equilibrium, it describes an economy that is always in motion, moving from one level of activity to another. The point of reference in this approach to macroeconomics is the **business cycle**.

The chapter opens with a discussion of **economic growth**. Being on a business cycle is not inconsistent with economic growth if, cycle after cycle, the economy's real GDP is increasing. What causes growth? Increases in the size of the labor force, with its specialization and division of labor, increases in the stock of capital, and improvements in technology are the principal factors we use to explain economic growth. Key variables that we track in studying the causes of economic growth include the **capital-labor ratio**, the **capital-output ratio**, and **labor productivity**.

Although economies grow over time, the growth path is by no means smooth and has many twists and turns. Economists have tried to figure out why the economy is subject to these twists and turns. Business cycle theorists offer a number of explanations, each of which can be viewed as belonging to either of two classes: **externally induced cycles** or **internally induced cycles**. Externally induced cycles are those triggered by causes that are external to the economy, such as wars, changes in climate, population booms, clustering of innovations, changes in consumer confidence, changes in government spending, or changes in the international scene. The internally induced cycle supposes that the economy is inherently cyclical. One theory that explains such an internally induced cycle shows how the multiplier and accelerator interact to create the cycle. The multiplier relates changes in investment to changes in income. The **accelerator** relates the level of investment to changes in income. A cycle can be triggered by a change in investment that changes income (the multiplier at work). That change in income changes the level of investment (the accelerator at work). That second round change in investment changes income (second round multiplier at work), and so on.

Not all economists accept the idea of the business cycle. **Real business cycle** theorists believe that there is no such thing as a business cycle marked by regular and distinct phases. Rather, the economy is highly dynamic, operating at full employment. What others diagnose as business cycles are, to them, really just sharp changes in the rate of economic growth that result from random changes in the rate of technological change.

Countercyclical fiscal policy can be used to moderate both the downturns and the prosperity phases of the cycle. The appropriate fiscal policy response to a downturn is to create a budget deficit by either raising government spending or lowering taxes, or both. To counteract inflationary pressures in the prosperity phase, the government should cut its spending, raise taxes, or both. Countercyclical fiscal policy is not always effective because it is not always clear where in the cycle the economy is positioned, or where it is heading. Anticipating the cycle's turning points is difficult. Moreover, even if it is clear what policy measure to use, there is still an **administrative lag** to overcome. The lag is the time interval between deciding on a policy and the execution of that policy. By the time a policy clears through the lag, it may no longer be appropriate.

After studying this chapter, you should be able to:

• Discuss the sources of long-run **economic growth**.
• Explain how the **capital-labor ratio**, **capital deepening**, and **labor productivity** are related to each other.
• Rank, according to their importance, the factors that have contributed to U.S. economic growth since World War II.
• Describe the **external theories of the business cycle.**
• Show how the multiplier and the **accelerator** can interact to generate an **internal cycle** in the economy.
• Contrast traditional theories of the business cycle with **real business cycle theory**.
• Discuss the design and implementation of **countercyclical fiscal policies**.

Concept Check — See how you do on these multiple-choice questions.

Think back to the sources of economic growth that we identified in Chapter 2 for this question.

1. Adam Smith identified all of the following as principal causes of **long-run economic growth** except the
   a. wage rate
   b. size of the labor force
   c. degree of labor specialization
   d. size of the capital stock
   e. level of technology

How do we define labor productivity? How would an increase in the capital-labor ratio affect labor productivity?

2. As the **capital-labor ratio** increases,
   a. labor productivity will decrease
   b. labor productivity will increase
   c. the capital-output ratio will increase
   d. saving will decrease
   e. consumption will decrease as resources are shifted to produce more capital goods

The accelerator relates the level of investment to changes in the level of national income.

3. The idea of the **accelerator** is that
   a. once economic growth begins, it continues to accelerate
   b. economic growth triggers an increase in expected sales and an increase in investment
   c. countercyclical fiscal policy can accelerate rates of long-run economic growth
   d. to justify more capital stock, economic growth must accelerate
   e. technological advances accelerate economic growth

Consider when specific types of fiscal policy are appropriate to implement.

4. The purpose of **countercyclical fiscal policy** is to
   a. eliminate large budget deficits
   b. experiment with changes in government spending
   c. learn precisely when turning points in the business cycle occur
   d. moderate the severity of the business cycle
   e. eliminate the real business cycle

Countercyclical fiscal policies are designed and implemented by government. Does government typically make decisions quickly?

5. **Administrative lag** stems from
   a. the inability to design appropriate countercyclical policies
   b. the delay between deciding on an appropriate policy and its execution
   c. a belief in the real business cycle among most government economists that prevents them from taking countercyclical measures soon enough to prevent recessions
   d. a reluctance by a budget-conscious Congress to pursue new spending programs
   e. difficulty calculating the precise value for the income and tax multipliers and the accelerator

Am I on the Right Track?

Your answers to the questions above should be **a, b, b, d,** and **b**. It may be useful for you to approach this chapter in three stages. First, you need to become comfortable with the terminology and methodology for examining economic growth. This is an extension of work we began in Chapter 2. Second, learn the various theories of the business cycle. Business cycle theory is a fascinating and colorful field. Finally, understand that countercyclical fiscal policy is intended to moderate the business cycle. To what extent is this possible given the difficulty of identifying business cycles and their phases and problems like administrative lag?

Key Terms Quiz — Match the terms on the left with the definitions in the column on the right.

1. economic growth

2. accelerator

3. labor productivity

4. countercyclical fiscal policy

5. capital-labor ratio

6. administrative lag

7. capital deepening

8. capital-output ratio

_____ a. the ratio of capital to labor, reflecting the quantity of capital used by each laborer in production

_____ b. a rise in the ratio of capital to labor

_____ c. the time interval between deciding on an appropriate policy and the execution of that policy

_____ d. an increase in real GDP, typically expressed as an annual rate of real GDP growth

_____ e. the ratio of capital stock to GDP

_____ f. the quantity of GDP produced per worker, typically measured in quantity of GDP per hour of labor

_____ g. fiscal policy designed to moderate the severity of the business cycle

_____ h. the relationship between the level of investment and the change in the level of national income

Graphing Tutorial

One new graph describing the relationship between the capital-labor ratio and labor productivity is presented in this chapter. The labor productivity curve is fairly easy to draw and to interpret. Best of all, it conveys considerable information about an economy. Suppose we have an economy with 1,000 workers and $300,000 of capital. The capital-labor ratio is equal to $K/L = \$300,000/1,000 = \$300$. On average, each worker has $300 of capital to use in production. Suppose that with $300 of capital each worker contributes $70 to GDP. Labor productivity in this case is equal to $70, since GDP/L = output per laborer = $70. We can compute GDP from this information. GDP is equal to $70 per worker times 1,000 workers, or $70,000.

Now suppose that a $30,000 investment raises the economy's capital stock from $300,000 to $330,000. The capital-labor ratio has increased from $300 to $330,000/1,000 = $330. With more capital, each worker is more productive. Suppose that output per laborer rises to $77. GDP also rises from $70,000 to $77,000. Let's plot the capital-labor ratio on the horizontal axis and the output per laborer ratio on the vertical axis to explore the relationship between them further.

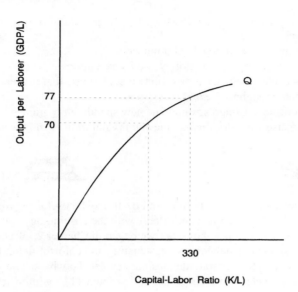

The graph shows that as the capital-labor ratio increases, output per laborer increases, but at a decreasing rate. The slope of the labor productivity curve becomes flatter as the capital-labor ratio increases, reflecting the law of diminishing returns. As each laborer has more capital to work with, labor productivity increases, but at a decreasing rate. Each additional unit of capital adds less and less to output per laborer. Economists refer to the rise in the capital-labor ratio along the horizontal axis as capital deepening.

The labor productivity curve can be used to show the effect of a change in technology. An improvement in technology can increase labor productivity without any change in the value of the capital stock. With better technology, the same dollar amount of capital per laborer results in a higher output per laborer. The impact of technological change is shown in the graph below. The labor productivity curve shifts from Q to Q' so that with $300 of capital, each laborer now generates $90 of output instead of $70.

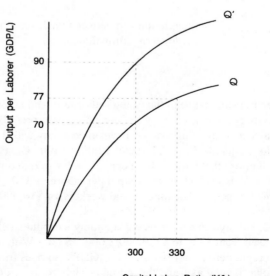

Graphing Pitfalls

Be certain that you draw the labor productivity curve with the correct slope. The slope should be positive and decreasing as *K/L* increases to reflect the law of diminishing returns — the fact that as capital is added for each laborer, output per laborer increases, but at a decreasing rate. It wouldn't make sense to have a labor productivity curve with a positive and increasing slope. Consider the example in the text where laborers are given double-bladed axes. Once each laborer has an axe, output per laborer will increase at a decreasing rate as the number of axes per laborer increases. So, the labor productivity curve won't look like the one drawn below.

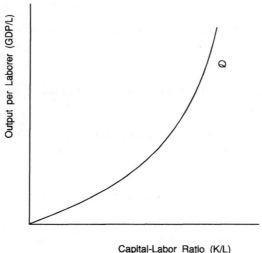

As the capital-labor ratio increases, output per laborer increases at a decreasing rate, not at an increasing rate as shown in this graph.

True-False Questions — If a statement is false, explain why.

1. External theories of economic cycles link cycles to external, random events. (T/F)

2. The U.S. economy grew faster from 1947 to 1973 than it did from 1973 to 1992. (T/F)

3. Our ideas about the causes of economic growth today are much different than those that were advanced by Adam Smith in 1776. (T/F)

4. The capital-output ratio tells us how many dollars' worth of capital are required to generate a dollar's worth of output. (T/F)

5. The model of economic growth based on the linkage between capital stock and GDP incorporates all the key factors associated with the growth process. (T/F)

6. Technological change contributed relatively less to economic growth in the period 1947-1973 than it did in the period 1973-1992. (T/F)

7. During the 20th century, the U.S. economic growth path traces out a steady, upward thrust in real GDP. (T/F)

8. There is a universal consensus among economists that business cycles exist. (T/F)

9. The sunspot theory associated movements through a business cycle with changes in solar activity. (T/F)

10. Marxists argue that governments use wars as a means to overcome economic recessions or depressions. (T/F)

11. New housing construction triggers the income multiplier that sparks the 15-to-20-year housing cycle. (T/F)

12. Simon Kuznets identified the innovation cycle which is linked to specific innovations that create major breakthroughs in technology that require massive investments. (T/F)

13. The multiplier-accelerator cycle is based on the premise that the economy is inherently cyclical. (T/F)

14. The accelerator principle states that an increase in the rate of innovation will induce a higher level of investment. (T/F)

15. Real business cycle theorists argue that what other economists believe to be the business cycle is really just variations in the rate of economic growth attributable to uneven variations in the rate of technological change. (T/F)

Multiple-Choice Questions

1. The effect of technological change on the labor productivity curve is to
   a. shift to a point further to the right on the curve
   b. shift to a point further to the left on the curve since less capital per laborer is required
   c. change the shape of the curve so that the slope is positive and increasing
   d. change the curve to a straight line as the law of diminishing returns is overcome
   e. cause the curve to shift upward

2. The sunspot theory of business cycles is most applicable to
   a. modern industrial economies
   b. an economy affected by global warming
   c. an agricultural economy
   d. an island economy like Great Britain
   e. an economy in a prolonged depression

3. The accelerator is the
   a. relationship between the level of investment and changes in the level of national income
   b. reciprocal of the multiplier
   c. rate of economic growth in the recovery phase of a business cycle
   d. relationship between changes in investment that cause changes in national income
   e. speed at which policy decisions are made in response to changes in the economy

4. The capital-output ratio
   a. describes how changes in investment affect the level of output in an economy
   b. describes how the level of investment affects changes in the economy's output
   c. describes the relationship between the economy's capital stock and its output
   d. is the key factor explaining why business cycles develop in an industrialized economy
   e. measures changes in output during one cycle, from peak to recession

5. All of the following are examples of external theories of business cycles except
   a. the sunspot theory
   b. war-induced cycles
   c. the housing cycle
   d. the innovation cycle
   e. the real business cycle theory

6. The real business cycle theory claims that
   a. business cycles occur because the economy is not competitive
   b. economic performance is linked to technological change that is totally random
   c. competition causes business cycles
   d. there are no adequate theories explaining why the economy experiences business cycles
   e. downturn phases of the cycle dominate the recovery phases

7. All of the following apply to the multiplier-accelerator model of the business cycle **except**
   a. the level of investment depends on changes in national income, which in turn depend on changes in investment
   b. the cycle is internally fueled, that is, it is inherent to the economic system
   c. the cycle dampens to a steady-state equilibrium in the long run
   d. the cycle, once triggered, will repeat
   e. it is not dependent on some external shock to the economic system, such as a war or population boom

8. Thomas Malthus believed that one of the most important factors contributing to "the wealth of nations" was
   a. rapid population growth
   b. increased capital per worker
   c. technological change
   d. the security of property
   e. the effective use of countercyclical fiscal policy

9. Most of the increase in GDP from 1947 to 1973 is explained by _____ while _____ explains most of the growth from 1973 to 1992.
   a. technological change; capital accumulation
   b. capital accumulation; increases in the labor force
   c. increases in the labor force; capital accumulation
   d. increases in the labor force; technological change
   e. technological change; increases in the labor force

10. War-induced cycles, sunspot-induced cycles, and the housing cycle have in common that they are
    a. triggered by misguided government policy
    b. triggered during the prosperity phase of the cycle
    c. internally induced; that is, each occurs because it is an integral part of the economic system
    d. caused by factors that are external to the economic system
    e. all by-products of the multiplier-accelerator cycle

11. The most important source of economic growth since 1973 has been
    a. increased labor inputs
    b. increased capital inputs
    c. technological change
    d. investment
    e. saving

12. The Kuznets cycle describes
    a. the relationship between cycles and housing construction
    b. volatile changes in GDP just prior to the Great Depression
    c. the relationship between changes in the real interest rate and changes in output
    d. how the economy's marginal propensity to consume can, by itself, generate cycles
    e. how immigration can trigger production booms in the economy that are soon followed by recession

13. Countercyclical fiscal policy is designed to
    a. moderate the severity of the business cycle
    b. create a balanced budget in each of the years of a cycle
    c. counter fiscal policies that create deficits, which trigger cycles
    d. curb the excessive powers of government's fiscal policy on cycles
    e. create a cycle whose phases are of equal length

14. An administrative lag
    a. reflects differences in the government's willingness to cope with inflation and unemployment
    b. is the time it takes fiscal policy to clear the bureaucratic channels of government
    c. is the time interval between making a fiscal policy decision and the actual execution of that policy
    d. the time interval between executing and later correcting inappropriate fiscal policy
    e. measures the number of government agencies required to approve any policy

15. A problem inherent in creating countercyclical fiscal policy when the economy is in a downturn is that
    a. the private sector may not go along with that policy, thus undermining the effort
    b. competition among firms in the economy creates a less-than-uniform response to any government policy
    c. government agencies fight among themselves — some want to curb unemployment, others inflation
    d. it is impossible to know whether the economy is heading into recession or toward its recovery phase
    e. lack of consumer confidence undermines any government effort to initiate the recovery phase

16. All of the following are associated with capital deepening **except**
    a. a rise in the ratio of capital to labor
    b. an increase in investment that exceeds an increase in the number of laborers
    c. a movement along the labor productivity curve
    d. a shift upward in the labor productivity curve
    e. an increase in output per laborer

17. Investment-induced growth is dependent on
    a. consumption
    b. fiscal policy
    c. low unemployment
    d. innovation
    e. saving that is automatically converted to investment

18. A major difference between real business cycle theory and the innovation business cycle theory associated with Joseph Schumpeter is that real business cycle
    a. theory predicts that real GDP grows through innovation while Schumpeter's theory predicts that nominal GDP grows through innovation
    b. theorists regard innovations as clustered and connected while Schumpeter believed that innovations are random and unconnected
    c. theory predicts growth will be faster because it is less dependent on innovation than Schumpeter thought
    d. theorists regard innovations as random and unconnected while Schumpeter believed that innovations are clustered and related
    e. theorists support the use of countercyclical fiscal policy but Schumpeter's innovation business cycle theory argues against the use of countercyclical fiscal policy

19. Real business cycle theorists believe that
    a. timing is crucial to the effective use of countercyclical fiscal policy
    b. technological changes are clustered and related to one another
    c. the economy is dynamic and competitive and operates at or close to full employment
    d. improvements in technology have little effect on labor productivity
    e. the growth rate for the economy will eventually fall to zero

20. Data for the United States from 1960 to 1999 suggest that saving as a percentage of GDP
    a. declined gradually until 1993 when it began to increase due to an increase in personal saving
    b. rose dramatically over the entire period
    c. declined gradually until 1993 when it began to increase due to an increase in government saving
    d. fell dramatically over the entire period due to large government budget deficits
    e. was steady over the entire period

The following questions relate to the interdisciplinary, theoretical, global, and applied perspectives in the text.

21. Which of the following is not a reason for developed countries to be reluctant about lending to or investing directly in a developing country?
    a. The developing country may renege on the loan.
    b. The developing country may seize the assets of a foreign company that has invested.
    c. The developing country may pass laws that make it more difficult for the foreign company to do business.
    d. The developing country may threaten to seize the assets of a foreign company if it does not pay bribes.
    e. The developed country may fear damage to its image for exploiting workers in the developing country.

22. The classical economists of the 19th century predicted that the rate of economic growth would gradually fall to zero in the long run because
    a. they failed to anticipate the impact of technological change and capital-deepening on labor productivity
    b. they believed the world would run out of nonrenewable resources
    c. of political instability that was experienced throughout Europe in the 19th century
    d. the economies of the 19th century were not growing
    e. they expected that people would choose to have very small families so the labor force would shrink over time

23. An examination of the growth performance of the world's industrialized economies from 1967 to 2003 shows that
    a. only a few have experienced significant economic growth over the period
    b. economic growth has slowed over the period in the way the classical economists predicted it would
    c. all have positive annual average percentage rates of growth over the period
    d. low savings rates have contributed to slow economic growth
    e. high rates of population growth have slowed economic growth in these countries

24. A comparison of economic growth rates between years when the Republicans held the White House and the Democrats held the White House from 1971-1996 shows that
    a. the economy grows more rapidly with Republicans in office than Democrats
    b. there is little or no correlation
    c. the economy grows more rapidly with Democrats in office than Republicans
    d. only under Reagan did the economy grow
    e. only under Clinton did the economy grow

25. Even if the correct countercyclical fiscal policy can be determined in order to moderate the severity of the business cycle, it is possible that the policy will not be implemented at the appropriate time because
    a. of the Congressional phase of administrative lag
    b. Congressional Republicans and Democrats rarely cooperate in such matters
    c. Congress is more concerned with maintaining a balanced budget rather than pursuing countercyclical fiscal policy
    d. the President usually vetoes bills containing changes in taxes and spending
    e. bureaucrats who administer the policy are highly inefficient

Fill in the Blanks

1. An economy's equilibrium may be more of a _____ than a specifically

   _____ GDP.

2. The four factors that Adam Smith identified as principal contributors to economic growth are

   _____, _____, _____, and

   _____.

3. Countercyclical fiscal policies are intended to moderate the _____ and the

   _____ phases of the business cycle.

4. Administrative lag is the time lapse between the government's _____ of a specific fiscal

   policy and the _____ of the policy.

Discussion Questions

1. How can economic cycles be related to the level of sunspot activity? Would you be comfortable predicting economic performance in the United States over the next five years based on sunspot activity? Why or why not?

2. Explain the innovation cycle.

3. How does real business cycle theory compare to the innovation business cycle theory?

4. Describe circumstances under which a countercyclical fiscal policy could be destabilizing even though it seemed to be the right thing to do when the policy was introduced.

Problems

1. Suppose the capital-output ratio is 4, and the initial level of income is $1,000, and the marginal propensity to consume is 0.80. Assume that there is no government and no foreign trade. Assume also that the dollar amount invested in one year increases the capital stock in the next year by the same amount. Compute values to fill the cells in the table below to show the level of income, the size of the capital stock, consumption, saving and investment for a four-year period. What is the rate of growth for this economy? What allows this economy to grow?

	Y	K	C	S	I
Year 1					
Year 2					
Year 3					
Year 4					

Everyday Applications

Since the brief recession in the early 1990s, economic growth in the United States has been quite robust. The signs of growth in all parts of the country are readily visible. What are some examples? Is there a particular business cycle theory that can explain this resurgence of growth? Consider the applicability of the various theories that we have examined.

Economics Online

Some analysts are opposed to active government intervention in the economy to counter the business cycle. The Cato Institute is home to some of these conservative analysts. You can visit the Cato Institute web site at (*http://www.cato.org/*). Under the heading *Cato Research Areas* go to the *fiscal policy* option and consider the Cato Institute position on countercyclical fiscal policy.

Answers to Questions

Key Terms Quiz

a. 5   **f.** 3
b. 7   **g.** 4
c. 6   **h.** 2
d. 1
e. 8

True-False Questions

1. True
2. True
3. False. Smith identified the same principal factors that we study today as the sources of economic growth.
4. True
5. False. Economic growth is a function of many other factors, such as labor inputs and technological change, that are left out of the growth model that links GDP to the size of the capital stock.
6. False. Technological change was relatively more important in the early period.
7. False. This period is marked by major fluctuations in real GDP.
8. False. Real business cycle theorists completely reject the idea of a business cycle.
9. True
10. True
11. True
12. False. Schumpeter is credited with the innovation business cycle theory.
13. True
14. False. The accelerator principle states that an increase in the rate of growth of GDP will induce a higher level of investment.
15. True

Multiple-Choice Questions

1. e	**6.** b	**11.** b	**16.** d	**21.** e
2. c	**7.** c	**12.** a	**17.** e	**22.** a
3. a	**8.** d	**13.** a	**18.** d	**23.** c
4. c	**9.** a	**14.** c	**19.** c	**24.** b
5. e	**10.** d	**15.** d	**20.** c	**25.** a

Fill in the Blanks

1. moving target; fixed
2. size of the labor force; degree of labor specialization; size of the capital stock; level of technology
3. recession; prosperity
4. choice; implementation

Discussion Questions

1. High levels of sunspot activity seem to be related to poor crop performance. This theory of the business cycle wouldn't be good for predicting cycles in the United States because agriculture accounts for such a small portion of our GDP. However, during the 19th century and earlier, when a larger percentage of the population farmed for a living, this theory was quite relevant.

2. The innovation cycle refers to technological changes that are clustered in particular industries and lead to high rates of investment in these industries. These innovations spur the economy into prosperity. When the innovations run their course, and the level of innovative activity falls, the economy slips into its downturn phase. A good example is the progress of transportation technology during the 19th century and into the 20th. New technologies and new industries replaced old ones as, for example, the automobile replaced the horse and buggy. These waves of investment can cause economic cycles.

3. Real business cycle theorists don't believe in a business cycle. Rather, they argue that the economy experiences periodic bursts of rapid growth associated with rapid technological changes that occur randomly in the economy. On the other hand, the innovation cycle focuses on technological changes that are significant enough to lead to major changes in investment, which starts the cycle process. The innovation business cycle theory maintains that innovations are clustered and related to one another, rather than random and unrelated.

4. Many answers are possible here. Suppose the economy was in recession and the president, hoping to moderate the economy's decline, decides on a massive spending program. By the time the program is approved by Congress and implemented, the economy has begun its recovery. But the program now takes effect, and instead of moderating the economy's fall, it contributes to the growing inflationary pressures. This is a classic example of administrative lag.

Problems

1. The completed table is shown below.

	Y	K	C	S	I
Year 1	1,000	4,000	800	200	200
Year 2	1,050	4,200	840	210	210
Year 3	1,102.5	4,410	882	220.5	220.5
Year 4	1,157.6	4,630.5	926.1	231.5	231.5

The cells are calculated as follows. In year 1, output is set at 1,000 and the capital-output ratio is 4. Therefore, the capital stock, K, is equal to 4,000. The MPC is given, equal to .8, so consumption is 800, saving is 200, and because saving is equal to investment, investment is equal to 200. In year 2, the $I = 200$ from year 1 is added to the capital stock, increasing K to 4,200. The capital-output ratio equal to 4 means that $Y = 4,200/4 = 1,050$ in year 2. Given the MPC = .8, consumption is .8(1,050) = 840, S = 210, and $I = 210$; add this to the capital stock, and follow the calculations for years 3 and 4.

This economy is growing at a constant 5 percent rate. Ultimately, it is saving that provides resources for investment that leads to capital accumulation, which allows this economy to grow.

Homework Questions

True-False Questions — If a statement is false, explain why.

1. New technology shifts the labor productivity curve upward. (T/F)

2. The classical economists of the 19th century believed that economic growth would eventually come to a halt. (T/F)

3. As expected sales in an economy decrease, investment in new capital equipment will increase, according to the idea of the accelerator. (T/F)

4. Real business cycle theorists believe that technological changes in the economy were random and unrelated. (T/F)

5. The existence of administrative lag makes countercyclical fiscal policy difficult to implement at the appropriate time. (T/F)

Multiple-Choice Questions

1. William Stanley Jevons's sunspot theory relates
   a. economic performance to nuclear storms on the sun
   b. investment behavior of firms to seasons of the year
   c. changes in consumers' propensities to consume to seasons of the year
   d. changes in economic performance to government's fiscal policy
   e. changes in economic performance to changes in the interest rate

2. In Schumpeter's innovation cycle,
   a. technological change dampens the cycle, forcing the economy to equilibrium
   b. government's randomly distributed investments in research and development trigger the cycle
   c. innovations cause uneven changes in labor productivity, which trigger the cycle
   d. clusters of innovations propel an economy into prosperity and, once exhausted, create a downturn
   e. innovations cause nominal GDP to depart from real GDP, which triggers the cycle

3. An examination of the sources of U.S. economic growth from 1947 to 1973, 1973 to 1992, and 1992 to 2003 shows that
   a. technological change was a relatively more important source of economic growth in the later two periods
   b. capital inputs were a relatively more important source of economic growth in the earliest period
   c. total growth was faster in the latest period
   d. technological change was a relatively more important source of economic growth in the earliest period
   e. labor inputs were the most important source of growth in all three periods

4. Long-run economic growth can be represented in a graph of aggregate demand and aggregate supply as a
   a. shift to the left of the aggregate supply curve
   b. shift to the right of the aggregate demand curve
   c. decrease in the equilibrium price level
   d. shift to the right in the aggregate supply curve
   e. decrease in the slope of the upward-sloping segment of the aggregate supply curve

5. Real business cycle theorists believe that the
   a. economy always operates close to full employment
   b. rate of economic growth is stable over time
   c. phases of the business cycle can be easily identified
   d. administrative lag is short
   e. economy's performance can be improved through government intervention

Discussion Questions/Problems

1. Why did the classical economists believe that economic growth would eventually cease?

2. Describe how interactions between the multiplier and the accelerator can create a business cycle.

PART 2 — EMPLOYMENT, INFLATION, AND FISCAL POLICY

COMPREHENSIVE SAMPLE TEST

Give yourself 50 minutes to complete this exam and see how you do. The answers follow. Don't look until you are finished!

True-False Questions — If a statement is false, explain why. Each question is worth two points.

1. The horizontal segment of the aggregate supply curve means that resources are fully employed. (T/F)

2. As the price level decreases, the quantity demanded of real goods and services increases because real wealth increases. (T/F)

3. The income and expenditure approaches to calculating GDP are equivalent. (T/F)

4. Modigliani's life-cycle hypothesis states that consumption varies exactly in proportion to income change over a person's lifetime. (T/F)

5. When the level of income is zero, consumption spending must be zero too. (T/F)

6. The accumulation of unwanted inventories is an indication that intended investment is greater than actual investment. (T/F)

7. In an economy with no government and no foreign trade the aggregate expenditure curve lies above and parallel to the consumption curve with the vertical distance between them equal to autonomous investment. (T/F)

8. An appropriate fiscal policy to close an inflationary gap is to cut taxes. (T/F)

9. A potential problem with increasing government spending to close a recessionary gap is that it is very difficult to cut government spending once it is introduced. (T/F)

10. The accelerator is an increase in investment causing income to increase, which is followed by the multiplier causing investment to increase further. (T/F)

Multiple-Choice Questions — Each question is worth two points.

1. Demand-pull inflation is the result of
   a. a leftward shift in the aggregate supply curve
   b. a rightward shift in the aggregate supply curve
   c. a leftward shift in the aggregate demand curve
   d. a rightward shift in the aggregate demand curve
   e. simultaneous shifts to the left in the aggregate demand and aggregate supply curves

2. A recession is defined as a period during which
   a. real GDP decreases for at least six months
   b. the GDP deflator decreases for at least six months
   c. nominal GDP decreases for at least six months
   d. real GDP decreases for at least a year
   e. the GDP deflator decreases for at least a year

3. If nominal GDP is $7 trillion in 1998 and the GDP deflator is 110, then real GDP is
   a. $7.7 trillion
   b. $6.89 trillion
   c. $7.11 trillion
   d. $6.36 trillion
   e. $7 trillion

4. If gross private domestic investment in the economy is less than depreciation, then
   a. GDP and NDP are equal
   b. the stock of capital is shrinking
   c. the stock of capital is growing
   d. unwanted inventories are accumulating
   e. the useful life for capital equipment is increasing

5. Of the following, the largest percentage component of national income is
   a. profits
   b. rents and royalties
   c. interest
   d. compensation to employees
   e. proprietors' income

6. For a country that has a large number of its citizens working abroad, the better measure of economic performance is
   a. the GDP deflator
   b. real GDP
   c. nominal GDP
   d. nominal GNP
   e. real GNP

7. Keynes's absolute income hypothesis for consumption behavior states that as income increases,
   a. consumption increases at a decreasing rate
   b. the consumption of leisure increases at an increasing rate
   c. consumption increases at an increasing rate
   d. the MPC increases
   e. the MPC is constant

8. All of the following are determinants of autonomous investment **except**
   a. the level of national income
   b. the level of technology
   c. the rate of capacity utilization
   d. the interest rate
   e. expectations of future economic growth

9. An increase in the marginal propensity to consume will cause
   a. the marginal propensity to save to increase
   b. autonomous consumption to increase
   c. autonomous consumption to decrease
   d. the marginal propensity to save to decrease
   e. the tax multiplier to increase

10. Keynes believed that saving would equal intended investment
    a. automatically, because saving and investment decisions are closely coordinated
    b. so that the economy can move toward equilibrium
    c. because unwanted inventories are equal to zero
    d. purely by chance because saving and investment decisions are made independently by different groups
    e. if the marginal propensity to save were sufficiently large

11. If saving is greater than intended investment, then
    a. aggregate expenditure is greater than national income
    b. national income will increase as the economy moves toward equilibrium
    c. national income is greater than aggregate expenditure
    d. wanted inventories are decreasing
    e. employment will increase

12. Suppose you read in the newspaper that the ratio of inventories to sales is increasing. It is likely that
    a. the economy is poised to experience a period of rapid growth
    b. employment, production, and national income will fall
    c. wanted inventories are decreasing
    d. the price level will rise significantly
    e. an inflationary gap will need to be closed

13. Suppose the consumption function is $C = 500 + .8Y$ and $I = 300$. The equilibrium level of national income is
    a. 4,000
    b. 400
    c. 40,000
    d. 40
    e. 1,600

14. Suppose there is a recessionary gap equal to $10 billion and the MPC is equal to .8. We know that the economy is in equilibrium at a level of income that is
    a. $80 billion below the full-employment level of income
    b. $80 billion above the full-employment level of income
    c. $40 billion below the full-employment level of income
    d. $50 billion above the full-employment level of income
    e. $50 billion below the full-employment level of income

15. One problem with using the balanced budget approach to close a recessionary gap is that
   a. full employment with a balanced budget happens purely by chance and cannot be achieved with conscious policy
   b. the increases in G and T necessary to achieve full employment may be quite large
   c. people will not tolerate the cuts in government spending necessary to balance the budget
   d. the tax increase necessary to balance the budget would cause a bigger recessionary gap
   e. the tax multiplier is very small

16. One conclusion to be drawn from our analysis of the income multiplier is that
   a. a recession due to a decrease in investment will be short-lived because of the income multiplier
   b. the decrease in national income due to a decrease in investment will be a multiple of the decrease in investment
   c. a decrease in investment will be matched by an increase in saving
   d. the income multiplier will guarantee a full-employment level of national income
   e. the value of the MPC and the multiplier are inversely related

17. Consider the following combinations of government spending and tax changes. The strongest policy to close an inflationary gap is a
   a. $100 billion increase in G; $100 billion decrease in T
   b. $100 billion increase in G; $100 billion increase in T
   c. $100 billion decrease in G; $100 billion increase in T
   d. $100 billion decrease in G; $100 billion decrease in T
   e. $100 billion decrease in G; no change in T

18. All of the following are examples of external theories of cycles **except**
   a. the sunspot theory
   b. war-induced cycles
   c. the housing cycle
   d. the innovation cycle
   e. the real business cycle

19. If we were to represent real business cycle theory using a production possibilities curve model, we would show
   a. shifts in the curve, some large, some small, that correspond to different rates of growth in the economy due to random and unrelated technological changes
   b. a continual shift in the curve to the right at a constant rate over time
   c. movements from points inside the curve to points on the curve that seem to happen randomly
   d. sequential shifts in the intercepts of the curve, first along the horizontal axis, then along the vertical axis
   e. an increase in the extent of the bowed-out shape of the curve as the economy becomes more specialized

20. The upward shift in the labor productivity curve over time is the result of
   a. capital deepening
   b. an increase in the capital-labor ratio
   c. technological change
   d. an increase in the capital-output ratio
   e. saving

Discussion Questions/Problems — Each question is worth 10 points.

1. a. What is aggregate demand? Draw an aggregate demand curve and explain its shape. What factors influence aggregate demand?

b. What is aggregate supply? Draw an aggregate supply curve and explain its shape. What factors influence aggregate supply?

c. What does macroequilibrium mean?

2. Describe Keynes's absolute income hypothesis to explain consumption spending behavior. Why is it incorrect? Present an alternative hypothesis to explain consumption behavior.

3. a. Suppose that consumption is $C = 600 + .75Y$ and $I = 400$ (all values are billions of dollars). Write an equation for aggregate expenditure, calculate the equilibrium level of national income, and sketch a graph of the aggregate expenditure curve to show the equilibrium level of national income.

    b. Suppose the full-employment level of income is $6,000 billion. Is there a recessionary or an inflationary gap? How large is the gap? By how much would government spending have to change to close the gap? Show your work.

4. Discuss the problems inherent in designing a countercyclical fiscal policy.

Answers to Sample Test on Part 2

True-False Questions

1. False. The horizontal segment of the aggregate supply curve corresponds to ample unemployed resources in the economy that can be brought into production without an increase in the price level.
2. True
3. True
4. False. Modigliani's life-cycle hypothesis states that consumption spending will rise gradually during a person's life as income rises. The marginal propensity to consume changes significantly over a person's life. Typically, young adults have a very high marginal propensity to consume, middle-aged individuals have a lower *MPC* as they save for retirement, and retirees have a higher *MPC*.
5. False. Autonomous consumption, consumption when income is zero, is positive when people spend out of accumulated saving.
6. False. If unwanted inventories accumulate, then actual investment is greater than intended investment.
7. True
8. False. An appropriate fiscal policy to close an inflationary gap would be to increase taxes.
9. True.
10. False. The multiplier is an increase in investment causing income to increase. It is followed by the accelerator causing investment to increase further in order to create the productive capacity to support a higher level of expected sales that is associated with a higher level of national income.

Multiple-Choice Questions

1. d	6. e	11. c	16. b
2. a	7. a	12. b	17. c
3. d	8. a	13. a	18. e
4. b	9. e	14. e	19. a
5. d	10. d	15. b	20. c

Discussion Questions/Problems

1. a. Aggregate demand is the total quantity of goods and services demanded by households, firms, foreigners, and government at varying price levels. The aggregate demand curve is downward sloping as the price level decreases. The aggregate demand curve slopes downward because of the real wealth effect, the interest rate effect, and the international trade effect. The real wealth effect states that as the price level decreases, real wealth increases, so consumption spending will increase. The interest rate effect states that as the price level decreases, the demand for loanable funds decreases, so the interest rate decreases, causing consumption spending and investment to increase. The international trade effect states that as the price level decreases in the United States relative to other countries, the demand for U.S. exports increases. The position of the aggregate demand curve is influenced by changes in consumption spending, changes in investment spending, changes in government spending, and changes in spending on exports and imports. Increases in spending shift the curve to the right and decreases in spending shift the curve to the left. A graph of the aggregate demand curve is shown on the following page along with a graph of the aggregate supply curve.

   b. Aggregate supply is the total quantity of goods and services that firms in the economy are willing to supply at varying price levels. The aggregate supply curve is drawn in three distinct segments — a horizontal segment at low levels of real GDP, an upward-sloping segment as real GDP increases, and a vertical segment that corresponds to a full-employment level of real GDP. The horizontal segment describes low levels of real GDP where resources are unemployed and can be brought into production with no increase in the price level. The upward-sloping segment describes an economy approaching full employment. As unemployed resources become scarcer, employers must pay more to hire them, and these cost increases are passed on in the form of price increases. Alternatively, an increase in the price level will increase profit margins for firms, which then expand production or enter profitable industries causing real GDP to increase. The vertical segment corresponds to full employment — no more resources are available for production so real GDP cannot increase. The position of the aggregate supply curve is influenced by resource availability. As labor, land, capital, and entrepreneurial energies become more available, the aggregate supply curve shifts to the right. As resources become less available, the aggregate supply curve shifts to the left.

   c. Macroequilibrium occurs at the level of real GDP and the price level that equate the aggregate quantity demanded and the aggregate quantity supplied. This point is represented by the intersection of the aggregate demand and aggregate supply curves drawn on the following page.

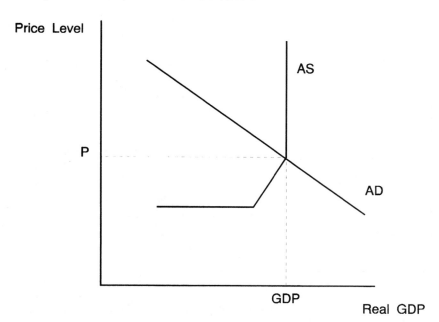

2. Keynes argued that consumption spending depended on the absolute level of national income. Consumption spending is a larger fraction on national income at low levels of national income than at high levels. Once income rises to a high enough level to meet the most pressing consumption needs, the desire to save a portion of income becomes more prominent. Therefore, the marginal propensity to consume decreases as income increases, according to Keynes. However, data examined by Simon Kuznets showed that consumption spending is a constant fraction of income. That is, the marginal propensity to consume is constant. The Duesenberry relative income hypothesis can explain this fact. People with low incomes spend nearly all of their income to meet immediate consumption needs. They have a marginal propensity to consume that is close to 1. Middle-income individuals also have a relatively high marginal propensity to consume. The rich are able to save a larger fraction of their income, so their marginal propensity to consume is lower. If each group's income level increases at approximately the same rate as national income over time, no group's relative position changes; therefore, the overall marginal propensity to consume is constant.

3. a. The aggregate expenditure equation is $AE = 1,000 + .75Y$. To solve for the equilibrium level of national income, set $AE = Y$. Thus, we have $1,000 + .75Y = Y$. Subtracting $.75Y$ from both sides gives $1,000 = .25Y$, so $Y = \$4,000$ billion. The graph on the following page illustrates this equilibrium level of national income.

   b. If the full-employment level of national income is $6,000 billion, then national income will have to rise by \$2,000. A recessionary gap exists. The multiplier is equal to $1/(1 - MPC) = 1/(1 - .75) = 4$. $\Delta Y = 2,000 = 4\Delta G$. Therefore, $\Delta G = 2,000/4 = \$500$ billion. The recessionary gap is $500 billion, and government spending must increase by this amount to achieve the full-employment level of national income.

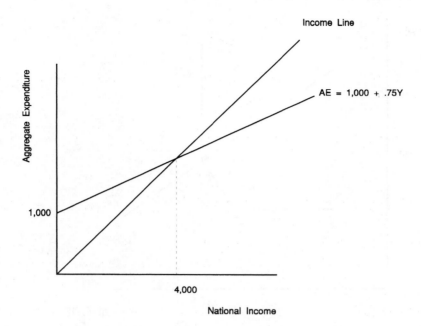

4. Countercyclical fiscal policy is designed to moderate the severity of the business cycle. Designing and implementing countercyclical fiscal policy is quite difficult. First, it takes time to recognize that a recession or inflation is beginning. Once a problem is recognized, a decision has to be made about whether policy action should be taken or not. This depends on the type of cycle the economy is entering. For example, if the economy dips into a recession, it could be very brief and largely self-correcting. If this is the case, no action is justified because a fiscal policy that increased spending might trigger inflation. However, perhaps the recession will deepen and be long-lasting. In this case, increased spending via a fiscal policy action is justified. How does one tell which way the cycle will go? No one can be certain. Suppose the decision is made to implement a fiscal policy to increase spending. The problem of administrative lag is then encountered — the time lapse between deciding on a policy and the implementation of the policy. A long administrative lag can result in a situation where the economy has already recovered before the policy takes effect, creating inflationary pressure. The problem of increased unemployment that is associated with a recession may be structural rather than cyclical unemployment. In that case, a job retraining program than fiscal policy would be more appropriate than fiscal policy. Finally, some believe there is no such thing as a business cycle — real business cycle theorists hold this view. If they are correct, then fiscal policy is never appropriate.

CHAPTER 10

MONEY

Chapter in a Nutshell

Although we know from experience that, under certain circumstances, **barter exchange** works, the complications associated with the requirements of a **double coincidence of wants** make the exchange of one good for another inefficient in the modern world. **Money** was invented to facilitate exchange. Money serves three functions. It is a **medium of exchange, a measure of value, and a store of value**. What properties must money have? It must be durable, portable, divisible, homeogeneous, and be relatively scarce. Gold has these characteristics and has long been used as money. Paper money — called fiat money — works as well, as long as it is universally accepted as the medium of exchange.

Let's look at our modern world of money. Money is described as a **liquid asset** because it exchanges easily for other assets. Our money supply is categorized according to its **liquidity**. **M1** is the most liquid. It includes currency and demand deposits (our checking accounts) and traveler's checks. **M2** is M1 money plus savings accounts, certificates of deposit, money market mutual funds, money market deposit accounts, repurchase agreements, and small-denomination time deposits. **M3** is M2 money plus other less liquid forms of money such as large denomination time deposits and large overnight repurchase agreements.

The relationship between an economy's prices and its money supply is expressed in the **quantity theory of money,** which derives from the **equation of exchange: $MV = PQ$**, where M is the money supply, V is the velocity of money, P is the price level, and Q the quantity of goods. The quantity theory of money restates the equation to read, assuming both V and Q are constant:

$$P = MV/Q.$$

We now see the direct relationship between money and prices (increase money, and the price level increases).

Economists hold different views concerning the velocity of money. **Classical economists** believe velocity is constant; **monetarists** believe it is not constant but stable and predictable; and **Keynesians** believe it is neither constant, stable, nor predictable. Economists' views on velocity affect their policy prescriptions. These show up in their theories of demand for money.

Classical economists believed that the demand for money is strictly a **transactions demand**, that is, a demand arising from the need to carry out transactions. They assume that since output is constant at full employment and velocity is constant, then the transactions demand for money depends on the price level. Monetarists accept the variability of velocity but believe that $MV = PQ$ can still be a good tool for analysis because even though velocity is variable, it is predictable.

Keynesians believe that there are three motives for demanding (holding) money: **the transactions motive, the precautionary motive, and the speculative motive.** The speculative demand for money is inversely related to the interest rate. A fall in the interest rate increases the quantity demanded of money. Therefore, if the money supply increases, interest rates will fall and investment will increase, causing aggregate demand and real GDP to increase. To Keynesians, money matters. Classical economists and monetarists, on the other hand, believe that increases in the money supply only cause the price level to increase because the economy is continuously at full employment.

After you study this chapter, you should be able to:

- Explain why **money** has replaced **barter**.
- List the functions of money.
- Explain the **liquidity characteristics** of our money supply.
- Describe the **classical view of money demand** and the **quantity theory of money**.
- Explain **monetarism**.
- Contrast the **Keynesian** and the **monetarist** views of **money demand**.
- Account for the Keynesian belief that money matters.

Concept Check — See how you do on these multiple-choice questions.

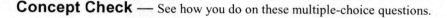

Barter is an exchange of one good for another. Why is barter problematic in a modern economy?

1. A significant problem with **barter exchanges** in a modern economy is that
   a. only one party benefits from barter exchanges
   b. converted into money terms, barter prices typically are lower
   c. converted into money terms, barter prices typically are higher
   d. barter requires a double coincidence of wants, which is often difficult to achieve
   e. only agricultural goods can be exchanged by barter

The more liquid an asset is, the easier it is to. . .

2. **Liquidity** refers to
   a. money flows in the circular flow model
   b. flows of goods and services in the circular flow model
   c. the fact that gold is easy to melt and purify
   d. the fact that flows of debased coins drive out flows of good coins according to Gresham's law
   e. the degree to which an asset can be easily exchanged for money

How did the classical economists view velocity compared to monetarists?

3. The main difference in viewpoints about **velocity** between the classical economists and monetarists is that classical economists believed that
   a. velocity was constant and monetarist believe that it is variable but predictable
   b. velocity was determined by the money supply and monetarists believe that velocity is determined by interest rates
   c. velocity was determined by the price level and monetarists believe that velocity determines the price level
   d. velocity is variable but predictable and monetarists believe that velocity is constant
   e. velocity increases as real GDP increases and monetarists believe that velocity is independent of GDP

The quantity theory of money focuses on the amount of money in circulation.

4. The **quantity theory of money** states that
   a. the quantity of money in circulation depends on the velocity of money
   b. the price level is proportional to the quantity of money in circulation
   c. velocity and real GDP fluctuate significantly in the short run
   d. the quantity of money in circulation is proportional to the price level
   e. velocity is not constant, but it is highly predictable

Why do people demand money?

5. The **transactions demand for money**
   a. is the quantity of money demanded by households and businesses to transact their buying and selling of goods and services
   b. decreases as the interest rate increases
   c. increases as the interest rate increases
   d. is the only determinant of the demand for money, according to Keynesians
   e. is money held as insurance against unexpected needs

Am I on the Right Track?

Your answers to the questions above should be **d**, **e**, **a**, **b**, and **a**. You can divide your study of this chapter into two parts. The first part focuses on the nature of money, its role in society, and the characteristics of the money supply. The material is largely descriptive. The second part of the chapter is more theoretical. Here, you need to learn the similarities and differences among the classical, monetarist, and Keynesian theories of money's role in the economy. The differences among these monetary theories are the source of enormous controversy and debate among economists.

Key Terms Quiz — Match the terms on the left with the definitions in the column on the right.

1. barter
2. M2 money supply
3. money
4. M3 money supply
5. fiat money
6. currency
7. equation of exchange
8. liquidity
9. quantity theory of money
10. transactions demand for money
11. M1 money supply
12. money supply
13. velocity of money

_____ a. coins and paper money

_____ b. the supply of the most immediate form of money that includes currency, demand deposits, and traveler's checks

_____ c. paper money that is not backed by or convertible into any good

_____ d. $P = MV/Q$ — the equation specifying the direct relationship between the money supply and prices, assuming V and Q are constant

_____ e. the M1 money supply plus savings accounts, money market mutual fund accounts, money market deposit accounts, repurchase agreements, and small-denomination time deposits

_____ f. the exchange of one good for another, without the use of money

_____ g. typically, the M1 money supply — currency, demand deposits, and traveler's checks used in transactions

_____ h. the quantity of money demanded by households and businesses to transact their buying and selling of goods and services

_____ i. the M2 money supply plus large-denomination time deposits and large-denomination repurchase agreements

_____ j. any commonly accepted good that acts as a medium of exchange, a measure of value, and a store of value

_____ k. $MV = PQ$

_____ l. the degree to which an asset can easily be exchanged for money

_____ m. the average number of times per year each dollar is used to transact an exchange

Graphing Tutorial

Keynesians view the demand for money as comprised of three parts — the transactions motive (the source of demand for money according to the classical and monetarist views), the speculative motive, and the precautionary motive. The speculative demand for money arises from the fact that people have a choice to hold their assets either as money, which earns little or no interest, or as other financial assets that do earn interest. How people choose to split their assets between money and interest-bearing assets depends on the interest rate. As the interest rate decreases, people choose to hold more money because the opportunity cost of holding money (what they give up in interest income from interest-bearing assets) has fallen. By holding a larger proportion of their assets in money, people are in a better position to take advantage of buying opportunities that might arise. That is to say, they put themselves in a better position to speculate by holding more cash. This logic allows us to graph the speculative demand for money as a downward-sloping function of the interest rate as shown below.

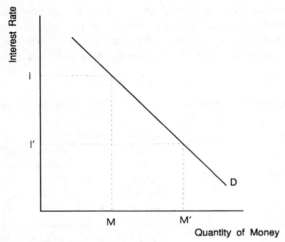

A decrease in the interest rate from i to i′ causes the quantity demanded of money to increase from M to M′. Now we are in a position to understand how money matters to a Keynesian. Suppose the money supply curve, shown as a vertical line labeled S in Panel A below, increases to S′. The increase in the money supply causes a decrease in the interest rate that results in an increase in the quantity of investment in Panel B. This increase in investment will cause the aggregate demand curve to shift to the right, raising the equilibrium level of real GDP if the economy is operating below the full-employment level.

A   B

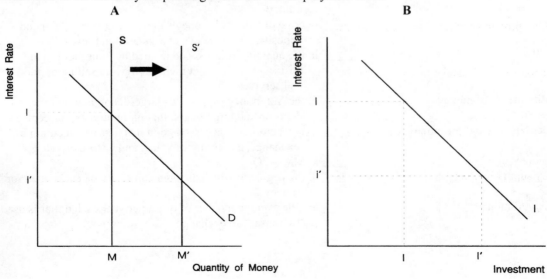

Graphing Pitfalls

As usual, labeling the axes incorrectly is a pitfall to avoid when graphing the speculative demand for money. The speculative demand for money is downward sloping — typical for a demand curve — and the quantity of money is measured on the horizontal axis — also typical — but the vertical axis doesn't measure price. The interest rate is the price of holding money in this case. The interest rate is what a person gives up in order to hold money rather than an interest-bearing asset. So label the vertical axis with the interest rate.

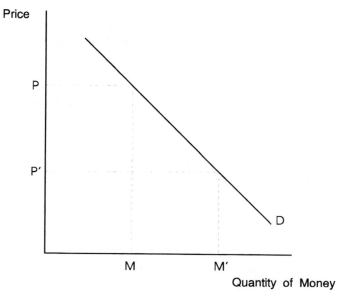

The interest rate is the opportunity cost of holding money, so the vertical axis is labeled with the interest rate, not price as shown above.

True-False Questions — If a statement is false, explain why.

1. Barter only works effectively when there is a double coincidence of wants. (T/F)

2. Gold has properties that make it a good form of money. (T/F)

3. Paper money that is backed by gold is called fiat money. (T/F)

4. According to Keynesians, when the economy is in a recession, an increase in the money supply would decrease the interest rate and, consequently, increase the level of investment and real GDP. (T/F)

5. An asset is considered to be liquid if it can be exchanged easily for money. (T/F)

6. As one compares the various forms of money supply in order — from M1, to M2, to M3 — increasingly liquid assets are included. (T/F)

7. Time deposits, such as people's savings accounts, are considered to be part of M1. (T/F)

8. The largest category of our M2 money supply is in the form of currency. (T/F)

9. The transactions demand for money refers to the amount of money necessary for people to transact the buying and selling of goods and services. (T/F)

10. If the velocity of money is equal to 1, then the transactions demand for money is equal to nominal GDP. (T/F)

11. The quantity of money demanded to satisfy people's speculative motive increases as the interest rate decreases. (T/F)

12. Assuming full employment and a constant velocity of money, an increase in the money supply will lead to a proportionate increase in the price level. (T/F)

13. Monetarists believe that the velocity of money is highly variable and impossible to predict. (T/F)

14. The three motives that Keynesians believe influence people's demand for money are transactions, precautionary, and speculative. (T/F)

15. Keynesians argue that money velocity is neither constant nor predictable, and is affected, in large measure, by changes in people's expectations of future prices. (T/F)

Multiple-Choice Questions

1. The most liquid form of money is
   a. M1
   b. M2
   c. M3
   d. gold
   e. barter

2. The creation of new financial innovations, such as NOW accounts and ATS accounts, has
   a. created distinct differentiations between M1 and M2 money
   b. created distinct differentiations between M2 and M3 money
   c. blurred the distinctions between M1 and M2 money
   d. blurred the distinctions between M2 and M3 money forms
   e. made credit cards, such as Visa and MasterCard, a new form of money

3. All of the following are included in the M3 money supply **except**
   a. currency
   b. corporate bonds
   c. savings accounts
   d. large-denomination time deposits
   e. large-denomination repurchase agreements

4. In order to serve as a medium of exchange, money must fulfill all of the following requirements **except**
   a. divisibility
   b. homogeneity
   c. scarcity
   d. attractability
   e. durability

5. According to Keynes, the demand for money
   a. is an increasing function of the interest rate, that is, as the interest rate rises, the demand for money rises
   b. depends on the supply of money, which is determined by the government
   c. is based solely on the amount of money needed to transact aggregate supply
   d. is based on people's transactions, speculative, and precautionary motives for holding money
   e. exceeds the money supply when real GDP is greater than nominal GDP

6. All of the following statements about M1 are correct **except**
   a. M1, compared to M2 and M3, is the most readily available money form
   b. M1 includes checking accounts, which are generally more liquid than savings accounts
   c. M1 excludes currency, which is the least liquid form of money
   d. travelers' checks are a form of M1 money
   e. the quantity of money ($ billions) that makes up M1 is less than the quantities that make up M2 and M3

7. The classical model of money demand holds that the demand for money is dependent on
   a. the money supply
   b. the interest rate
   c. nominal GDP and the velocity of money
   d. the precautionary and speculative motives for holding money
   e. changes in the velocity of money

8. According to the equation of exchange, $MV = PQ$, a short-run increase in the money supply equal to 10 percent will cause the price level to increase by 10 percent if V is
   a. variable and Q is below full employment
   b. variable and Q is at full employment
   c. constant and Q is at full employment
   d. constant and Q is below full employment
   e. variable but predictable and Q is close to full employment

9. The main difference between the classical view of money's role in the economy and the monetarist view of money is that the classical school
   a. held that the economy was very competitive while monetarists saw the economy as dominated by monopoly power
   b. held that velocity was variable but predictable while monetarists argued that velocity was constant
   c. thought that the economy was always at full employment while the monetarists argued that persistent unemployment could arise
   d. saw money demand as solely a transactions demand while monetarists viewed money demand as stemming from precautionary and speculative motives
   e. held that the velocity was constant while monetarists argued that velocity could vary over time in ways that are predictable

10. The value of money diminishes as
    a. it becomes more divisible
    b. society abandons gold and silver for paper currency
    c. it becomes more plentiful relative to other goods
    d. an economy becomes more advanced
    e. credit cards come into widespread use

11. According to Keynesians, an easy way to illustrate that velocity is not constant is to suppose people expect the price level to increase and begin to make purchases in advance. If the money supply is constant, then velocity will
    a. increase to accommodate the spending increase
    b. decrease to accommodate the spending increase
    c. decrease and the price level will increase
    d. decrease and the price level will decrease
    e. increase and the price level will decrease

12. According to the classical view of the quantity theory of money,
    a. an increase in the money supply causes real output to increase
    b. velocity is highly variable in the short run
    c. an increase in the money supply causes nominal GDP to fall
    d. an increase in the money supply causes the price level to increase proportionately
    e. the impact of an increase in the money supply is impossible to predict

13. If nominal GDP is $5 trillion, and the money supply is $500 billion, then, according to the equation of exchange, the velocity of money is
    a. 5
    b. 0.5
    c. 10
    d. 100
    e. 2.5

14. John demonstrates the speculative motive for holding money by
    a. holding money, waiting for stock prices to rise
    b. holding money, "for a rainy day"
    c. not spending money in May because he plans to get married and honeymoon in June
    d. borrowing money from the local bank to finance his college education
    e. buying a large quantity of lottery tickets because he speculates "today's the day"

15. John demonstrates the precautionary motive for holding money by
    a. holding money "for a rainy day"
    b. borrowing money from the local bank to finance his college education
    c. sleeping with his cash under the mattress
    d. not spending money in May because he plans to get married and honeymoon in June
    e. holding money, waiting for stock prices to rise

16. According to Keynesians, changes in the money supply can affect real GDP in the following way:
    a. a money supply increase when the economy is at full employment
    b. a money supply decrease when the price level increases
    c. a money supply increase when the economy is below full employment
    d. a money supply decrease shifts the investment curve to the left, which increases real GDP
    e. a money supply decrease creates an excess demand for holding money, which raises real GDP

17. The speculative demand for money curve is downward sloping because as the interest rate decreases,
    a. the opportunity cost of investing increases
    b. the opportunity cost of holding money decreases
    c. saving increases
    d. the opportunity cost of holding interest-paying assets decreases
    e. the opportunity cost of holding money increases

18. Barter exchange refers to
    a. exchange of one good for another
    b. the equilibrium price that arises after much bargaining and bartering occur in the market
    c. exchange of a good for a unit of currency other than gold
    d. exchange of a good for a unit of gold
    e. the sum of all values buyers and sellers place on the goods exchanged in an economy during a calendar year

19. Keynesians believe that money matters because an increase in the money supply causes the interest rate to
    _____ and the quantity of investment to _____ while monetarists
    believe that an increase in the money supply only causes the _____ to increase.
    a. increase; decrease; nominal GDP
    b. decrease; increase; real GDP
    c. decrease; increase; price level
    d. decrease; decrease; price level
    e. increase; increase; real GDP

20. According to classical economists, a 5 percent increase in the money supply coupled with a 5 percent increase in real GDP will create
    a. a 5 percent increase in the velocity of money
    b. a 5 percent increase in the price level
    c. no change in the price level
    d. a 25 percent increase in the price level
    e. a 10 percent increase in the velocity of money

The following questions relate to the historical, applied, and interdisciplinary perspectives in the text.

21. Gresham's Law is the idea that if debased coins and pure coins circulate together, very quickly
    a. only the pure coins will circulate because no one will accept the debased coins
    b. both types of coins will circulate equally well
    c. only the debased coins will circulate because people will hoard the pure coins
    d. good money drives out bad
    e. a government can solve its budget problems by reducing the amount of gold or silver in its coins

22. Of the various means of payment available to people to complete transactions, the most commonly used is
    a. cash
    b. checks
    c. debit cards
    d. credit cards
    e. barter

23. The introduction of money market mutual funds by investment houses, negotiable order of withdrawal accounts by savings and loan associations, and share-draft accounts by credit unions since the late 1970s has caused
    a. most traditional banks to go out of business
    b. a rapid increase in the M1 money supply
    c. a blurring of the distinction between M1 and M2
    d. a decrease in the M2 money supply
    e. greater regulation of all types of financial institutions

24. The concept of the velocity of money can be illustrated by students selling used textbooks after the semester is over because
    a. the velocity of money is equal to one just as each student taking a course buys one textbook for the course
    b. textbooks are sold after the semester to new students who use them again, just as money is used over and over
    c. as textbook sales increase the velocity of the author's money decreases
    d. as textbook sales increase the velocity of the author's money increases
    e. the velocities of money and of textbooks are roughly the same between 7 and 8

Fill in the Blanks

1. Barter requires a _____.

2. Money serves three functions. It is a _____, a _____, and a _____.

3. Monetarists view the demand for money as a _____ demand while Keynesians think

   that the demand for money consists of the _____ demand in addition to the

   _____ motive and the _____ motive.

4. The equation of exchange is written as $MV = PQ$ where M is _____, V is

   _____, P is _____, and Q is _____.

Discussion Questions

1. Discuss the advantages of money over barter.

2. Does a $100 nominal GDP imply a $100 money supply? Explain.

3. What's the difference between the equation of exchange and the quantity theory of money?

4. Suppose the economy is at full employment and that consumers increase their saving, causing aggregate expenditure to decrease. Explain what happens to real GDP and the transactions demand for money.

5. Using graphs, show how a decrease in the money supply could eliminate an inflationary gap. Label and explain your graphs carefully.

Everyday Applications

Consider the implications of eliminating currency from our economic life. Many people have already adopted purchasing habits that allow them to function without using currency. How would this affect your daily life? What would be the advantages and drawbacks of a world without currency?

Economics Online

The history of money is a fascinating topic. You can easily review the history of money from ancient times to the present on the Web at a site maintained by Roy and Glyn Davies titled, *A Comparative Chronology of Money from Ancient Times to the Present Day*. The address is (*http://www.ex.ac.uk/~RDavies/arian/amser/chrono.html*).

Answers to Questions

Key Terms Quiz

a. 6	**f.** 1	**k.** 7
b. 11	**g.** 12	**l.** 8
c. 5	**h.** 10	**m.** 13
d. 9	**i.** 4	
e. 2	**j.** 3	

True-False Questions

1. True
2. True
3. False. Fiat money is not backed by gold or any other good.
4. True
5. True
6. False. Less liquid assets are included as we move from M1 through M2 and M3.
7. False. Time deposits are part of M2.
8. False. The largest category of the M2 money supply is savings accounts.
9. True
10. True
11. True
12. True
13. False.   Monetarists believe that velocity is fairly constant and predictable.
14. True
15. True

Multiple-Choice Questions

1. a	**6.** c	**11.** a	**16.** c	**21.** c
2. c	**7.** c	**12.** d	**17.** b	**22.** a
3. b	**8.** c	**13.** c	**18.** a	**23.** c
4. d	**9.** e	**14.** a	**19.** c	**24.** b
5. d	**10.** c	**15.** a	**20.** c	

Fill in the Blanks

1. double coincidence of wants
2. medium of exchange; measure of value; store of value
3. transactions; transactions; speculative; precautionary
4. the money supply; velocity; the price level; the quantity of goods produced

Discussion Questions

1. The problem with barter is that it requires a double coincidence of wants in order to accomplish an exchange. In an economy with many people trading a wide variety of goods, finding double coincidences of wants to accomplish all the desired exchanges would be enormously difficult. That is why money is introduced as a universally accepted good for use in exchanges. Money becomes, as Adam Smith put it, a kind of universal pledge. Less time and energy are required to make exchanges with money instead of barter.

2. A $100 nominal GDP would imply a $100 money supply only when velocity is equal to 1. Typically, velocity is greater than 1. If the velocity were 2, a $100 nominal GDP could be supported with a $50 money supply.

3. The equation of exchange, $MV = PQ$, is an identity that shows that nominal GDP is equal to the money supply multiplied by the velocity of money. The quantity theory of money expresses a causal relationship: the price level is a function of the money supply, $P = MV/Q$ where V and Q are assumed to be constant.

4. Real GDP will decrease since the aggregate expenditure curve will shift down. This is an example of the paradox of thrift. At a lower level of real GDP, the transactions demand for money will be lower.

5. Panels A and B on the following page show the decrease in the money supply from S to S′, an increase in the interest rate from i to i′, and a decrease in the quantity of investment from I to I′. Panel C on the following page shows the aggregate demand curve shifting downward along the vertical portion of the aggregate supply curve to lower the price level to P′, thus reducing inflation.

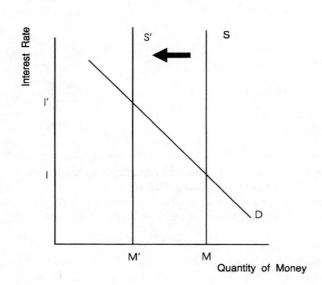

Panel A

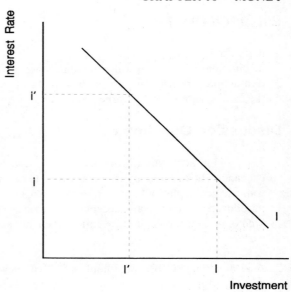

Panel B

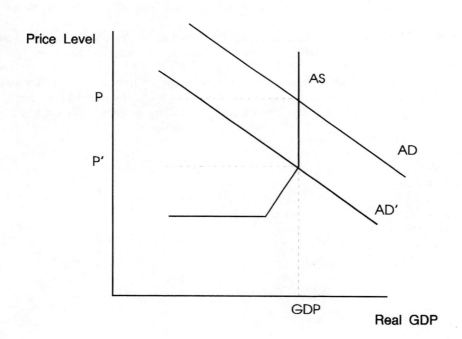

Panel C

Homework Questions

True-False Questions — If a statement is false, explain why.

1. In the quantity theory of money, when the money supply grows faster than real GDP, the price level must decrease. (T/F)

2. Gold was a poor choice for use as money in ancient societies because its supply fluctuated dramatically from year to year. (T/F)

3. Keynesians believe that the demand for money is a transactions demand, but that the demand for money includes the speculative and precautionary motives as well. (T/F)

4. If the economy is in equilibrium below full employment, then an increase in the money supply can lead to an increase in the interest rate, which causes an increase in investment and an increase in real GDP. (T/F)

5. According to Keynesians, changes in the money supply can affect the level of real GDP. (T/F)

Multiple-Choice Questions

1. In 2003, the M3 money supply was approximately _____ the size of the M1 money supply.
   a. 7 times
   b. equal to
   c. 10 times
   d. twice
   e. 5 times

2. The equation of exchange, $MV = PQ$, suggests that if we assume that velocity is constant and the economy is at full employment or moving toward it quickly, then in the short run
   a. an increase in the money supply will cause interest rates to fall and spending to increase
   b. an increase in government spending will increase real GDP
   c. an increase in taxes will cause real GDP to decrease
   d. an increase in the money supply will cause a proportionate increase in the price level
   e. monetary policy can influence the level of real GDP

3. A Keynesian believes that velocity is
   a. constant
   b. variable but predictable
   c. constant but only in the short run
   d. decreasing over time
   e. highly variable and unpredictable

4. The speculative demand for money curve is downward sloping because as interest rates
   a. decrease, the opportunity cost of investing increases
   b. increase, the opportunity cost of holding money decreases
   c. decrease, saving increases
   d. decrease, the opportunity cost of holding money decreases
   e. decrease, the opportunity cost of holding money increases

5. Monetarists believe that even though the velocity of money is not constant, the equation of exchange is still a useful tool because
   a. velocity is predictable and independent of the money supply
   b. the money supply is relatively constant and offsets fluctuations in velocity
   c. an increase in the money supply only causes the price level to increase
   d. the economy is always at full employment
   e. the economy grows very slowly

Discussion Questions/Problems

1. Sketch the speculative demand for money and explain why it slopes down.

2. Should the money supply be allowed to grow? At what rate? How might the answer to this question differ between monetarists and Keynesians?

CHAPTER 11

MONEY CREATION AND THE BANKING SYSTEM

Chapter in a Nutshell

The fundamental idea that explains how banks create money is the **fractional reserve system**. Fractional reserve simply means that banks have to keep in their vaults or at the Federal Reserve Bank only a fraction of what people deposit in their banks, even though these people have the right to withdraw their deposits on demand (which is why their deposits are called **demand deposits**). How can banks honor a promise to return deposits to people when their deposits aren't there? The answer is that customarily people don't ask for their deposits, certainly not all, and not all at one time. That's what banks count on and, most of the time, it works.

What do banks do with the deposits, if they're not there? That's the "creation" story. When a bank receives a new deposit, it can loan out a portion of the deposit, keeping a fraction of the deposit on hand as reserves. How large that fraction held in reserves must be is determined by the **Federal Reserve System (the Fed)**. That's why they are called **required reserves**. When the borrower who took out the loan spends it on, say, building a house, the housebuilder now has the money and deposits it in his own bank. This second bank is now able to loan a portion of this new deposit, keeping on hand a fraction as required reserves. Its own loan provides income for someone else who deposits it in a third bank, and so on. The process repeats and the money supply expands.

This money creation process doesn't go on forever because each round of deposits is smaller as more reserves must be set aside. Stretching it out, the new deposits eventually become close to zero. How much, then, does an initial deposit create in terms of total new deposits? The answer is found by using the **potential money multiplier** which is $1/LRR$, where **LRR is the legal reserve requirement** (in percentage terms).

The money supply is unlikely to expand to the extent indicated by the potential money multiplier for two reasons. First, banks may prefer to hold reserves in excess of those required. These are called **excess reserves**. Second, and more important, people may simply not borrow sufficiently to exhaust the full amount of the available reserves.

The money creation process can also run in reverse gear. When someone makes a withdrawal, it means the bank's loans are more than its new and lower deposits can support. It must reduce its loans. But that creates its own round-after-round sequence of loan and deposit reductions.

Banks sometimes fail when a large portion of the loans they made are not repaid. When people learn that someone else's bank is failing, they become nervous about their own deposits and may choose to withdraw them. If many people behave this way, they may cause a "run on the bank." If an exceptionally large number of withdrawals take place in a short period of time, loans must be called in, reducing the money supply and real GDP. **The Federal Deposit Insurance Corporation** was created to insure depositors' deposits up to $100,000 so they would be less anxious about the security of their deposits.

However, in spite of the FDIC and regular bank audits, banks do fail. During the 1980s and the early 1990s, bank failure rates rose significantly. A variety of causes account for these increased rates of bank failure. Savings and loans associations (S&Ls) also went through a difficult period during the 1980s as banks began to compete with them in the home mortgage market. Savings and loans failures were so extensive in the 1980s that a special government-sponsored corporation, the Resolution Trust Corporation, had to be established to handle the claims of depositors and creditors of the failed S&Ls.

In the absence of intervention by a central bank like the Fed, banking practice would tend to exacerbate the phases of the business cycle. During recession, a bank is less likely to lend for fear of not being repaid. The money supply shrinks as outstanding loans are called in, causing the interest rate to rise and the quantity of investment to fall, just when investment is needed the most. During prosperity, banks are more inclined to lend, which causes the money supply to grow more rapidly than otherwise, resulting in lower interest rates and more borrowing. With the economy near or at full employment, it creates an upward pressure on the price level. The Fed can counteract these outcomes by using some of its monetary tools.

After you study this chapter, you should be able to:

•   Explain the concept of a **fractional reserve banking system**.
•   Describe how **banks can create money** by making loans based on new deposits.
•   Calculate the amount of money a banking system can create given a new deposit and the **legal reserve requirement**.
•   Explain why banks may keep **excess reserves**.
•   Show how the money supply shrinks when loans are repaid.
•   Present reasons for **bank failures**.
•   Justify the need for **deposit insurance** and bank audits.
•   Recount events associated with the **savings and loan crisis** of the 1980s.
•   Explain how a **central bank** can help to stabilize the banking system and manipulate the money supply to dampen the business cycle.

Concept Check — See how you do on these multiple-choice questions.

Are depositors likely to withdraw all of their deposits from a fractional reserve banking system at any given moment?

1. A **fractional reserve banking system** operates so that
    a. a fraction of depositors' money is available to them at any given time
    b. a fraction of depositors' money is held in reserve by banks
    c. banks lend the full amount of people's deposits
    d. all deposits are insured by FDIC
    e. the potential money multiplier is equal to 1

Which two groups are linked through the activities of banks?

2. The role of **financial intermediaries** in the economy is to
    a. provide loans to depositors and accept deposits from borrowers
    b. aid entrepreneurs by finding potentially profitable investment opportunities
    c. control the money supply so that inflation does not result
    d. conduct examinations of banks and savings and loans to make certain they will not fail
    e. provide loans to borrowers and accept deposits from depositors

What is the difference between required reserves and excess reserves?

3. When a bank has **excess reserves**, it is
    a. operating with assets equal to liabilities
    b. able to make new loans if it chooses to do so
    c. required to call in loans to increase its required reserves
    d. contributing to the Federal Deposit Insurance Corporation
    e. causing the potential money multiplier to increase

What is the maximum amount by which demand deposits can be increased from an initial deposit?

4. The **potential money multiplier** is equal to
   a. $1/LRR$
   b. $1/1 - LRR$
   c. the legal reserve requirement
   d. $1/ID$
   e. $1/1 - ID$

What is the rationale for bank deposit insurance?

5. **Federal deposit insurance** is intended to assure depositors that
   a. they will earn the maximum possible interest on their savings accounts
   b. the bank holding their deposits has made sound loans
   c. their deposits are safe so they won't be easily inclined to withdraw their funds
   d. regular audits of banks will be conducted
   e. banks will continue to make loans during downturns in the business cycle

Am I on the Right Track?

Your answers to the questions above should be **b**, **e**, **b**, **a**, and **c**. The money creation process is fairly clear if you follow the sequence of events — new deposits followed by new loans that are spent and become income, new deposits, and new loans. The logic behind the potential money multiplier is the same as the logic behind the income multiplier. Just as the income multiplier can run in reverse, so can the potential money multiplier, with money being destroyed rather than created. Make certain that you understand why a banking system without a central bank can exacerbate the recession and prosperity phases of the business cycle.

Key Terms Quiz — Match the terms on the left with the definitions in the column on the right.

1. fractional reserve system

_____ a. the percentage of demand deposits banks and other financial intermediaries are required to keep in cash reserves and deposits at the Fed

2. potential money multiplier

_____ b. the quantity of reserves held by a bank in excess of the legally required amount

3. balance sheet

_____ c. a banking system that provides people with immediate access to their deposits but allows banks to hold only a fraction of those deposits in reserve

4. excess reserves

_____ d. a government insurance agency that provides depositors in FDIC-participating banks 100 percent coverage on the first $100,000 of deposits

5. legal reserve requirement

_____ e. firms that accept deposits from savers and use those deposits to make loans to borrowers

6. Federal Deposit Insurance Corporation

_____ f. the bank's statement of liabilities and assets

7. financial intermediaries

_____ g. the increase in the money supply that is potentially generated by a change in demand deposits

True-False Questions — If a question is false, explain why.

1. Banks keep all of their deposits on hand as reserves. (T/F)

2. The legal reserve requirement is the amount of capital that a bank must have in order to be chartered by the state. (T/F)

3. The legal reserve requirement is determined by the president. (T/F)

4. Banks may fail when an exceptionally large number of borrowers default on the loans they received from the bank, destroying, in this way, a large part of the bank's financial assets. (T/F)

5. One of the causes of the savings and loan crisis of the 1980s was the increased regulation of the banking industry. (T/F)

6. Increases in the legal reserve requirement increase the amount of money the banking system can create. (T/F)

7. Banks are eager to provide loans, thereby expanding the money supply, during a recession. (T/F)

8. The cave illustration in the text shows how a fractional reserve system came into being. (T/F)

9. A demand deposit is the bank's asset; the loan it makes possible is the bank's liability. (T/F)

10. If a bank is allowed to lend $900 on a new deposit of $1,000, then the legal reserve requirement is 0.10. (T/F)

11. The potential money creation associated with a new deposit may be larger than the actual money creation because not all of the money that is made available for loans is actually loaned out. (T/F)

12. If the legal reserve requirement is 0.50, then a $100 deposit in the Paris First National Bank will allow the bank to create loans of $50. (T/F)

13. An unregulated banking system without a central bank will tend to create too little money during a prosperity phase and too much money during a recession phase. (T/F)

14. Excess reserves accumulate in a bank when the bank, intentionally or unintentionally, does not loan out the full potential of its assets, subject to the legal reserve requirement. (T/F)

15. The principal role of financial intermediaries, such as banks, savings and loan associations, and credit unions is to accept deposits from savers and make loans to borrowers. (T/F)

Multiple-Choice Questions

1. A fractional reserve banking system is one in which banks within the system
   a. can lend out all of their reserves
   b. keep on hand all of their reserves to honor depositors' needs for cash
   c. can lend out only a fraction of their reserves
   d. try to maximize their excess reserves
   e. pay higher rates of interest to depositors than they charge borrowers to maximize deposits

2. The potential money multiplier is equal to
   a. the income multiplier
   b. the interest rate
   c. one divided by the legal reserve requirement
   d. the legal reserve requirement
   e. one

3. The actual money multiplier is less than the potential money multiplier because
   a. borrowers never save any of the money they are loaned by banks
   b. banks may not lend all of their excess reserves
   c. the legal reserve requirement is constantly increasing
   d. bank failures destroy money as other banks create new money
   e. all money that is borrowed is typically redeposited in other banks after it is spent

4. Prior to the 1980s, S&Ls were fairly stable financial institutions because they
   a. invested heavily in a buoyant stock market that produced relatively stable rates of return
   b. invested in high-risk, high-yielding bonds that earned higher than average rates of return
   c. were successful competing against commercial banks and credit unions for mortgage loans
   d. were able to open branches in more than one state, thereby diversifying their risks
   e. did not face competition from commercial banks in the home mortgage lending business

5. Suppose you deposit $1,000 in a bank and the reserve requirement is 0.25. Suppose also that the banking system has zero excess reserves. The total amount of new money (not counting your deposit) that can be created by the banking system is
   a. $3,000
   b. $4,000
   c. $1,000
   d. $250
   e. $750

6. If the Federal Reserve raises the legal reserve requirement from 0.10 to 0.20, then
   a. banks will lower the interest rate to make up for the loss of their loan volumes
   b. the potential money multiplier increases
   c. banks will reduce the loans they make and the money supply in the economy will fall
   d. banks will increase the loans they make and the money supply in the economy will rise
   e. excess reserves will increase by 10 percent

7. If the Federal Reserve sets the legal reserve requirement at 1.00, then
   a. banks could loan out as much money as they want
   b. banks could loan out only the amount they hold in deposit
   c. all bank deposits would be held as required reserves
   d. the potential money multiplier would be infinite
   e. each bank's liabilities would equal its assets

8. When you deposit $100 in your local bank, even though you can withdraw that amount at any time
   a. the bank becomes the legal owner of that $100 deposit
   b. it automatically and instantaneously creates $100 in the bank's reserves
   c. the bank's assets become $100 more than its liabilities
   d. the bank's balance sheet remains unchanged because its new asset equals its new liability
   e. the potential money multiplier increases by $100 times the legal reserve requirement

9. If you withdraw $100 from the bank the following month
   a. the bank's assets become $100 less than its liabilities
   b. it automatically and instantaneously creates $100 in the bank's excess reserves
   c. the potential money multiplier decreases by $100 times the legal reserve requirement
   d. the money supply will eventually decrease
   e. the money supply will eventually increase

10. On a bank's balance sheet, _____ are assets and _____ are liabilities.
    a. demand deposits; loans
    b. demand deposits; reserves
    c. demand deposits; cash deposits
    d. loans; reserves
    e. loans; demand deposits

11. Bank runs are most likely to occur when
    a. depositors discover that other depositors were not able to withdraw their deposits from their own banks
    b. borrowers who borrowed at high interest rates learn that interest rates are falling and will stay low for some time
    c. banks are forced by government to become part of the FDIC
    d. the Federal Reserve announces a series of upcoming bank audits
    e. borrowers outnumber savers

12. The Federal Deposit Insurance Corporation (FDIC) is designed to
    a. protect depositors from losing all their deposits in the event of bank failure
    b. protect banks from being sued by depositors in the event of bank failure
    c. protect banks against the possibility of bank failure
    d. insure the deposits in the Federal Reserve System
    e. safeguard the banking system against bank fraud

13. During the 1970s, banks provided farmers with significant amounts of new debt because
    a. banks had considerable excess reserves they wished to divest
    b. farmers were more willing than urban businesses to pay the high rates of interest banks demanded
    c. prices of grain and land were rising, providing farmers with higher-valued collateral to back the loans
    d. the government encouraged banks to make these loans in order to stabilize a sluggish farm economy
    e. they knew that Willie Nelson would bail them out with Farm Aid

14. Loans that U.S. bankers made to Mexico and Venezuela during the 1970s
    a. became very high-risk loans when the price of oil fell in the early 1980s
    b. were quickly repaid in the 1980s, providing U.S. banks with considerable excess reserves
    c. were at interest rates substantially higher than the U.S. rate, which caused many Latin American projects to fail
    d. were transformed by the Federal Reserve to outright grants in the 1980s
    e. were made at low rates of interest because of their commitment to fight poverty in Latin America

15. Prior to the 1980s, savings and loan associations were able to pay depositors relatively low rates of interest on their deposits because
    a. these rates were dictated by commercial banks
    b. mortgage lending was relatively unprofitable for them
    c. Regulation Q set ceilings on these rates
    d. the S&Ls were monopolists
    e. interest rates were falling dramatically in the early 1980s

16. Contrary to what the economy really needs, the banking system tends to _____ during periods of recession and _____ during periods of prosperity
    a. increase the money supply; decrease the money supply
    b. lower interest rates; raise interest rates
    c. decrease its liabilities; increase its assets
    d. increase its liabilities; decrease its assets
    e. decrease the money supply; increase the money supply

17. One argument opposing the FDIC is that by insuring deposits, banks are encouraged to engage in moral hazard, meaning that they will tend to
    a. make too few loans during a recession
    b. charge borrowers interest rates that are too high
    c. engage in race and gender discrimination when they evaluate loan applications
    d. make loans that are riskier than they otherwise would
    e. increase the fees charged to small depositors for routine bank services

18. If I find $1 million in my backyard and deposit the money in my local bank that has a legal reserve requirement equal to .2, then the banking system can create a maximum amount of **new money** (excluding the original deposit) equal to
    a. $1 million
    b. $10 million
    c. $5 million
    d. $4 million
    e. $2 million

19. When loans are paid back, checks are written, which decreases deposits so that banks may be forced to reduce their loans in order to maintain their legal reserve requirement thus causing
    a. the money supply to grow
    b. bank failures
    c. a push for lower legal reserve requirements in the banking community
    d. the money supply to decrease
    e. an increase in the price level

20. Waves of bank failures like those that occurred during the Great Depression exacerbate downturns in economic activity because
    a. with no banks to borrow from, the government cannot pursue a fiscal policy of increased spending
    b. as deposits are withdrawn, the money supply shrinks, interest rates increase, and the investment associated with failed loans is halted
    c. the money supply increases as people withdraw cash from banks and this causes inflation
    d. the Federal Reserve typically increases the legal reserve requirement
    e. failed banks are prevented from re-opening by stringent audit requirements

The following questions relate to the theoretical, interdisciplinary, and global perspectives in the text.

21. The biggest concern associated with the advent of electronic banking, or banking in cyberspace, is
    a. job losses in the banking industry as fewer workers are required to run banks
    b. longer hours for bankers because banking can now be done 24 hours per day, 7 days a week
    c. the reliability of the Web and the security of transactions carried out via cyberspace
    d. the sense of loss people will have not coming into physical contact with money and checks
    e. the inability of people to write checks then put money in the bank to cover them

22. Suppose the Fed introduces a 100 percent reserve requirement for banks. The effect of this policy would be to
    a. increase the ability of banks to make loans since the banking system will be more stable
    b. slightly reduce the amount of lending banks are able to do
    c. increase the money supply and lower the interest rate
    d. prevent money creation from happening in the banking system
    e. increase GDP and the volatility in GDP

23. The term "moral hazard," as it is applied to the Federal Deposit Insurance Corporation that insures bank deposits, means that
    a. insuring bank deposits is inherently risky and hazardous because of bank robberies
    b. banks may be inclined to make riskier loans because deposits are insured
    c. banks will be inclined to make loans to individuals with little prospect of repaying them so that the banks can seize their assets
    d. the risk of bank failures is reduced
    e. the risk of bank failures has been shifted from the United States to our major trading partners like Japan

24. The fact that deposit insurance has spread to numerous countries other than the United States over time suggests that
    a. deposit insurance is relatively low-cost since bank failures are rare and usually involve small sums
    b. banks and consumers are quite willing to pay for deposit insurance
    c. banks make risky loans whether or not deposits are insured
    d. people in other countries are less concerned about problems of moral hazard than are people in the United States
    e. the benefits from increased stability in the banking system must outweigh the costs of riskier loans

Fill in the Blanks

1. Fractional reserve banking is based on the idea that a bank need not keep all of its _____ on

   hand as _____.

2. If banks hold loans up to their _____ and checks are written on their deposits,

   then the banks must _____.

3. During an economic expansion, banks are more inclined to _____, which causes the

   _____ to grow and _____ to fall.

4. An increase in the legal reserve requirement will cause the potential money multiplier to _____.

Discussion Questions

1. Why is the potential money multiplier probably larger than the actual money multiplier?

2. Suppose you hear someone remark that "If there were no legal reserve requirement, banks would keep sufficient reserves anyway." Evaluate.

3. Why is the money supply too important to be left to the banks?

4. Outline the problems faced by financial intermediaries in the United States during the 1980s and early 1990s.

Problems

1. Suppose that Springfield National Bank has reserves totaling $100,000 on $1,000,000 of deposits. The reserve requirement is 10 percent. Can this bank make any new loans? Explain.

2. Suppose that Jeff Ankrom, fearing an impending financial crisis, withdraws $20,000 from his account at Springfield National Bank and buries the cash in his backyard. By how much will the bank have to reduce its loans? Calculate the maximum amount the money supply may contract as a result. Show your work.

Everyday Applications

Have you seen "*It's a Wonderful Life*" — the classic Jimmy Stewart film? If not, rent it so you can see a marvelous depiction of a run on a small-town savings and loan. If you've seen it, watch it again, this time from the perspective of someone who understands fractional reserve banking.

Economics Online

The FDIC has its own Web site providing information of interest to the banking industry, public information, laws and regulations, and consumer news, along with other topics. To learn more about the FDIC visit the site (*http://www.fdic.gov/*).

Answers to Questions

Key Terms Quiz

a.	5	**f.**	3
b.	4	**g.**	2
c.	1		
d.	6		
e.	7		

True-False Questions

1. False. Banks keep a fraction of their deposits on hand and at the Federal Reserve Bank to satisfy the legal reserve requirement. They lend the remaining reserves, assuming excess reserves equal zero.
2. False. The legal reserve requirement is the fraction of deposits that must be kept as reserves.
3. False. The legal reserve requirement is determined by the Federal Reserve.
4. True
5. False. The savings and loan crisis followed the deregulation of the banking industry.
6. False. Increases in the legal reserve requirement decrease the amount of money the banking system can create.
7. False. Bankers will be reluctant to make loans during a recession because economic conditions are bad.
8. True
9. False. A demand deposit is a liability for a bank and a loan is an asset.
10. True
11. True
12. True
13. False. An unregulated banking system tends to create too much money during periods of prosperity and too little money during a recession.

14. True
15. True

Multiple-Choice Questions

1. c	**6.** c	**11.** a	**16.** e	**21.** c
2. c	**7.** c	**12.** a	**17.** d	**22.** d
3. b	**8.** b	**13.** c	**18.** d	**23.** b
4. e	**9.** d	**14.** a	**19.** d	**24.** e
5. a	**10.** e	**15.** c	**20.** b	

Fill in the Blanks

1. deposits; reserves
2. legal reserve requirement; reduce their loans
3. lend; money supply; interest rates
4. decrease

Discussion Questions

1. The potential money multiplier equal to $1/LRR$, where LRR is the legal reserve requirement, is probably larger than the actual money multiplier for three reasons. First, banks may choose to hold excess reserves over and above their legal reserves in an effort to be cautious. Second, potential borrowers may choose not to borrow the excess reserves that banks have to lend. Finally, not all the money that is loaned by banks is redeposited in other banks, and this will limit the extent of the money creation process.

2. It is correct, in most cases, that even without a legal reserve requirement, banks would keep sufficient reserves to cover the day-to-day needs of depositors. After all, a bank does not want to be vulnerable to a possible run on its deposits. The bank is in business to make a profit, and its stability is critical to achieving profitability. However, in some cases, in an effort to make a profit more quickly or out of sheer recklessness, banks may not keep sufficient reserves, find themselves vulnerable to runs on their deposits, and fail if the runs materialize. Also, a legal reserve requirement enables the Fed to directly influence the money supply and, as a result, the state of the economy. It is for this reason that a legal reserve requirement is imposed on banks.

3. Just as war is too important to be left to the generals, the money supply is too important to be left to the bankers. An uncontrolled banking system without a central bank will tend to create too little money during the recessionary phase of the business cycle and too much money during the prosperity phase. This pattern stands to reason. Bankers are self-interested people who will be disinclined to risk loans in a period when economic conditions are bad. Their natural tendency will be to increase their excess reserves during a recesssion as unemployment rises, incomes fall, and businesses fail. As a result, the money supply will contract, interest rates will rise, and the recession will be made worse. Just the opposite is observed during the prosperity phase of the business cycle. Bankers observe healthy economic growth and feel confident that any new loans they can make will be repaid in a timely manner. Hence, lots of lending occurs, the money supply grows more rapidly than it would otherwise, interest rates fall, spending increases, and the economy may be subject to higher inflation.

4. The rate of bank failures in the United States grew markedly during the early 1980s as a result of severe shocks to specific sectors in the economy. One of these was agriculture. Higher prices for agricultural products during the 1970s led to rising values for farmland that provided farmers with collateral on which they could borrow. Many farmers purchased land and machinery at inflated prices on borrowed funds. When farm prices and land values collapsed in the early 1980s, these same farmers began to default on

loans, putting pressure on the banks that owned the loans.

Some large urban banks were hit during the same period by a decrease in oil prices that led to the need to restructure loans made to oil-exporting countries such as Venezuela and Mexico. A large number of bank failures occurred in states with oil-based economies such as Texas, Oklahoma, and Louisiana.

Finally, there is the Savings and Loan crisis of the 1980s and 1990s. S&Ls faced new competition from commercial banks in the home mortgage lending business as a result of deregulation in the banking industry. Also, Regulation Q, which had set a ceiling on interest rates paid on deposits, was discarded. S&Ls had to increase the interest rates they paid to depositors in order to compete with banks and other financial institutions like investment houses, which meant that the lower rates at which they had loaned money to homebuyers were no longer profitable. Therefore, S&Ls moved into new loan markets that were riskier, and fraud became evident in many of the operations. As a result, many S&Ls failed. Even though depositors were protected by the Federal Savings and Loan Insurance Corporation, the FSLIC was unable to cover all of the failed S&Ls' deposits, forcing the government to create the Resolution Trust Corporation to handle the disposal of the failed S&Ls.

Problems

1. No, it cannot because with a 10 percent reserve requirement, the $100,000 in actual reserves is exactly equal to the $100,000 in required reserves it must hold on deposits of $1,000,000.

2. Springfield National's reserves decrease by $20,000 to $80,000 when Jeff withdraws the $20,000 in cash. Its deposits fall to $1,000,000 – $20,000 = $980,000. Springfield National should have $98,000 in reserves to cover deposits equal to $980,000. Therefore, Springfield National must reduce its loans by $18,000, causing the money supply to contract by as much as $180,000 — the money multiplier multiplied by the amount by which loans must be reduced. Note that deposits can contract by as much as $200,000, including the initial reduction in deposits equal to $20,000.

Homework Questions

True-False Questions — If a statement is false, explain why.

1. A fractional reserve banking system keeps a fraction of its deposits on hand and lends the rest. (T/F)

2. A loan is an asset for a bank. (T/F)

3. Borrowers demand money in the form of loans from banks in order to cover losses from failed business ventures. (T/F)

4. Federal Deposit Insurance makes it less likely that banks will lend to people with little prospect of paying back the loan. (T/F)

5. The number of bank failures in the United States has declined steadily since the Great Depression. (T/F)

Multiple-Choice Questions

1. The amount of money created in the banking system by a new deposit may be less than the amount generated by multiplying the initial deposit by the potential money multiplier because
   a. many banks, intentionally or unintentionally, may end up holding excess reserves
   b. many banks may end up with more liabilities than assets
   c. many banks may end up with more assets than liabilities
   d. the legal reserve requirements may be less than the requirements associated with the potential money multiplier
   e. double counting of deposits may occur among banks in the system

2. If the legal reserve requirement is .20 and banks hold $40 million in excess reserves, then the maximum amount that the money supply can increase is
   a. $8 million
   b. $80 million
   c. $800 million
   d. $20 million
   e. $200 million

3. Suppose that total reserves = $1,000,000, demand deposits = $5,000,000, and the legal reserve requirement is 10 percent. How large are the bank's excess reserves?
   a. $4,000,000
   b. $6,000,000
   c. $500,000
   d. $1,000,000
   e. $4,900,000

4. Given a legal reserve requirement equal to 0.25, if a new deposit of $1 million is made, the maximum amount by which the money supply could increase is
    a. $4 million
    b. $3 million
    c. $2 million
    d. $1 million
    e. cannot be computed with the information presented

5. Assuming that every bank in the banking system holds substantial excess reserves, a decision by the Federal Reserve to increase the legal reserve requirement will
    a. cause the money supply to contract, but only slightly
    b. cause the money supply to increase, but only slightly
    c. force banks to decrease their excess reserves
    d. create a wave of bank failures
    e. cause the potential money multiplier to increase

Discussion Questions/Problems

1. Discuss the pros and cons of deposit insurance.

2. Suppose that FirstStar Bank in Yellow Springs, Ohio has $10,000,000 in deposits and holds no excess reserves with a legal reserve requirement of 20 percent. Calculate the required reserves for this bank. Suppose that the reserve requirement is increased to 30 percent. By how much will the bank have to increase its reserves. Assuming the original potential money multiplier of 5, by how much will FirstStar's increase in required reserves cause the money supply to contract.

CHAPTER 12

THE FEDERAL RESERVE SYSTEM AND MONETARY POLICY

Chapter in a Nutshell

The experiences of our early banking system cried out for the invention of central banking. Overindulging banks chronically overissued currency, kept too few reserves, and engaged in too many high-risk loans, all of which tended routinely to undermine the fragile, fledgling money economy in the United States. The Federal Reserve System came into existence in 1913 only after a history of failed attempts at central banking.

The money supply in 18th-century colonial America consisted of a variety of foreign currencies and coins. A paper money — the Continental, American money for the first time — was introduced during the revolutionary period, only to be devalued quickly by massive overprinting. After independence, the number of **state-chartered banks** grew dramatically. Many people feared that these state banks would overissue **bank notes** (promissory notes that could be redeemed for gold or silver) and renew inflation. In order to counter this fear, the **First Bank of the United States was established in 1791.**

But it didn't last long. Opponents of the First Bank saw it as unconstitutional and a feared money monopoly. Congress refused to recharter it. Soon after, the number of state banks and the amount of currency in circulation rose dramatically. Again, the money system was in trouble and a second try at central banking — the **Second Bank of the United States** — followed. Although widely regarded as having done a credible job, it too was unceremoniously discarded by Andrew Jackson during his second administration in the mid-1830s. Apart from the **National Bank Act** during the Civil War, the history of banking in the United States from the 1830s to the eve of World War I is one of growing banking power over the economy but without control or direction.

The Panic of 1907 that followed the **Knickerbocker Trust disaster** prompted U.S. political leaders to reconsider the need for a central bank. What emerged in **1913 was the Federal Reserve System (the Fed).** The Fed is composed of **twelve district Federal Reserve banks,** each owned by **member banks** that contribute 3 percent of their capital to the district bank. The main purpose of the Fed is to safeguard our money system. The Fed's **Board of Governors** consists of seven members appointed by the President for fourteen-year terms. The chairman of the board is a member who is appointed for a four-year term. The district banks are also headed by boards of directors. **The Federal Open Market Committee**, one of the Fed's most important operating bodies, consists of twelve members, including the seven-member Board of Governors, the president of the New York Fed, and four other district presidents who rotate. The Federal Open Market Committee controls the money supply via **open market operations**, the purchase and sale of government bonds.

Among the Fed's tasks is to decide how much money to have printed by the Bureau of Engraving and Printing. The Fed also serves as a **bankers' bank**, keeping much of the commercial banks' reserves on deposit in its vaults, providing them with currency and loans, and clearing many of the billions of checks that travel cross-country through the banking system.

However, the Fed's principal goal is to manage the money supply. It has three operating tools at its disposal to achieve that goal. They are changing the **legal reserve requirement**, changing the **discount rate**, and engaging in **open market operations**. Suppose the Fed, worried about inflationary pressures in the economy, decides to decrease the money supply. What does the Fed do? It can raise the legal reserve requirement, which would force banks to hold a greater proportion of their deposits on reserve. In this way, banks lend out less, and the money supply decreases. Or the Fed can raise the discount rate (the rate it charges member banks who borrow from the Fed), which makes banks' borrowing from it less attractive. If they borrow less, the money supply decreases. Or the Fed may resort to its most effective and most frequently used monetary tool, open market operations. The Fed can sell government securities to the public, to member banks, and to corporations, which draws money out of the banking system, thereby decreasing the money supply.

These same instruments can be used to increase the money supply, although their effectiveness in this direction is somewhat weaker. The Fed can lower the legal reserve requirement, making more reserves available for loans. Note, though, that the Fed can make reserves available, but it can't make people borrow. Similarly, the Fed can lower the discount rate, but banks still have to want to borrow to make that policy work. The Fed's best move here is to buy government securities on the open market, which will put more money in the hands of the securities' sellers. They may deposit the money in their banks, but someone still has to borrow.

An alternative to controlling the money supply in order to manage the money economy is for the Fed to control the interest rate, allowing the money supply to take its course. It uses these same tools — the reserve requirement, discount rate, and open market operations — to increase or decrease the interest rate. A number of ancillary tools, including **stock market margin requirements** and moral suasion, are available to the Fed.

The Fed tends to be more effective at fighting inflation in high employment periods than it is at combating unemployment during recessions. Occasionally, the Fed and the government pursue conflicting policies, one encouraging economic expansion while the other discourages it. Remember, the Fed is charged with managing the money economy. If it senses inflationary pressures mounting, it may curb economic activity even if that means creating unemployment. That's where the government steps in if it wants to protect jobs. It can use its fiscal policy to lower rates of unemployment at the same time the Fed uses its monetary policy to contain inflation. In this situation, they work at cross purposes. They did so through the mid-1980s when the Fed tended to maintain high interest rates while the government ran large, expansionary budget deficits.

After you study this chapter, you should be able to:

- Provide an account of the **history of money and banking** in the United States.
- Describe the **organizational structure of the Federal Reserve System**.
- List the **functions of the Fed**.
- Discuss the **tools of monetary policy** at the Fed's disposal.
- Contrast a **money supply target** with an **interest rate target** as policy options for the Fed.
- Show how the Fed can use **countercyclical monetary policy** to influence the macroeconomy.
- Explain how the Fed and the government can have **conflicting economic policy goals**.

Concept Check — See how you do on these multiple-choice questions.

In which market does the Open Market Committee make trades?

1. The principal function of the **Federal Open Market Committee** is to
   a. set the discount rate
   b. determine the reserve requirement
   c. purchase goods and services required by the Federal Reserve System on the open market
   d. buy and sell U.S. government bonds to influence the money supply
   e. set the federal funds rate

Should the money supply increase or decrease if we are in the downturn phase of the business cycle?

2. If the Fed pursues a **countercyclical monetary policy** in the downturn phase of the business cycle, then the Federal Open Market Committee will
   a. lower the discount rate
   b. lower the reserve requirement
   c. purchase U.S. government bonds
   d. lower the federal funds rate
   e. sell U.S. government bonds

Sometimes banks find it convenient to borrow. The Fed is the bankers' bank. What is the discount rate?

3. The **discount rate** is
   a. a lower interest rate that commercial banks charge their best customers
   b. the interest rate banks are charged when they borrow from the Fed
   c. the same as the federal funds rate
   d. the interest rate that district Federal Reserve banks charge each other for loans
   e. the interest rate that commercial banks charge each other for loans

As you think about this question, remember that lowering the reserve requirement makes excess reserves available for banks to lend.

4. If the Fed lowers the **reserve requirement**, we can be certain that the intention is to
   a. increase the money supply and lower interest rates
   b. decrease the inflation rate
   c. increase the money supply and increase interest rates
   d. lower the price of government bonds
   e. decrease the excess reserves held by member banks

What are the functions of the Fed?

5. All of the following are functions of the **Federal Reserve System except**
   a. printing money
   b. holding the reserves of member banks
   c. controlling the money supply
   d. setting stock market margin requirements
   e. printing state bank notes

Am I on the Right Track?

Your answers to the questions above should be **d, c, b, a**, and **e**. Approaching this chapter in a step-wise fashion, you should first learn the basics of U.S. monetary history and the reasons for the creation of the Federal Reserve System in 1913. It is important to understand the structure of the Fed. Then you should become well-versed in the tools of monetary policy that the Fed uses. Be certain that you are clear about how each tool should be used under different economic circumstances. Finally, it is important to understand how monetary policy and fiscal policy relate to each other. The economic goals of the Fed are sometimes in conflict with those pursued by Congress and the president.

Key Terms Quiz — Match the terms on the left with their definitions in the column on the right.

1. bank note
2. countercyclical monetary policy
3. state-chartered bank
4. reserve requirement
5. nationally chartered bank
6. federal funds market
7. Federal Reserve System (the Fed)
8. federal funds rate
9. Federal Open Market Committee
10. open market operations
11. discount rate
12. margin requirement

_____ a. policy directives used by the Fed to moderate swings in the business cycle

_____ b. the central bank of the United States

_____ c. the interest rate on loans made by banks in the federal funds market

_____ d. a commercial bank that receives its charter from the comptroller of the currency subject to federal law

_____ e. the buying and selling of government bonds by the Federal Open Market Committee

_____ f. the Fed's principal decision-making body, charged with executing the Fed's open market operations

_____ g. the minimum amount of reserves the Fed requires a bank to hold, based on a percentage of the bank's total deposit liabilities

_____ h. a promissory note, issued by a bank, pledging to redeem the note for a specific amount of gold or silver

_____ i. the market in which banks lend and borrow reserves from each other for very short periods of time, usually overnight

_____ j. the maximum percentage of the cost of a stock that can be borrowed from a bank or any other financial institution, with the stock offered as collateral

_____ k. a commercial bank that receives its charter or license from a state government subject to the laws of that state

_____ l. the interest rate the Fed charges banks that borrow reserves from it

True-False Questions — If a statement is false, explain why.

1. Continental notes, issued by the Continental Congress to finance the American Revolution, were paper money backed by gold. (T/F)

2. Alexander Hamilton was in favor of a central bank, while the idea of a central bank was opposed by Jefferson and Madison. (T/F)

3. The Fed's primary goal, as mandated by Congress, is to promote full employment in the economy. (T/F)

4. At the very top of the Federal Reserve System is the Open Market Committee. (T/F)

5. Open market operations refer to the Fed's intervention in the stock market when it perceives that a decrease in stock prices might endanger the stability of the economy. (T/F)

6. In the event that a bank, at the close of a banking day, discovers it is short of required reserves, it can borrow the needed reserves from its district Federal Reserve bank, paying the discount rate. (T/F)

7. The biggest money problem faced in the United States from the late 18th century through the 19th century was the reluctance of banks to issue enough paper money. (T/F)

8. The most effective and frequently used tool the Fed has at its disposal to change the money supply is its open market operations. (T/F)

9. When the Fed sells a $1000 government security to your local bank, the only change in your bank's balance sheet is in the composition of its assets; its liabilities remain unchanged. (T/F)

10. The Fed is often called the bankers' bank because commercial banks can make deposits in it and borrow from it. (T/F)

11. District Federal Reserve banks play a vital role in clearing the millions of checks that are written daily by people and businesses. (T/F)

12. A newly elected president has the opportunity to appoint a new chairman of the Federal Reserve Board of Governors and to replace the board with new members. (T/F)

13. The Federal Open Market Committee can increase the money supply by buying government securities. (T/F)

14. Because the Fed gets its policy cues from government, its monetary policy is always coordinated with the government's own fiscal policy. (T/F)

15. Because the Fed does not know the exact position of the demand curve for money in the money market, it cannot target both the money supply and the interest rate at the same time. (T/F)

Multiple-Choice Questions

1. When the United States' first central bank, the First Bank of the United States, was established in 1791
   a. no other country had a central bank
   b. the U.S. monetary system was plagued by the hoarding of bank notes
   c. unanimous support for the bank was given by Congress
   d. there were many other nationally chartered banks that served the functions of a central bank
   e. there were already central banks functioning in England, Holland, and Sweden

2. The National Bank Act of 1864, passed during the Civil War, legislated
   a. the establishment of an early version of the Fed
   b. funds for the South to reconstruct
   c. the creation of the comptroller of the currency
   d. a significant increase in taxes to win the Civil War
   e. greater competition in the banking industry

3. One source of instability in the banking system, prior to the establishment of the Fed, was the relationship between country banks and city banks, where country banks would deposit excess reserves in the city banks in the fall and, in the spring,
    a. the city banks would force the country banks to borrow from them at high interest rates
    b. country banks would fail since they could not meet demands for specie from their depositors over the winter
    c. city banks would find lending opportunities in manufacturing activities
    d. country banks would withdraw their deposits to provide loans to farmers, leaving city banks unstable
    e. the money supply would grow enormously due to all the new lending

4.. The Fed must choose either an interest rate target or a money supply target because it cannot control the
    a. money supply
    b. interest rate
    c. money demand
    d. supply of government bonds
    e. the margin requirement

5. All of the following are characteristics of the Fed **except**
    a. it is owned by its member banks
    b. all nationally chartered banks must be members of the Fed
    c. there are 12 district Federal Reserve banks
    d. it is better at combating recessions than inflation
    e. the Fed chairman is appointed by the president

6. All of the following are mechanisms the Fed can use to increase the money supply **except**
    a. selling government bonds on the open market
    b. buying government bonds on the open market
    c. lowering the reserve requirement
    d. lowering the discount rate
    e. lowering the margin requirement on loans to purchase stocks

7. The Federal Reserve Act of 1913 created the Federal Reserve System, not the Federal Reserve Bank, because
    a. the United States already had experience with a central bank, and it didn't work
    b. the government wanted to keep the entire money system, not just the banks, under its control
    c. Congress wanted a decentralized central bank
    d. state-chartered and nationally chartered banks were already operating in the economy
    e. the government planned to link the central bank to the Department of the Treasury

8. The discount rate is determined by
    a. supply and demand in the money market
    b. supply and demand in the federal funds market
    c. nationally chartered banks, although it applies as well to state-chartered banks
    d. the Fed
    e. the Department of the Treasury

9. Monetary policy is more effective at curbing inflation than reducing unemployment because during periods of high unemployment
    a. banks are more reluctant to lend to businesses and businesses are more reluctant to borrow
    b. businesses may wish to borrow, but banks are reluctant to lend
    c. the Fed can rely on the self-correcting behavior of the labor market
    d. providing easier credit never stimulates borrowing
    e. the government will act, making the Fed's participation unnecessary and even interfering

10. When the government tries to finance a deficit by issuing new government securities while, at the same time, the Fed pursues policies to encourage more borrowing by businesses,
    a. the government and the Fed should raise the interest rate
    b. the Fed should buy the government's new securities issues
    c. the government's policy and the Fed's policy have opposite effects on the interest rate
    d. the new government securities issues will lower the interest rate, which is what the Fed wants anyway
    e. the Fed should lower the interest rate, which will allow the government to sell the new securities more easily.

11. During a period of inflation, an appropriate pair of policies for the Fed to implement would be to
    a. lower the discount rate and purchase government securities
    b. increase the discount rate and purchase government securities
    c. raise the legal reserve requirement and lower the discount rate
    d. sell government securities and raise the discount rate
    e. raise the discount rate and lower the legal reserve requirement

12. Moral suasion and controlling stock market margin requirements are two of the
    a. strongest tools used by the Fed to control the money supply
    b. ancillary tools used by the Fed to control the money supply
    c. tools that are quite effective at fine-tuning monetary policy
    d. tools used only to decrease the money supply
    e. tools used only to increase the money supply

13. When the Fed raises the legal reserve requirement, it
    a. may force banks to call in loans and convert them to reserves
    b. decreases the amount of reserves banks are obligated to hold
    c. creates the conditions for bank loan expansion
    d. makes government securities more attractive because interest rates fall
    e. lowers the discount rate that the Fed charges commercial banks

14. When the Fed buys government securities in the open market, the effect on the asset positions of commercial banks is
    a. negative, forcing banks to call in loans and converting them to reserves
    b. positive, decreasing the amount of reserves banks are obligated to hold
    c. to increase bank reserves, which allow banks to increase lending
    d. a substitution of stocks and corporate bonds for government securities
    e. to increase banks' assets, but, at the same time, their liabilities

15. The most likely place for a commercial bank to go to increase its reserves for short periods is
    a. its district Federal Reserve bank
    b. the federal open market committee
    c. the federal funds market
    d. the Department of the Treasury
    e. Knickerbocker Trust

16. All of the following are roles played by the Fed as a bankers' bank **except**
    a. clearing checks
    b. providing currency
    c. providing loans
    d. providing customers for commercial loans
    e. holding the reserves of member banks

17. A central bank could moderate the extremes in the business cycle by _____ during an economic downturn and _____ during an upswing in the business cycle.
    a. decreasing the money supply; increasing the money supply
    b. raising interest rates; lowering interest rates
    c. increasing the money supply; decreasing the money supply
    d. closely examining bank balance sheets; largely ignoring bank regulation
    e. setting prices higher; decreasing the price level

18. The U.S. Bureau of Printing and Engraving in Washington, D.C., prints our currency
    a. but the Department of the Treasury determines when and how much to put into the economy
    b. and determines how much of it should be introduced into the economy
    c. but district Federal Reserve banks determine when and how much to put into the economy
    d. but the Federal Open Market Committee determines when and how much to put into the economy
    e. but the government, through fiscal policy, determines when and how much to put into the economy.

19. A Fed policy to increase the money supply in order to increase real GDP works best when the money demand
    a. and investment demand curves are steep
    b. and investment demand curves are flat
    c. curve is flat and the investment demand curve is steep
    d. curve shifts to the right and the investment demand curve shifts to the left
    e. curve is steep and the investment demand curve is flat

20. The Fed's use of moral suasion to control inflation
    a. is very effective because people know that fiscal policy doesn't work
    b. is always tried before the Fed resorts to other tools of monetary policy
    c. is inherently weak because it relies on voluntary compliance
    d. is preferred by banks because they might otherwise have to pay a higher discount rate at the Fed
    e. is only used in combination with the Fed's other tools of monetary policy

The following questions relate to the global, applied, and interdisciplinary perspectives in the text.

21. Canada opted for a zero reserve requirement for its commercial banks in the 1990s because
    a. Canadian bankers are risk lovers
    b. the United States has a zero reserve requirement and Canada typically mimics U.S. policy
    c. banks are able to end each day with zero cash reserves
    d. if the bank ends up with negative cash balances, it can borrow from the Bank of Canada
    e. Canada is conducting economic experiments by changing the reserve requirement over time

22. The Department of Treasury determines the interest rate on government securities by
    a. fixing it at the same level that European securities earn
    b. auctioning securities to those who will accept the lowest interest rates
    c. taking advice from the Fed Chairman
    d. open market operations
    e. matching the rate established in the federal funds market

23. The largest asset for United States commercial banks is
    a. loans
    b. cash
    c. government securities
    d. gold
    e. foreign securities

24. The impression one gets on reading an account of how the FOMC makes monetary policy decisions is that
   a. they are highly autocratic, dominated by the Fed Chairman
   b. they are highly technocratic, dominated by staffers who are highly skilled econometricians
   c. the approach is different in every meeting
   d. there is much discussion, questioning, careful study of options, and a vote on which policy to adopt
   e. heated arguments are the rule rather than the exception

25. The basic reason that 75 percent of U.S. currency is held in $100 and $50 bills in foreign countries is that
   a. dollars are an excellent store of value compared to many foreign currencies that are highly unstable
   b. drug transactions are typically conducted in U.S. currency
   c. foreign tourists who have visited the U.S. take the bills home as souvenirs
   d. American tourists in foreign countries spend their dollars there
   e. Americans hardly use currency any longer, so it is more useful in foreign countries that lack cash

Fill in the Blanks

1. The failure to renew the charter for the First Bank of the United States was due primarily to opposition from

   _____ and _____ states.

2. The main goal of the Fed is to provide the economy with an appropriate _____ consistent

   with a stable _____.

3. The Fed tends to be more effective in controlling _____ during periods of

   _____ than in combating _____ during periods of

   _____.

4. If the Fed chooses to target the money supply, then it cannot simultaneously target the

   _____ because it cannot control _____.

Discussion Questions

1. How stable were financial institutions in the United States prior to the establishment of the Federal Reserve System? Provide examples.

2. Why is monetary policy a more effective tool for controlling inflation than for controlling unemployment?

3. Outline the institutional structure of the Federal Reserve System. Why are there 12 district banks in the Fed instead of one central bank?

4. Describe the tools used by the Fed to influence the money supply and interest rates.

5. When might the Fed use a money supply target? When is it more likely to employ an interest rate target? Why?

Everyday Applications

Suppose we were considering the establishment of a central bank in the United States now just as we did in the period from 1907 to 1913. Would there be as much political pressure to create 12 district banks today as there was in the early part of this century? Consider the ways that changes in banking technology have reduced the need for decentralization in a central banking system even for a large country like the United States.

Economics Online

The Federal Reserve Board of Governors has an extraordinarily extensive Web site (*http://www.federalreserve.gov/*). Among the items that you can browse at this site are the transcripts of Federal Open Market Committee meetings, speeches by Federal Reserve Board members, press releases, enforcement actions, consumer information, and reports to Congress. There is a lot to explore. Have fun.

Answers to Questions

Key Terms Quiz

a. 2	**f.** 9	**k.** 3
b. 7	**g.** 4	**l.** 11
c. 8	**h.** 1	
d. 5	**i.** 6	
e. 10	**j.** 12	

True-False Questions

1. False. Continental notes were not backed by gold or silver so as the quantity of notes in circulation increased, their value depreciated. In 1777 they traded 2 for 1 against silver, but by 1781 they traded 1,000 to 1 against silver.
2. True
3. False. The primary goal for the Fed is to provide a money supply that is consistent with stable prices.
4. False. At the very top of the Fed is the Board of Governors.
5. False. Open market operations refer to the purchase and sale of bonds by the Federal Open Market Committee in order to influence the money supply and interest rates.
6. True
7. False. The greater problem for banks in the United States during the late 18th and 19th centuries was their tendency to overissue paper money.
8. True
9. True
10. True
11. True
12. False. The chairman of the Fed serves a 4-year term and can be reappointed for up to 14 years.
13. True
14. False. The Fed's policies and the policy favored by Congress and the president may be different. For example, the Fed's primary concern is maintaining low or zero inflation, while Congress and the president may want to keep unemployment at a low level. Monetary and fiscal policy would then work in opposite directions.
15. True

Multiple-Choice Questions

1. e	6. a	11. d	16. d	21. d
2. c	7. c	12. b	17. c	22. b
3. d	8. d	13. a	18. c	23. a
4. c	9. a	14. c	19. e	24. c
5. d	10. b	15. c	20. c	25. a

Fill in the Blanks

1. southern; western
2. money supply; price level
3. inflation; prosperity; unemployment; recession
4. interest rate; money demand

Discussion Questions

1. The banking system was chronically unstable prior to the establishment of the Federal Reserve System. Among the most notable examples of instability are the suspension of specie payments by most banks in 1814 prior to the establishment of the Second Bank of the United States and the Knickerbocker Trust crisis in 1907. The problem that a central bank could have helped to solve was the tendency of banks to issue more currency than their reserves could support. A central bank could have forced banks to effectively back their notes with specie — that is, to redeem bank notes with specie on presentation. A central bank could also have provided loans of specie to banks when depositors' demand for specie exceeded the banks' reserves. Without a central bank, bank failures tended to occur in waves with no mechanism for stopping the withdrawal of deposits from the nation's banks. For example, as a result of withdrawals of deposits sparked by the Knickerbocker Trust disaster, investment projects had to be suspended and sound businesses

were left without credit and forced into bankruptcy. A severe recession was the result.

2. In order to lower the unemployment rate, the Fed would have to increase the money supply and lower the interest rate so that investment increases. There are two possible stumbling blocks in this process. First, while the Fed can make reserves for lending available to banks, it cannot force banks to lend these reserves. As we learned in the previous chapter, it is by lending that the money supply increases. The second potential stumbling block is that the reserves may not be borrowed. Neither the Fed nor banks can make investors borrow funds to pursue productive projects.

   Controlling inflation is easier. In this case, the Fed simply reduces the money supply, causing interest rates to rise, investment and consumption spending to fall, and aggregate demand to fall as a result. If the aggregate demand curve intersected the aggregate supply curve along its vertical segment, a decrease in aggregate demand would lower the price level and inflation.

3. The Fed is controlled by a seven-member board with one member appointed as the chair. The board members have 14-year terms, and the chair serves for four years with the potential for reappointments for up to 14 years. The Fed Open Market Committee consists of the board and five of the district Fed Presidents, one of whom must be the New York Fed president. District Fed presidents rotate on and off the Open Market Committee. Open market operations are the purchase and sale of government securities by the Fed. There are 12 district Feds to better serve the regions of the United States and to diffuse power throughout the Federal Reserve System.

4. The Fed can change the legal reserve requirement. An increase in the legal reserve requirement reduces the reserves available to banks to make loans and so decreases the money supply. A decrease in the legal reserve requirement makes more reserves available to banks for lending. The Fed can change the discount rate, the rate at which banks borrow from the district banks. An increase in the discount rate makes it more expensive for banks to borrow, so it has the effect of decreasing the money supply and increasing interest rates throughout the economy. A decrease in the discount rate has the opposite effect. The Fed can use open market operations to change the money supply and interest rates. By selling government bonds, the Fed reduces reserves available to banks to make loans, so the money supply shrinks and interest rates increase. By purchasing government bonds, the Fed increases reserves available to banks to make loans, so the money supply can increase and interest rates will fall. The margin requirement is the maximum percentage of a stock's value that can be borrowed when the stock is being purchased. By increasing the margin requirement, the Fed reduces the amount of borrowing to buy stocks and limits the money supply somewhat. Moral suasion is a technique that relies on people's voluntary compliance to the Fed's wishes. The Fed chair may urge banks to restrict lending, or firms to hold the prices of their goods constant, to combat inflation.

5. The Fed is most inclined to use a money supply target when inflation is a serious problem. By restricting the money supply, the interest rate will rise, the quantity of investment and aggregate demand will fall, and the price level should fall. An interest rate target is preferred to fight unemployment since, by lowering interest rates, investment and aggregate demand can be stimulated. The Fed's countercyclical policy works in either case no matter which target it chooses. However, in that last few decades, the money supply target has been preferred for battling inflation, and the interest rate target has been preferred for reducing unemployment.

Homework Questions

True-False Questions — If a statement is false, explain why.

1. The impetus for the establishment of the Federal Reserve System came as a result of the Civil War in 1865. (T/F)

2. The twelve district banks in the Federal Reserve System are owned by member banks in the district. (T/F)

3. The tool used most frequently by the Fed to control the money supply is the reserve requirement. (T/F)

4. If the Fed Open Market Committee deems that a decrease in interest rates is appropriate, then it will recommend open market sales of government securities. (T/F)

5. The Fed can simultaneously control the money supply and the interest rate. (T/F)

Multiple Choice Questions

1. Which of the following actions by the Fed would cause the money supply to decrease?
   a. a decrease in the discount rate
   b. open market sales of government securities
   c. a decrease in the federal funds rate
   d. a decrease in the legal reserve requirement
   e. a statement by the Fed Chairman that he expects next year's corporate profits to be higher than anticipated

2. The main role of the Federal Reserve System is to safeguard the country's money system by
   a. controlling the money supply, interest rates, and the price level
   b. doing thorough monthly audits of all nationally chartered banks
   c. encouraging district Feds to monitor all business transactions that exceed $1,000,000
   d. putting in place monetary policy that helps Congress cut the deficit
   e. keeping very conservative bankers on the Board of Governors

3. Financial panics in the United States in the late 19th century were sometimes started by country banks that
   a. made risky loans to farmers who had purchased land and equipment at inflated prices
   b. failed because they kept inadequate reserves
   c. had abandoned their national charters for state charters
   d. issued too many Greenbacks
   e. withdrew deposits at city banks in the spring to make loans to farmers

4. If the economy is headed into a recession, then the Federal Reserve should
   a. purchase government securities (bonds)
   b. lower bond prices
   c. raise interest rates and raise bond prices
   d. cut taxes
   e. stop loaning money to banks whose reserves are dwindling

5. It is impossible for the Fed to target both the interest rate and the money supply simultaneously because
   a. the money supply is hard to calculate precisely
   b. the Fed can't control money demand
   c. the interest rate is determined on the money market, not by the Fed
   d. Congress has veto power over the Fed's decision-making process
   e. this would be unconstitutional

Discussion Questions/Problems

1. Sketch a graph of the business cycle and list the monetary policies that are appropriate during downturns and during periods of prosperity.

2. What are open market operations? How do they work?

PART 3 — MONEY, BANKING, AND MONETARY POLICY

COMPREHENSIVE SAMPLE TEST

Give yourself 50 minutes to complete this exam and see how you do. The answers follow. Don't look until you are finished.

True-False Questions — If a statement is false, explain why. Each question is worth two points.

1. The quantity theory of money states that the price level is directly related to the money supply in the short run because velocity is constant and the quantity of goods produced is constant. (T/F)

2. Monetarists believe that velocity is constant. (T/F)

3. According to Keynesians, as the interest rate decreases, the opportunity cost of holding money decreases, so the speculative demand for money is downward sloping. (T/F)

4. The potential money multiplier is equal to $1/(1 - LRR)$. (T/F)

5. One factor contributing to the savings and loan crisis during the 1980s was the increasingly risky loans that S&Ls began to make in order to stay profitable. (T/F)

6. The banking system could create more money if the legal reserve requirement were reduced. (T/F)

7. The Fed can decrease the money supply by open market purchases of government bonds. (T/F)

8. All of the banks in the United States are required to be part of the Federal Reserve System. (T/F)

9. The primary goal for the Fed is to close recessionary gaps. (T/F)

10. In order for the Fed to be able to lower the unemployment rate, banks must be willing to lend reserves and borrowers must be willing to borrow and invest them. (T/F)

Multiple-Choice Questions — Each question is worth two points.

1. An asset is more liquid if it is
   a. more durable and portable
   b. more homogeneous
   c. closer to universally acceptable
   d. more easily exchanged for money
   e. fixed in supply and easily divisible

2. The largest measure of the U.S. money supply is
    a. M1
    b. currency
    c. demand deposits
    d. M2
    e. M3

3. If velocity increases while the money supply and real GDP remain constant, then the
    a. quantity theory of money predicts that interest rates will increase
    b. speculative demand for money will increase
    c. the equation of exchange predicts that the price level will increase
    d. the equation of exchange predicts that the price level will decrease
    e. the quantity theory of money predicts that interest rates will decrease

4. Keynesians reject the monetarist view that the equation of exchange is a useful predictive tool because they
    believe that
    a. aggregate expenditure determines the equilibrium level of national income
    b. the aggregate supply curve is vertical at full employment
    c. money only affects the price level
    d. velocity is neither constant nor predictable and real GDP can be in equilibrium at levels below full
       employment
    e. velocity is not constant but it is predictable and real GDP is always moving toward equilibrium at the
       full-employment level

5. Monetarists believe that the investment demand function is _____ to changes in the interest rate
    and that the economy always operates on the _____ segment of the aggregate supply curve.
    a. very sensitive; vertical
    b. insensitive; vertical
    c. very sensitive; upward-sloping
    d. insensitive; upward-sloping
    e. very sensitive; horizontal

6. According to Keynesians, the demand for money is comprised by
    a. the transactions motive
    b. the speculative motive
    c. the transactions and the speculative motives
    d. the transactions, speculative, and investment motives
    e. the transactions, speculative, and precautionary motives

7. Suppose a bank accepts a new deposit of currency equal to $1,000 and the legal reserve requirement is .2.
    The money supply has
    a. increased by $1,000
    b. increased by $800
    c. not changed
    d. decreased by $1,000
    e. decreased by $800

8. If the bank in the previous question loans $800 based on the original deposit of $1,000, then it has created _____ of new money and the banking system can create a maximum of _____ new money (excluding the original deposit).
   a. $800; $4,000
   b. $1,800; $5,000
   c. $1,000; $5,000
   d. $800; $5,000
   e. $1,000; $4,000

9. All of the following contributed to the increased number of bank and savings and loan failures during the 1980s and early 1990s **except** the
   a. fall in agricultural prices
   b. rise of the stock market
   c. repeal of Regulation Q
   d. fall in oil prices
   e. entry of banks into home mortgage lending

10. An important function served by financial intermediaries is linking savers with borrowers so that people's savings can
    a. generate interest income for bankers
    b. generate profits for borrowers
    c. earn the maximum amount of interest
    d. be available for withdrawal
    e. be used to produce the maximum amount of goods and services

11. Suppose that the Federal Reserve increases the reserve requirement from 10 percent to 20 percent. If a bank holds loans up to its legal reserve requirement at 10 percent, the increase in the reserve requirement will force the bank to
    a. extend more loans to generate interest income to increase reserves
    b. stop meeting the demands of depositors for currency
    c. raise interest rates on loans
    d. wait for loans to be paid back to increase reserves
    e. convert demand deposits into reserves

12. The impact of an increase in the legal reserve requirement from 10 percent to 20 percent will be to
    a. cause an increase in lending
    b. cause an increase in the money supply
    c. shrink the money supply
    d. force banks to purchase government bonds to hold as reserves
    e. cause depositors to withdraw their deposits

13. The potential money multiplier equal to $1/LRR$ is called potential because
    a. banks never exceed the legal reserve requirement
    b. the legal reserve requirement is merely a suggested value and banks typically hold fewer reserves
    c. the actual reserve requirement is given by $1/(1 - LRR)$
    d. the FDIC creates moral hazard
    e. banks may not lend all of their excess reserves, borrowers may not borrow them, and loans may not be redeposited

14. The First Bank of the United States was created in 1791 in response to a proposal by _____ for a central bank to _____ .
    a. Thomas Jefferson; make certain the paper dollars issued were backed by gold and silver
    b. James Madison; make certain that debts from the Revolutionary War were paid
    c. Alexander Hamilton; control the money supply and provide credit to the government
    d. George Washington; collect taxes to pay for the Revolutionary War
    e. the British; make certain the new nation had a stable price level

15. The Federal Reserve System, comprised of 12 district banks owned by member banks in each district, was created in 1913 instead of just one Federal Reserve Bank because
    a. 12 banks were necessary to create enough money for such a large economy
    b. Congress wanted a decentralized central bank
    c. central banking was poorly understood in the United States
    d. large regional banks demanded that they be designated District Banks
    e. the large number of bank failures had created a need for many new banks across the country

16. If the Fed Open Market Committee purchases government bonds from banks, the intention is to
    a. raise interest rates
    b. avoid increasing the discount rate
    c. make reserves more available to banks so that loans can be made to increase the money supply
    d. combat inflation
    e. allow the Treasury to finance a deficit government budget

17. A decision by the Fed Open Market Committee to sell government bonds is an appropriate policy when the economy is in equilibrium
    a. on the vertical segment of the aggregate supply curve
    b. on the horizontal segment of the aggregate supply curve
    c. below a full-employment level of national income
    d. with unwanted inventories of government bonds
    e. and the investment demand curve is very steep, close to vertical

18. Among the alternative tools available to the Fed for controlling the money supply, the one that has the greatest potential to immediately alter the reserves available to banks for lending is
    a. changing the legal reserve requirement
    b. changing the discount rate
    c. changing the federal funds rate
    d. open market operations
    e. changing the margin requirement for stock purchases

19. If the Fed chooses to target the interest rate, it cannot at the same time control the money supply because
    a. it has difficulty reducing unemployment if it controls the money supply
    b. it has difficulty combating inflation if it targets the interest rate
    c. interest rates and the money supply are directly related to each other
    d. it cannot control money demand
    e. there are several interest rates to target, e.g., the discount rate and the federal funds rate

20. If the government and the Fed have policies that work in unison during a period of high unemployment and recession, then a possible combination is a fiscal policy with a
    a. surplus budget and a monetary policy to purchase government bonds
    b. deficit budget and a monetary policy to sell government bonds
    c. deficit budget and a monetary policy to purchase government bonds
    d. surplus budget and a monetary policy to lower the discount rate
    e. deficit budget and a monetary policy to raise the discount rate

Discussion Questions/Problems — Each question is worth 10 points.

1. a. Use graphs to show why a Keynesian believes that an increase in the money supply can increase employment and the equilibrium level of real GDP with little impact on the price level. Explain your graphs carefully.

   b. Would a monetarist or classical economist agree with the Keynesian? Why or why not?

2. Suppose that a bank starts with zero excess reserves and the Fed purchases $10,000 in government bonds from the bank. What is the maximum amount of money that can be created as a result of this bond purchase if the legal reserve requirement is 20 percent? Show your work.

3. Why is it easier for the Fed to limit growth in the money supply than to increase the money supply? How does this influence the Fed's relative effectiveness at combating inflation and unemployment?

4. Why is the speculative demand for money downward sloping as the interest rate decreases?

Answers to the Sample Test on Part 3

True-False Questions

1. True
2. False. Monetarists believe that velocity may vary, but in predictable ways.
3. True
4. False. The potential money multiplier is equal to 1/*LRR*.
5. True
6. True
7. False. The Fed can reduce the money supply by open market sales of government bonds.
8. False. Banks with national charters are members of the Federal Reserve System while state-chartered banks may choose, but are not required, to be part of the Fed.
9. False. The primary goal for the Fed is to provide a money supply that is consistent with a stable price level.
10. True

Multiple-Choice Questions

1. d	6. e	11. d	16. c
2. e	7. c	12. c	17. a
3. c	8. a	13. e	18. a
4. d	9. b	14. c	19. d
5. a	10. e	15. b	20. c

Discussion Questions/Problems

1. a. The graph in Panel A shows a shift in the money supply curve that causes the interest rate to fall from i to i′. The decrease in the interest rate causes investment to increase from I to I′, as shown in Panel B. In Panel C, on the following page, the increase in investment causes the aggregate demand curve to shift to the right along the horizontal segment of the aggregate supply curve. Therefore, the equilibrium level of real GDP increases from GDP₁ to GDP₂, but the price level stays fairly constant because the aggregate supply curve is flat. Keynesians believe that there are ample unemployed resources in the economy so that an increase in aggregate demand will increase real GDP rather than the pri

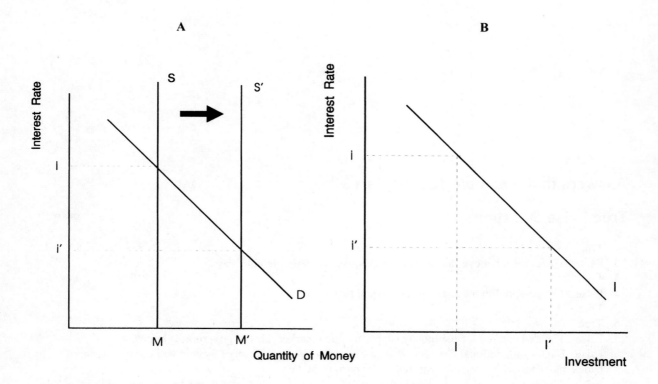

A

B

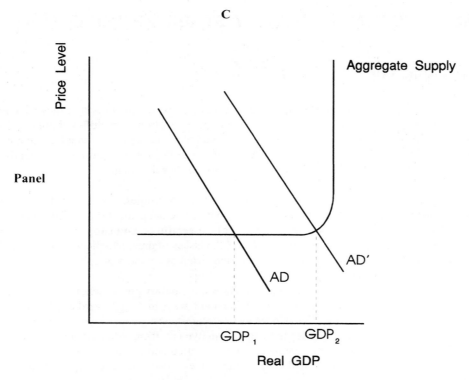

b. Monetarists and classical economists would disagree with the analysis in part a of this question because they believe the economy is always at a full-employment level of GDP along the vertical segment of the aggregate supply curve. An increase in the money supply would cause a shift in the aggregate demand curve upward along the vertical segment of the aggregate supply curve, causing the price level to increase with no increase in real GDP.

2. The reserves created by this purchase would all be excess reserves for the bank; thus, the full $10,000 can be loaned. The potential money multiplier is equal to $1/LRR = 1/.2 = 5$. The maximum amount by which the money supply can expand is 5 x $10,000 = $50,000.

3. The Fed can effectively limit the ability of banks to lend by limiting their access to reserves. The Fed can do this by raising the legal reserve requirement, raising the discount rate, and selling government bonds. If banks don't have new reserves, they can't make new loans, and new money cannot be created. Increasing the money supply is harder to accomplish because the Fed can only make reserves more available to banks. It cannot make banks lend these reserves, nor can it force people to borrow the reserves. Only by lending and borrowing the reserves will the money supply grow. Therefore, combating inflation is easier for the Fed than combating unemployment. By limiting growth in the money supply, the Fed pushes up interest rates and reduces aggregate demand, which will lower the price level and lower inflation. It is harder for the Fed to increase the money supply, lower interest rates, and increase aggregate demand to increase employment and real GDP.

4. The speculative demand for money is downward sloping as the interest rate decreases because at a lower interest rate, the opportunity cost of holding money (the interest sacrificed by holding money rather than an interest-bearing asset like a bond) is lower, so people will hold more money. They hold more money because that puts them in a better position to speculate. It is easier for them to purchase an asset at an attractive price if the chance arises.

CHAPTER 13

CAN GOVERNMENT REALLY STABILIZE THE ECONOMY?

Chapter in a Nutshell

There is little consensus among economists on macroeconomic policy, not only because they have imperfect information to work with, but because they approach economic issues from very different political perspectives. It is not altogether surprising, then, that liberal economists tend to be more inclined to advocate government intervention in the economy than do conservative economists. The fact that our presidents typically choose economic advisers who share their political ideologies is also hardly surprising.

Macroeconomic theorists, who represent a wide range of ideologies, have focused most of their attention on why unemployment and inflation occur and what can be done about them. Different schools of thought — **classical, Keynesian, neo-Keynesian, rational expectations, and supply-side economics** — reflecting differences in ideology, have developed around the issues of unemployment, inflation, and policies to prevent them. Even within schools of thought there are significant differences of opinion.

The **classical school** believes that unemployment is a temporary phenomenon. Classical economists believe that markets are competitive, so prices are flexible and always moving toward equilibrium where quantity demanded equals quantity supplied. Under these circumstances, labor markets will always generate full employment. The appropriate policy for dealing with unemployment, then, is to not intervene. To classical economists, inflation is purely the result of too much money in circulation. The rate of growth of the money supply should match the rate of growth of real GDP so that prices remain stable, consistent with the quantity theory of money.

Keynesian economists see the world very differently. They argue that prices are rigid and markets are not competitive. A decrease in demand leads to a decrease in output rather than a decrease in price. Under these circumstances, unemployment can persist indefinitely if nothing is done to prevent it. Increases in government spending, decreases in taxes, and increases in the money supply are all appropriate policies for combating unemployment according to Keynesians. As long as the economy is at or below full employment, inflation poses no problems for Keynesians.

To the Keynesians' dismay, the 1970s and 1980s generated both high rates of unemployment and high rates of inflation. The term *stagflation* was coined to describe this unpleasant event. If the policy to cure unemployment was exactly the opposite of the policy to cure inflation, how could both be cured at the same time? Many Keynesians conceded that it just couldn't be done. Then what? Enter the **Phillips curve**. It was used to explain how a higher rate of inflation could be traded for a lower rate of unemployment. **Neo-Keynesians** developed a new version of the aggregate supply curve with an upward-sloping segment that depicts price level increases as full employment is approached.

Neo-Keynesians developed a new stabilization policy based on the Phillips curve. Suppose the government wants to lower the rate of unemployment. It increases its spending (that's what Keynesians would do), which raises GDP and employment. Workers now feel more comfortable to press for higher wages, which creates cost-push inflation. When cost-push inflation occurs because of the initial government spending to lower unemployment, workers discover that their real wages are falling and react by demanding wage increases to make up for the loss. If successful, these wage increases cut into firms' profit, discouraging production so that GDP falls and unemployment increases. Neo-Keynesians now concede that while government can lower unemployment rates in the short run, it is much less successful in keeping them low in the long run.

Rational expectations theorists deny even these temporary short-run gains. They argue that the trade-off between unemployment and inflation suggested by the Phillips curve does not exist. Why? The reason is that workers are rational and can translate past experience into expectations about the future. Let's go back to the first announcement by government that it will increase spending to lower the rate of unemployment. Workers expect such a policy to create inflation so, before suffering the expected real wage erosion, they demand wage increases to compensate for the expected inflation. Their success undermines the government's employment policy because firms, paying the higher wages, have no incentive to increase production. The unemployment rate doesn't fall. According to rational expectations theorists, the government can't lower unemployment rates even in the short run. Any attempt to do so will only cause inflation.

Supply-side economists argue that the best way to attack the problem of unemployment and inflation is by implementing policies that will move the aggregate supply curve to the right more rapidly over time. Such policies include lower tax rates, less government regulation, and less government spending. In their criticisms of demand-side Keynesian policy, supply-siders emphasize the **crowding-out effect of fiscal policy**. To finance its spending and deficits, government resorts to selling its own securities (savings bonds, for example) on the securities market, competing directly with private firms that try to sell their own securities to finance private investment. The interest rate increases and some private investment is crowded out as a result.

Stabilization policy is described as discretionary, meaning that policy is a matter of judgment. However, to some extent, the economy automatically stabilizes. Unemployment insurance is one type of **automatic stabilizer**. During a recession, when unemployment increases, unemployment insurance payments increase and prop up aggregate demand somewhat. At full employment, these payments are lower, thus relieving inflationary pressure. The income and corporate profits taxes work similarly, adding to aggregate demand when the economy is in recession and tax revenues decrease and subtracting from aggregate demand when the economy is inflationary and tax revenues increase. If these automatic stabilizers are effective, then the need for active government intervention to stabilize the economy diminishes.

After you study this chapter, you should be able to:

- State why the **classical school** believes **stabilization policy** is unnecessary.
- Present the **Keynesian** argument for the existence of unemployment.
- Draw a **Phillips curve** and explain its shape.
- Discuss **neo-Keynesian** policies to cope with unemployment and inflation.
- Justify the vertical shape of the **long-run Phillips curve**.
- Explain what is meant by **rational expectations**.
- Contrast **supply-side** and Keynesian policies for economic stabilization.
- Describe how **automatic stabilizers** work.

Concept Check — See how you do on these multiple-choice questions.

Recall from previous chapters that classical economists believe markets are competitive and prices are flexible.

1. The **classical economics** view of the economy is that
   a. without government interference, the economy will move toward an equilibrium rate of growth with full employment and zero inflation
   b. a central bank like the Fed is necessary to introduce a countercyclical monetary policy
   c. the Phillips curve provides policymakers with a menu of combinations of inflation and unemployment rates
   d. prices in the economy are flexible upward, but not downward
   e. the money supply should grow faster than the annual rate of growth of full-employment real GDP

On the other hand, Keynesian economists believe markets are not competitive and wages and prices are not flexible.

2. The **Keynesian economics** view of the economy is that
   a. without government interference, the economy will move toward an equilibrium rate of growth with full employment and zero inflation
   b. tax cuts and increases in government spending do little to increase aggregate demand
   c. the money supply should never grow faster than the annual rate of growth of full-employment real GDP
   d. wages and prices are flexible upward and downward
   e. equilibrium at full employment without inflation can be achieved by managing aggregate demand

What happens to inflation as unemployment decreases?

3. The **Phillips curve** is a graph showing
   a. combinations of government spending and taxation that generate a full-employment GDP without inflation
   b. the inverse relationship between the economy's rate of unemployment and rate of inflation
   c. the direct relationship between the economy's rate of unemployment and rate of inflation
   d. the inverse relationship between the economy's rate of employment and rate of inflation
   e. the direct relationship between the rate of growth of the money supply and the rate of inflation

According to the rational expectations school, how do workers react immediately after learning that the Fed will increase the money supply? Why?

4. A fundamental idea behind the **rational expectations** school of thought is that
   a. the Phillips curve is downward sloping
   b. the Phillips curve is upward sloping
   c. by anticipating the consequences of announced government policy and incorporating these consequences into their decision making, people undermine the policy
   d. most people know too little about economic theory to be able to anticipate the consequences of announced government policy
   e. policies designed to close recessionary gaps work quickly with no inflation, but policies designed to close inflationary gaps reduce inflation at the expense of a recession

If the government borrows large sums, is it easier or more difficult for people to borrow in the private sector?

5. **Crowding out** is
   a. the decrease in the number of state banks that happened when the Fed was established
   b. a fall in government spending caused by an increase in private investment spending
   c. a fall in private investment spending caused by an increase in government spending
   d. a fall in government spending caused by increased deficit spending during the 1980s
   e. a decrease in inflationary pressure that occurs when government spending is cut

Am I on the Right Track?

Your answers to the questions above should be **a**, **e**, **b**, **c**, and **c**. The key to success with this chapter is to ask the questions "Why unemployment?" and "Why inflation?" for each school of thought presented. The answers to these questions will help you to distinguish among the various schools. As you answer these questions for each school, you will gain an appreciation for the role played by the Phillips curve in different theories and the varying views on the usefulness of the Phillips curve as a tool for designing economic policy. The meaning of automatic stabilization and crowding out should also become clear to you.

Key Terms Quiz — Match the terms on the left with the definitions in the column on the right.

1. rational expectations

_____ a. the use of countercyclical monetary and fiscal policy by the government and the Fed to stabilize the economy

2. classical school

_____ b. the school of thought that argues that people anticipate the consequences of announced government policy and incorporate these anticipated consequences into their decision making, thus undermining the policy

3. stabilization policy

_____ c. a graph showing the inverse relationship between the economy's rate of unemployment and rate of inflation

4. supply-side economics

_____ d. a fall in private investment spending caused by an increase in government spending

5. Keynesian economics

_____ e. the school of though that argues that through tax reductions, spending cuts, and deregulation, government creates the proper incentives for the private sector to increase aggregate supply

6. crowding out

_____ f. any unemployment rate lower than this will cause the inflation rate to rise

7. Phillips curve

_____ g. the school of thought that emphasizes the possibility that an economy can be in equilibrium at less than full employment with inflation

8. automatic stabilizers

_____ h. the school of thought that emphasizes the natural tendency for an economy to move toward equilibrium at full employment without inflation

9. neo-Keynesian economics

_____ i. structures in the economy that tend to add to aggregate demand when the economy is in recession, and subtract from aggregate demand when the economy is inflationary

10. non-accelerating inflation rate of unemployment (NAIRU)

_____ j. the school of thought that argues that government can achieve the most acceptable combination of unemployment and inflation by managing aggregate demand

Graphing Tutorial

The Phillips curve is used to show the inverse relationship between the percentage rate of unemployment and the percentage rate of inflation. The Phillips curve originated with the economist A. W. Phillips who first observed the inverse relationship between the two variables in a study of British inflation and unemployment between 1861 and 1957. Phillips's study showed clearly that for Great Britain over this long time period, as unemployment decreased, inflation increased. A hypothetical Phillips curve is shown below.

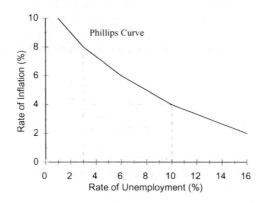

The Phillips curve relationship suggests that in order to decrease unemployment, it is necessary to accept a higher rate of inflation. For example, given the Phillips curve drawn on the previous page, to cut unemployment from 10 percent to 3 percent, one would have to be willing to tolerate an increase in inflation from 4 percent to 8 percent. This happens because a fiscal or monetary policy designed to increase aggregate demand and lower unemployment would do so with the cost of increased inflation. The Phillips curve suggests that inflation and unemployment can coexist and that there is a trade-off between the two — high inflation and low unemployment, or low inflation and high unemployment, or somewhere in between with moderate rates of inflation and unemployment.

The idea of a Phillips curve trade-off between unemployment and inflation was incorporated into the neo-Keynesian version of the aggregate supply curve with its upward-sloping segment as the economy approaches a full-employment level of GDP. The neo-Keynesian aggregate supply curve is drawn below.

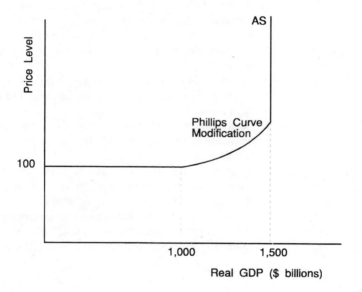

The Phillips curve modification shown in the neo-Keynesian aggregate supply curve suggests that as the economy approaches full employment, the price level will begin to rise. In the context of the Phillips curve, the upward-sloping aggregate supply curve corresponds to the rise in inflation that accompanies a fall in unemployment from, say, 10 percent to 3 percent.

Why does the economy behave this way? Neo-Keynesians argue that as the economy grows faster, approaching full employment, firms attempt to increase production by hiring more workers. Workers who are secure in their jobs begin to demand higher wages. Firms acquiesce to these demands for higher wages and pass the higher costs on as price increases. As a result, the price level rises as real GDP increases along the upward-sloping segment of the aggregate supply curve.

Graphing Pitfalls

Be sure that the Phillips curves you draw to represent the neo-Keynesian short-run view are caved in toward the origin, not bowed-out. Most of the data we have for the Phillips curve relationship suggest that as unemployment decreases, inflation increases at an increasing, not at a decreasing, rate. If the Phillips curve is drawn so that it is bowed-out from the origin, it would show an inflation rate that increases at a decreasing rate. An incorrectly drawn Phillips curve is shown on the following page.

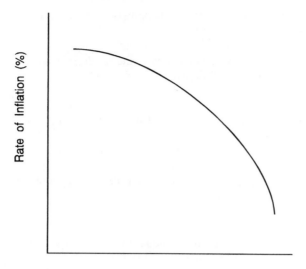

The Phillips curve relationship drawn above shows that the rate of inflation increases at a decreasing rate as unemployment decreases, not at an increasing rate as most data indicate.

True-False Questions — If a statement is false, explain why.

1. Political ideology may influence the way economists believe the economy works. (T/F)

2. A basic assumption underlying the classical school's view of the economy is that firms are highly competitive. (T/F)

3. The Keynesian idea of fine-tuning the economy rests on the belief that it is possible through fiscal and monetary policies to decrease rates of unemployment and inflation simultaneously. (T/F)

4. The Phillips curve shows the direct relationship between unemployment and inflation. (T/F)

5. If the long-run Phillips curve is vertical, then fiscal and monetary policy can permanently lower both inflation and unemployment. (T/F)

6. The Humphrey-Hawkins Act of 1978 defined 10 percent inflation and 10 percent unemployment as reasonable targets for fiscal and monetary policy. (T/F)

7. A beneficial effect of lowering the budget deficit is that government borrowing will decline, causing interest rates to decline as well. (T/F)

8. One advantage to automatic stabilizers is that no decision making is necessary for them to work. (T/F)

9. The classical school explains unemployment in the economy as the result, in part, of interference from unions and minimum wage laws in labor markets. (T/F)

10. A classical school economist would agree with a Keynesian that the cause of inflation is most likely a horizontal aggregate supply curve. (T/F)

11. A rational expectations theorist believes that only temporary victories over unemployment are possible through the use of fiscal and monetary policy. (T/F)

12. The main idea of rational expectations is that consumers and producers anticipate the effects of announced fiscal and monetary policy and react before it has time to influence aggregate demand, thus undermining the policy. (T/F)

13. If workers are successful in bargaining for wage increases to offset the increase in inflation associated with government policies to combat unemployment, then the long-run Phillips curve will be vertical. (T/F)

14. Raising tax rates to curb inflation is a cornerstone of supply-side economics. (T/F)

15. The upward-sloping segment of the aggregate supply curve suggests that as the economy approaches full employment, a higher price level must be tolerated, just as the Phillips curve suggests a trade-off between lower unemployment and higher inflation. (T/F)

Multiple-Choice Questions

1. An economist who states that the cause of inflation is excessive growth in the money supply is probably a
   a. Keynesian
   b. neo-Keynesian
   c. classical school economist
   d. supply-side economist
   e. rational expectations theorist

2. In a world characterized by rational expectations, if the Fed announces that interest rates will be decreased, then workers will respond by
   a. withdrawing bank deposits
   b. bargaining with employers for a wage increase
   c. requesting that wages be cut to preserve employment
   d. increasing saving
   e. decreasing consumption

3. Supply-side economists argue that policies designed to make firms more profitable
    a. shift the aggregate supply curve to the right
    b. cause a decrease in tax revenue
    c. cause aggregate demand to shift to the right and aggregate supply to shift left
    d. lower unemployment but cause higher inflation
    e. cause the Phillips curve to shift up

4. All of the following are sources of inflation according to a neo-Keynesian economist **except**
    a. the influence of unions
    b. dramatic increases in prices of critical inputs like oil
    c. crop failures throughout much of the world
    d. the money supply growing at the same rate as real GDP
    e. excessive government spending

5. Classical economists believe that the economy will automatically adjust to full employment because
    a. aggregate demand will increase, causing real GDP and employment to increase
    b. aggregate supply will decrease, causing inflation to fall and employment to increase
    c. the economy is highly competitive and wages and prices are flexible
    d. successful unions will effectively promote higher levels of employment
    e. employers will raise wages to retain employees as real GDP and employment increase

6. The main difference between Keynesians and neo-Keynesians is that Keynesians believe it is possible to eliminate unemployment _____ and neo-Keynesians believe that in the battle against unemployment _____.
    a. permanently with zero inflation; only temporary victories with some inflation are possible
    b. only temporarily with some inflation; permanent victories with zero inflation are possible
    c. permanently with some inflation; only temporary victories are possible but with no inflation
    d. with great difficulty because of structural unemployment; structural unemployment is of little concern
    e. without government intervention; government intervention is necessary

7. An essential component of the rational expectations model is that
    a. wages are rigid, at least when aggregate demand falls
    b. unions' leaders can be made to see why stabilizing wages stabilizes prices
    c. unions are not very powerful
    d. wages are quite flexible
    e. monetary policy is quite effective when used to combat unemployment

8. Consider the following statement: "Tax rates are so high that incentives to work and invest are stifled. In fact, a reduction of income tax rates would actually increase, not decrease, tax revenues by giving encouragement to work and investment." This statement was likely made by a
    a. classical economist
    b. Keynesian
    c. monetarist
    d. rational expectations theorist
    e. supply-side economist

9. The Humphrey-Hawkins Act of 1978
    a. called on government to pursue zero unemployment and zero inflation policies
    b. acknowledged the impossibility of pursuing zero unemployment and zero inflation
    c. put rational expectations policies into effect
    d. forced unions to accept lower wage rate increases to keep unemployment rates low
    e. created wage and price controls to control both inflation and unemployment

10. All of the following are characteristics of the classical model of the economy **except**
    a. flexible wages
    b. monopoly power
    c. increases in the price level that are proportionate to increases in the money supply
    d. competitive markets
    e. flexible prices

11. Keynesians do not view inflation as a chronic problem because
    a. the aggregate supply curve shifts to the right at the same rate as aggregate demand
    b. central banks monitor the money supply
    c. the aggregate supply curve is horizontal until full employment is reached
    d. technology shifts the aggregate supply curve to the left, raising real GDP and lowering inflation
    e. the long-run Phillips curve is vertical

12. The neo-Keynesian view of the Phillips curve is that the curve
    a. is vertical in the short run, but becomes less steep in the long run
    b. is constant, although government policy may shift the economy's position on the curve
    c. shows no correlation between rates of unemployment and rates of inflation
    d. shifts upward over time because government keeps trying to lower the rate of unemployment
    e. is horizontal, so unemployment can be reduced to low levels without causing inflation

13. A rational expectations theorist believes that the Phillips curve is
    a. downward-sloping in the short run but vertical in the long run
    b. vertical in both the short run and the long run
    c. shifting over time
    d. horizontal in the short run but downward sloping in the long run
    e. downward-sloping in both the short run and the long run

14. Many economist believe that the NAIRU has
    a. been constant for many decades
    b. increased during the 1990s
    c. been reduced as a result of supply-side policies
    d. been constant because workers have rational expectations
    e. decreased dramatically from the six percent rate that held for the 1980s

15. An example of an automatic stabilizer is
    a. fiscal policy
    b. the Laffer curve
    c. the Phillips curve
    d. the Full Employment Act of 1946
    e. unemployment insurance

16. Consider the following statement: "The economy is very close to full employment at the present time. A reduction in tax rates may result in a reduction in the unemployment rate below 5 percent, however, this decrease in unemployment must be traded-off against an increase in inflation." This statement was likely made by a
    a. classical economist
    b. Keynesian
    c. neo-Keynesian
    d. rational expectations theorist
    e. supply-side economist

17. The school of macroeconomic thought most closely associated with the idea that government can stabilize an economy that is in equilibrium below full employment without causing inflation is the
    a. Keynesian
    b. classical
    c. neo-Keynesian
    d. rational expectations
    e. supply-side

18. The Full Employment Act of 1946 made it government policy to ensure that
    a. real wages rise steadily over time
    b. there will be employment for all those willing and able to work
    c. deficit spending be used to increase aggregate demand
    d. unions represent workers who lose their jobs
    e. Keynesian economists be consulted before government makes economic policy decisions

19. One of the reasons why the coexistence of inflation and unemployment in the late 1960s and 1970s was a surprise to Keynesian economists was that
    a. Keynesians didn't think inflation would arise with high unemployment rates
    b. Keynesians didn't think inflation was possible in a modern economy
    c. fiscal policies to increase aggregate demand are naturally anti-inflationary
    d. inflation could be stopped successfully with wage-price controls
    e. inflation was viewed as only a temporary phenomenon with wages and prices adjusting back downward automatically once full employment was reached

20. The progressive income tax is an example of an automatic stabilizer because
    a. when GDP increases, tax revenues increase at a faster rate, reducing the upward pressure on prices
    b. the progressive income tax is a permanent structure in our economy
    c. taxes are withheld on paychecks so people automatically pay them
    d. people tend to forget their tax obligations when they consume, so aggregate demand is always high
    e. people pay taxes from saving, so consumption spending is unaffected

The following questions relate to the theoretical, historical, and global perspectives in the text.

21. The natural rate of unemployment in the United States is
    a. 6 percent
    b. 4 percent
    c. between 4 and 6 percent
    d. falling over time
    e. a concept that increasingly is called into question by economists

22. *Ceteris paribus*, the longer the time between a peak and the following trough in the business cycle, the more it makes sense for the government to
    a. introduce a policy to reduce inflation
    b. avoid introducing a stabilization policy
    c. wait until the downturn has ended to intervene with stabilization policy
    d. intervene aggressively to avoid persistently high rates of unemployment
    e. make sure the budget is balanced

23. Which of the following statements is most correct?
    a. Keynesians always support policies to reduce unemployment even if large budget deficits result.
    b. Supply-side economists always advocate policies that balance the budget and focus on aggregate supply.
    c. Keynesians and supply-side economists both depart from their ideologies in order to pursue their agenda.
    d. Keynesians never balance the budget.
    e. Supply-siders never run deficits.

24. The NAIRU estimates for Western European countries from 1990-1997, with the exception of the Netherlands, show that they are
    a. falling over the period
    b. rising over the period
    c. much lower than the NAIRU for the United States and Japan
    d. falling to a rate lower than for the United States and Japan
    e. stable and higher than the NAIRU for the United States and Japan

Fill in the Blanks

1. The five schools of macroeconomic thought related to the analysis of employment and inflation are the

   _____, _____, _____,

   _____, and _____.

2. Keynesian economists argue that markets are not _____ and that prices are downward

   _____.

3. The coexistence of _____ and _____ is referred to as

   stagflation.

4. Neo-Keynesians believe that a government policy that successfully reduces _____ will be

   followed by demands for _____ by unions, which, if successful, lead to

   _____ and an increase in unemployment.

Discussion Questions

1. Compare and contrast the Keynesian and classical school views on pricing in the economy. Use graphs in your analysis.

2. Sketch the Phillips curve diagram and explain the logic behind the relationship between inflation and unemployment that is represented.

3. Why is the long-run Phillips curve vertical?

4. How well do fiscal and monetary policies designed to lower unemployment rates work in a world of rational expectations? What about policies designed to reduce inflation? Explain.

5. Give some examples of supply-side policies. Critique the argument that supply-side economists make about the impact of their policies on the economy.

6. What is meant by the term "crowding out"? How could crowding out act as a drag on economic growth over time?

Everyday Applications

The late 1990s have been characterized by low and falling unemployment and virtually nonexistent inflation. Which of the schools of macroeconomic thought you have studied in this chapter is able to explain this remarkable bill of economic good health? Think creatively about this question. Several of the models we have worked with may be applicable.

Economics Online

The President's Council of Economic Advisers (CEA) is a group of distinguished economists who advise the president about what they think are appropriate stabilization policies given current and anticipated economic conditions. To find out the latest thoughts on stabilization policy at the White House, visit the CEA's Web site (*http://www.whitehouse.gov/cea/about.html*).

Answers to Questions

Key Terms Quiz

a.	3	**f.**	10
b.	1	**g.**	9
c.	7	**h.**	2
d.	6	**i.**	8
e.	4	**j.**	5

True-False Questions

1. True
2. True
3. False. Fine-tuning involved developing policies to deal with either unemployment or inflation, not both at the same time.
4. False. Rates of unemployment and inflation are inversely related according to the Phillips curve.
5. False. Policies to increase aggregate demand will be ineffective at decreasing unemployment in the long run if the long-run Phillips curve is vertical.
6. False. The targets specified in the Humphrey-Hawkins Act were 3 percent inflation and 4 percent unemployment.
7. True
8. True
9. True
10. False. Classical economists associate inflation with excessive growth in the money supply. Keynesians, who believe the economy is operating on the horizontal segment of the aggregate supply curve do not see inflation as a problem.
11. False. Rational expectations theorists believe that even temporary victories over unemployment are impossible.
12. True
13. True
14. False. Supply-side economics favors tax cuts in order to shift the aggregate supply curve to the right.
15. True

Multiple-Choice Questions

1. c	**6.** a	**11.** c	**16.** c	**21.** e
2. b	**7.** d	**12.** d	**17.** a	**22.** d
3. a	**8.** e	**13.** b	**18.** b	**23.** c
4. d	**9.** b	**14.** e	**19.** a	**24.** e
5. c	**10.** b	**15.** e	**20.** a	

Fill in the Blanks

1. classical; Keynesian; neo-Keynesian; rational expectations; supply-side
2. competitive; inflexible
3. inflation; unemployment
4. unemployment; wage increases; a decrease in GDP

Discussion Questions

1. The Keynesian and classical views can be compared using the following graphs. The left panel, depicting the classical view, shows a labor market in which wages are flexible. As the demand for labor falls from D to D', the wage rate falls from $10 to $8. Note that at the $8 wage rate, everyone willing to work has a job. That describes full employment. In the right panel, showing the Keynesian view, a fall in demand for automobiles from D to D' causes output and employment to decrease. Employment in the automobile industry will remain at lower levels as long as demand is lower. In the classical case, wages (and prices in goods markets are flexible), and in the Keynesian case, wages and prices are downward inflexible.

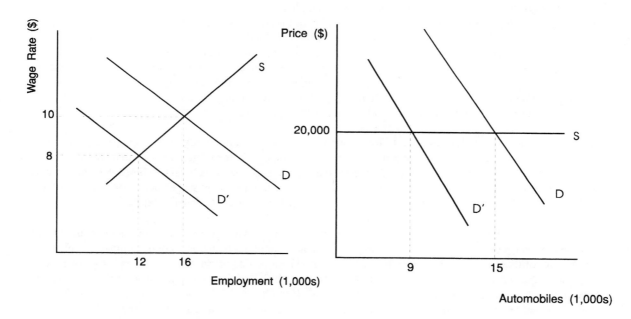

2. The Phillips curve shows the inverse relationship between rates of unemployment on the horizontal axis and rates of inflation on the vertical axis. As the economy approaches full employment, upward pressure on wages and prices causes inflation to rise, and vice-versa. A hypothetical Phillips curve is shown on the following page.

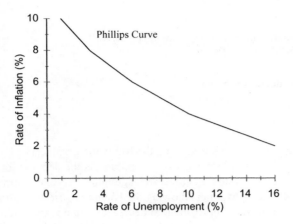

3. Suppose the government wants to lower the rate of unemployment. Government spending is increased, which raises GDP and employment. Unions now feel comfortable pressing for higher wages, which creates cost-push inflation. Workers and unions now discover their real wages eroding and react by demanding wage increases to make up for the loss. If successful, these wage increases cut into firms' profit, discouraging production so that GDP falls and unemployment increases. In other words, while government can lower unemployment rates in the short run, it is much less successful in keeping them low in the long run. If government keeps trying to lower unemployment rates, it can only succeed in raising the rate of inflation. On a graph, these attempts map out a vertical Phillips curve.

4. Fiscal and monetary policies designed to lower unemployment rates don't work at all because workers anticipate the increase in inflation the policies will cause and bargain for wage increases in advance, preventing the policy from having any effect other than to increase the price level. Policies designed to cut aggregate demand to fight inflation work well. Workers immediately accept wage cuts in anticipation of a lower price level, so the unemployment rate does not increase as aggregate demand falls.

5. Tax cuts are at the heart of supply-side policies. Supply-siders also advocate less government spending and less government regulation. In short, any policy that makes suppliers happy is a good supply-side policy. One impact of these policies is to increase their profits. The intended effect of the policies is to move the aggregate supply curve to the right more rapidly over time. If the aggregate supply curve shifts to the right, lower unemployment and lower inflation can be achieved simultaneously. One problem in the supply-side analysis is that tax cuts will also have the effect of shifting the aggregate demand curve to the right, negating to some extent the inflation reduction accomplished by the supply-side policy. Another problem with supply-side tax cuts is that they may increase the budget deficit if they aren't accompanied by sufficiently large cuts in government spending, as happened during the Reagan administrations during the 1980s.

6. Crowding out is the idea that government finance of deficit spending by borrowing pushes up interest rates. The government borrowing causes private investment to be crowded out of the economy in a manner that will slow down the accumulation of capital and create a lower rate of economic growth over time.

Homework Questions

True-False Questions — If a statement is false, explain why.

1. A Keynesian believes that the economy can be in equilibrium at a level of GDP below that necessary to achieve full employment. (T/F)

2. The experience of the 1990s suggests that the natural rate of unemployment has risen from the 6 percent rate agreed upon by many economists in the 1980s. (T/F)

3. Rational expectations theorists believe that workers will bargain immediately for a wage cut in anticipation of higher inflation given a Fed announcement of a decrease in the discount rate. (T/F)

4. The supply-side tax cuts implemented early in the first Reagan Administration led to dramatic increases in the deficit. (T/F)

5. Unemployment insurance and the progressive income tax tend to destabilize the economy. (T/F)

Multiple-Choice Questions

1. Which of the following is not consistent with supply-side policies?
   a. a cut in income taxes
   b. cuts in subsidies for research and development
   c. cuts in corporate profits taxes
   d. tax credits for firms that pursue research and development
   e. an increase in the capital gains tax

2. In an attempt to prevent wage and price increases from undermining the cuts in unemployment resulting from government fiscal and monetary policy, neo-Keynesians advocated
   a. moral suasion
   b. wage-price controls
   c. raising interest rates
   d. cutting corporate profits taxes
   e. outlawing unions

3. According to rational expectations theorists, the main effect of fiscal and monetary policy designed to increase aggregate demand is to
   a. lower the level of unemployment at the cost of somewhat higher inflation
   b. create a shift to the right in the aggregate supply curve
   c. cause workers to bargain for a wage increase in advance of an increase in the price level, causing inflation
   d. raise the rates of both autonomous and induced investment
   e. create a larger pool of savings from which investors can borrow

4. The most appropriate stabilization policy, according to the classical school, is to
   a. do nothing
   b. rely on monetary policy, not fiscal policy, in order to keep government interference minimal
   c. rely on aggressive fiscal policy immediately when problems arise to keep the problem from expanding
   d. make sure the Phillips curve does not shift in either direction
   e. apply wage and price controls to stabilize employment and inflation

5. Classical economists believe that the aggregate supply curve is
   a. vertical
   b. horizontal
   c. upward-sloping
   d. downward-sloping
   e. a right-angle curve

Discussion Questions/Problems

1. What are the main differences in belief between Keynesians and neo-Keynesians?

2. How do automatic stabilizers work to keep the economy close to full employment with low inflation?

CHAPTER 14

GOVERNMENT SPENDING

Chapter in a Nutshell

The level and composition of government spending will always be topics for debate. Decisions about government spending are value judgments, as well as economic decisions. Government spending is more than an instrument of fiscal policy. Even if the economy was always at full employment without inflation, there would still be a role for government. After all, we do need city streets, interstate highways, schools, environmental protection, and national defense. These goods are not typically provided by markets, at least not in sufficient quantities. Economists call them **public goods** because they are basically nonexclusive and nonrival. Nonexclusive means that no one can be excluded from consuming the good, and nonrival means that any person's consumption of that good does not diminish the good for others. By contrast, milk is not a public good because the owner can exclude others from consuming it, and when one consumes it, it is not available for someone else to drink.

Aside from its stabilization and public-goods-provider roles, the government also legislates and administers **transfer payments**. Transfer payments are payments by government to particular groups in society. These are usually in the form of government services, price subsidies, or cash payments. In 2001, approximately 55.8 percent of federal spending was on transfer payments and interest, and only 27.3 percent was for provision of public goods. By contrast, 76.9 percent of state and local government spending was for the purchase of goods and services.

The chapter describes federal, state, and local spending item by item. Security is an important spending item. Most federal spending on security is for national defense. State and local spending is split among police, corrections, and fire protection. Federal spending on security has been falling as a percentage of total federal spending over the last quarter century.

There has always been strong support for public schools. Public education is one of Thomas Jefferson's cherished legacies. Over the period 1980 - 2001, the annual rate of increase in real government spending on education at all levels was approximately 3 percent, slightly above the annual rate of increase in real GDP.

Transportation, natural resources, energy, and space are all areas receiving government support. These areas exhibit the characteristics of public goods, though to varying degrees. In each area, competing groups press for different levels of spending. Though the debate over the appropriate level of spending in these areas is fierce, each has its own history and reasons for existence.

Spending programs for agriculture and public assistance are more people-specific than spending on defense, education, or transportation. Agriculture receives public money because it is felt that farm incomes might suffer significantly otherwise, jeopardizing the health of regional economies. Public assistance shows up as spending on **Medicaid**, **Temporary Assistance for Needy Families**, **Supplemental Security Income**, and **food stamps**. Public assistance spending by the federal government totaled $107.3 billion in 2001, while state and local governments added another $97.2 billion.

Since the 1930s, government has taken on the job of providing social insurance. The best known of these insurance programs is **Social Security**. Social Security is a compulsory program that transfers income across income and age groups. Low-wage earners tend to receive more benefits relative to their contributions than do high-wage earners. Younger workers paying Social Security taxes subsidize people in retirement who receive benefits. **Unemployment insurance** is another type of government social insurance program. **Medicare** provides health insurance for the elderly. Even though Social Security transfer payments in the United States accounted for 16.5 percent of GDP in 1996, they are still somewhat below average for the group of industrialized countries.

Interest payments on the government debt grew significantly during the 1980s. In 2001, the public debt reached $5.8 trillion, and $238.1 billion was spent on interest payments.

Government spending was about 28.3 percent of GDP in 1970 and was 31.6 percent of GDP in 2001. Among the major industrialized countries, the United States allocates a smaller share of GDP to government than any other country except Japan. As a share of GDP, federal, state, and local purchases of goods and services (excluding transfer payments) amounted to about 14.9 percent in 2001. To the extent that government spending moves resources away from the provision of private goods to the provision of public goods, resource allocation is affected.

After studying this chapter, you should be able to:

- Present a **public goods** argument to justify government spending.
- Give examples of **transfer payments**.
- Describe the relative size of different components of government spending.
- List the areas of **public assistance** provided by the government.
- Discuss how **Social Security** operates in the United States.
- Contrast the level of Social Security payments in the United States with levels in other countries.
- Rank levels of government spending as percentages of GDP for major industrialized countries.
- Explain the impact of government spending on the allocation of resources.

Concept Check — See how you do on these multiple-choice questions.

Does your consumption of national defense exclude someone else from enjoying the benefits? Are the benefits still there for someone else to enjoy after you consume national defense?

1. A **public good** is a good for which consumption is
    a. limited by scarcity
    b. expensive
    c. exclusive
    d. rival
    e. nonexclusive and nonrival

"More public money is needed to support higher education," said Professor Gottheil.

2. **Merit goods** are goods that the market
    a. produces in large amounts because of their high value
    b. does not produce enough of in some people's opinion
    c. produces even though they are public goods
    d. will not produce in sufficient quantities
    e. cannot create like art and music

What changes were made in the welfare program during the second Clinton Administration in the late 1990s?

3. Cash-payment **welfare** in the United States
   a. is an entitlement program for all who qualify
   b. is administered under the Aid to Families with Dependent Children program
   c. requires that those who are able participate in work activities within two years of receiving it
   d. is the food stamp program
   e. supports Medicaid

Who contributes to Social Security?

4. **Social Security** is first and foremost a pension system where
   a. contributions are optional for all workers
   b. each worker contributes to his/her own retirement fund
   c. contributions are mandatory for wage earners
   d. the benefits are a larger percentage of contributions for the rich than for the poor
   e. the benefits are the primary source of income for most retirees

How do Americans typically feel about "big" government?

5. In the United States, **government spending as a percentage of GDP**
   a. is rising dramatically
   b. is less than in most other industrialized countries
   c. is quite volatile
   d. has declined since 1980
   e. rose from 1970 to 1980 but has declined since

Am I on the Right Track?

Your answers to the questions above should be **e, b, c, c,** and **b**. If you can organize your thinking about government spending so that you distinguish between spending on public goods, spending on merit goods, and transfer payments, you'll be on the right track. Then it is a matter of learning the categories into which the different programs fit.

Key Terms Quiz — Match the terms on the left with the definitions in the column on the right.

1. Medicaid

2. Social Security

3. unemployment insurance

4. Medicare

5. food stamp program

6. welfare

7. merit good

_____ a. a good whose benefits are not diminished when additional people consume it and whose benefits cannot be withheld from anyone

_____ b. government-provided assistance — cash payments and goods and services — to the poor, the elderly, and the disabled

_____ c. an aid program that provides low-income people with stamps that can be redeemed for food and related items

_____ d. a health care program administered through Social Security that is applicable to low-income and disabled people

_____ e. a social insurance program that provides benefits subject to eligibility to the elderly, the disabled, and their dependents

_____ f. a program of income support for eligible workers who are temporarily unemployed

_____ g. a health care program administered through Social Security that is applicable to everyone over 65 years old

8. public good   _____ h. a good that market demand and supply do not produce enough of, in some people's opinion

True-False Questions — If a statement is false, explain why.

1. Government spending on goods and services is strictly an economic decision. (T/F)

2. Your consumption of a public good does not exclude others from consuming it as well. (T/F)

3. The nonrival characteristic of a public good means your consuming it does not lessen the enjoyment others can get from it. (T/F)

4. If there was no government, no public goods would be available because the market would not produce them. (T/F)

5. Social Security doesn't really help those in retirement because they had to pay for what they receive earlier in their careers. (T/F)

6. Interest payments on the government debt declined after 1980. (T/F)

7. The largest share of federal government spending is on transfer payments. (T/F)

8. Determining the optimal amount to spend on national defense is extremely complex. (T/F)

9. The space program represents the most recent addition to the federal government's transfer payments program. (T/F)

10. The federal government's farm program represents transfer payments (from nonfarmers) to farmers. (T/F)

11. Food stamps can be legally converted to cash at most grocery stores. (T/F)

12. Medicare is available to those over 65 years old while Medicaid is a health care program for the poor. (T/F)

13. Social Security benefits go only to those who are over 65 years old. (T/F)

14. A legitimate argument for cutting government spending is that the private market will provide sufficient amounts of the sorts of goods and services that government provides and do it more efficiently. (T/F)

15. As a percentage of GDP, government spending in the United States is less than government spending in West European economies. (T/F)

Multiple-Choice Questions

1. Government spending includes all of the following categories **except**
    a. public goods
    b. transfer payments
    c. merit goods
    d. interest payments on the national debt
    e. Social Security contributions

2. To say that a good is nonexclusive means that
    a. everyone will consume it
    b. no one can be denied its use
    c. it is easily privatized
    d. it is of low quality
    e. only the poor purchase it

3. A nonrival good is one such that
    a. my consumption of the good doesn't deplete it for others to consume
    b. it is the best of its kind on the market
    c. the good has no close substitutes
    d. its price is very low
    e. private firms will be likely to offer it in abundant quantities

4. One of the problems associated with a public good is that
    a. people who work in the private sector have low demands for it
    b. the market will provide too much of it
    c. chronic excess demand for it exists
    d. people feel that because others want it, they personally won't have to pay for it
    e. the market will provide too little of it

5. A case can be made that the U. S. international aid program serves all of the following roles **except**
    a. national security
    b. Social Security
    c. an expression of our humanitarian concern
    d. jobs creation
    e. transfer payment

6. The largest percentage of federal government spending is on
    a. purchases of goods and services
    b. grants-in-aid to state and local governments
    c. transfer payments
    d. foreign aid
    e. defense

7. As a percentage of total federal spending, from 1970 to 2001, spending on national defense in the United States
   a. rose significantly
   b. fluctuated wildly between presidential administrations
   c. stayed the same
   d. fell significantly
   e. failed to keep up with inflation

8. Most of the spending for education comes from
   a. the federal government
   b. transfer payments in the form of student loans and grants
   c. state and local governments
   d. private donations
   e. tuition payments by students and their parents

9. The largest share of spending on transportation is handled at the
   a. municipal level
   b. state and local level
   c. federal level
   d. regional level
   e. international level

10. Government spending on agriculture is an example of
    a. government purchases of goods and services
    b. a merit good
    c. a public good
    d. a transfer payment
    e. public assistance

11. One difference between Medicaid and Temporary Assistance for Needy Families (TANF) is that
    a. Medicaid serves the elderly and TANF serves the poor
    b. Medicaid provides in-kind benefits while TANF provides cash grants
    c. TANF guarantees that the poor will get jobs while Medicaid provides limited medical education
    d. TANF is an entitlement and Medicaid is not
    e. Medicaid is an entitlement and TANF is not

12. Government insurance protects individuals from all of the following **except** income losses due to
    a. retirement
    b. unemployment
    c. disability
    d. unexpected deaths of breadwinners
    e. fires

13. When Social Security transfers in the United States are compared to those in other developed countries as a percentage of GDP, the United States is spending
    a. somewhat less
    b. about the same
    c. an adequate amount
    d. an inadequate amount
    e. far more

14. When government spending in the United States is compared to spending in other industrialized countries as a percentage of GDP, it is clear that spending levels in the United States
    a. are well above those in other countries
    b. are near the bottom of the range that is observed
    c. have risen much faster than in other countries
    d. need to be cut
    e. need to be increased

15. Throughout the 1970-2001 period, government spending in the United States was
    a. within a few percentage points of half of GDP
    b. a much higher share of GDP than government spending in Canada
    c. slowly falling
    d. approximately 30 percent of GDP
    e. rising much faster than GDP

16. Government spending on public goods shifts resource allocation
    a. toward private goods
    b. away from private goods
    c. to less productive uses
    d. to more productive uses
    e. to transfer payments

17. All of the following are examples of merit goods **except**
    a. National Public Radio
    b. the Public Broadcasting System
    c. state universities
    d. private universities
    e. the National Endowment for the Arts

18. Both the size of the government debt and the annual interest payments on it grew considerably in the
    a. 1950s
    b. 1960s
    c. 1970s
    d. 1980s
    e. 1990s

19. One reason that Aid to Families with Dependent Children was eliminated is
    a. the feeling that the program had served its function
    b. that it was bankrupting the nation
    c. the feeling that it undermined the recipients' motivation to work
    d. the rising cost of Social Security
    e. that food stamps served the same function

20. One reason for concern about the future of the Social Security and Medicare systems is
    a. that people no longer contribute to them
    b. the falling ratio of retirees to working people
    c. that people retire later in life now
    d. the rising ratio of retirees to working people
    e. that the trust fund is virtually depleted

The following questions relate to the global and applied perspectives in the text.

21. When government spending on the arts is compared among OECD countries, the United States ranks
    a. highest in total spending but lowest in per capita spending
    b. highest in per capita spending but lowest in total spending
    c. lowest in per capita spending and spending as a percentage of GDP
    d. highest in per capita spending and spending as a percentage of GDP
    e. lowest in total spending and spending as a percentage of GDP

22. Prescription drugs are a likely candidate for merit good status because the
    a. cost of prescription drug coverage is rising dramatically as baby-boomers approach retirement
    b. government is moving toward a nationalized system of health care
    c. George W. Bush's administration has favored greater government intervention in the health industry
    d. prescription drugs are plentiful and cheap
    e. Medicare provides no prescription drug coverage

23. Which of the following is **not** an option for maintaining enough funds to support Social Security as the baby-boomers retire?
    a. raise the social security tax
    b. reduce future Social Security benefits
    c. increase the number of years of earnings used to determine benefits
    d. lower the retirement age to 59
    e. allow the Social Security system to invest its funds in the private sector

Fill in the Blanks

1. Public goods are _____ and _____.

2. Transfer payments represent a _____ of income from taxpayers to

   _____.

3. Approximately 60 percent of all government spending is done by the _____ and the

   remaining 40 percent is done by _____.

4. Government decides what goods and services will be produced for approximately _____ percent of

   GDP.

Discussion Questions

1. What distinguishes government spending on public goods from transfer payments?

2. Explain why the government spends on agriculture. Is this spending a public good, a transfer payment, or part of the government's countercyclical fiscal policy?

3. How is Social Security financed in the United States? How is this system different from a private pension fund?

4. Discuss the recent changes in the welfare program in the United States.

Everyday Applications

How would your life change if government spending went to zero?

Economics Online

The Social Security Administration has a Web site (*http://www.ssa.gov/*). The page provides considerable information about the issue of social security's solvency in the coming decades as the baby boomers retire. This is an important matter for you — you'll be paying the taxes to support Social Security benefits for my generation.

Answers to Questions

Key Terms Quiz

a. 8   f. 3
b. 6   g. 4
c. 5   h. 7
d. 1
e. 2

True-False Questions

1. False. There is a political element to the choice of which public goods to purchase and how transfer payments should be allocated among various recipients and at what level.
2. True
3. True
4. False. The market would not supply enough of public goods.
5. False. People in retirement receive Social Security benefits that are paid for by those who are currently employed. Retirees' contributions to Social Security supported an earlier generation of retirees.
6. False. Interest payments on the national debt grew significantly during the 1980s.
7. True
8. True
9. False. The space program has characteristics of a public good and a merit good. It is not a transfer program.
10. True
11. False. Food stamps can only be legally exchanged for food.
12. True
13. False. Eligibility for benefits extends to the disabled and dependents of beneficiaries.
14. False. The market would not provide adequate quantities of public goods, and transfer payments would rarely occur without government.
15. True

Multiple-Choice Questions

1. e	6. c	11. b	16. b	21. c
2. b	7. d	12. e	17. d	22. a
3. a	8. c	13. a	18. d	23. d
4. e	9. b	14. b	19. c	
5. b	10. d	15. d	20. d	

Fill in the Blanks

1. nonexclusive; nonrival
2. redistribution; particular groups
3. federal government; state and local governments
4. 15

Discussion Questions

1. Purchases of public goods by government correspond to the use of public money to buy specific amounts of goods and services that the market would not provide in sufficient quantities. These goods are nonexclusive and nonrival to some degree. Merit goods are also purchased by government. These are goods that the market would not provide enough of, according to some people. Determining the quantity of public goods to be purchased is a matter of controversy and debate in many cases. The decision to purchase public goods shifts the allocation of resources from one that is determined by consumer sovereignty in the private market toward an allocation that is partially determined by government. In the case of transfer payments, consumer sovereignty determines the allocation of resources because income is shifted from taxpayers to particular groups in society. Private individuals then decide what to purchase with the income that is redistributed.

2. Government spending on the farm community is essentially a transfer payment. Government farm programs end up taxing nonfarming populations and giving the income to the farming population. The agricultural sector has substantial political clout, which helps to maintain the transfer payment. The primary justification for government aid to farmers is that instability in the agricultural economy could contribute to instability in the national economy.

3. Social Security is financed by taxes paid jointly by employers and employees. Current employees pay for the benefits received by the current generation of retirees. Social Security differs from a private pension fund in three ways. First, Social Security is mandatory. Second, Social Security transfers income across income and age groups. A pension fund keeps funds that an individual deposits for that individual. Third, Social Security is a pay-as-you-go system financed by a payroll tax, half of which is paid by the employee with the remainder paid by the employer.

4. The major recent change in the welfare system in the United States has been the elimination of Aid to Families with Dependent Children. On August 22, 1996, the Personal Responsibility and Work Opportunity Reconciliation Act was enacted by Congress. This act created the Temporary Assistance for Needy Families program, which was to abolish entitlement in the welfare program. The federal government now provides states with capped block grants to administer their own welfare programs. Welfare recipients must participate in work activities within two years of receiving aid or risk losing it. Eligibility for a family on welfare runs out after five years of benefits. The idea behind the new program is to create incentives for people on welfare to gain skills and enter the labor force. However, many of these individuals have few skills, and the question remains whether enough low-skill jobs will be available to employ those going off the welfare rolls.

Homework Questions

True-False Questions — If a statement is false, explain why.

1. The benefits from a public good cannot be withheld from people. (T/F)

2. To environmentalists, the preservation of natural areas is an issue of national security. (T/F)

3. Under current law, individuals who receive aid through the Temporary Assistance for Needy Families program can receive benefits for up to five years. (T/F)

4. Government spending as a percentage of GDP is lower in the United States than in other industrialized countries, with the exception of Japan. (T/F)

5. Transfer payments are a much larger fraction of total government spending at the state level than are government purchases of goods and services by states. (T/F)

Multiple-Choice Questions

1. Spending on education in the United States
   a. is greater at the federal level than at the state and local level
   b. fell from 1980 to 1996
   c. was constant from 1980 to 1996
   d. rose in nominal terms but fell in real terms from 1980 to 1996
   e. is greater at the state and local level than at the national level

2. When compared to total government spending in other industrialized economies, government spending in the United States measured as a percentage of real GDP is
   a. about average
   b. above average
   c. below average
   d. the lowest
   e. the highest

3. Government spending on agriculture has been justified on the grounds that
   a. without aid, the farm economy and the national economy would be destabilized
   b. farm prices are rising so research and development need to be financed
   c. food prices can be kept low this way
   d. no one would farm otherwise
   e. farming is harder work than other occupations

4. During the 1980s, interest payments on the national debt
   a. rose
   b. fell
   c. were constant
   d. were offset by increased tax revenue due to supply-side policies
   e. were halted for a time when the government defaulted

5. Government spending on goods and services, leaving out transfer payments and interest payments on the government debt was _____ percent of GDP in the year 2001.
   a. 8.5
   b. 10.7
   c. 14.9
   d. 21.3
   e. about 30

Discussion Questions/Problems

1. Contrast public goods and merit goods. Are public goods always merit goods? Are merit goods always public goods? Give examples to go along with your explanation.

2. Explain how government spending affects resource allocation between the private and public sector.

CHAPTER 15

FINANCING GOVERNMENT: TAXES AND DEBT

Chapter in a Nutshell

Public goods are not free goods. Resources are needed to produce city streets, just as they are needed to produce automobiles that drive up and down those streets. The opportunity cost of producing public goods — measured by how much we must give up of private goods — is always a matter of public debate. But even if we know how many public goods we want and are willing to make the sacrifice to acquire them, the question still remains: How does the government get the money it needs to provide those public goods?

In pre-modern societies, a government would often simply **commandeer** the resources it needed. If it needed labor to construct roads, it simply rounded up people to make the roads. The roads were built, but not necessarily in the most efficient way. In modern societies, government has shifted from commandeering resources to commandeering money. That's the essence of a tax system.

There are a number of ways to tax. Perhaps the simplest is a **poll (or head) tax**, say, $100, that is levied on every adult in a population. If there are 1,000 people, then the government's tax revenue is $100,000. An alternative way of taxing the population is by levying the tax on the person's income, rather than on the person. This is the income tax. An income tax structure can be **regressive** (the rich are taxed a lower percentage of their income than are the poor), **proportional** (the rich and poor are taxed the same percentage) or **progressive** (the rich are taxed a higher percentage). The government can also levy **taxes on corporate profits**, or on wealth (such as a **property tax** or estate and gift taxes). Perhaps the most widely used tax is levied not on a person's income or wealth, but on the person's consumption (**sales and excise taxes**). Contributions to the Social Security system are another form of taxation, but these are earmarked to finance the benefits the Social Security system is obligated to pay.

What does the U.S. tax structure look like? At the federal level, the income tax is the most important source of revenue. Its structure is progressive, with five tax brackets. The richer you are, the higher the tax rate on your higher income. If you are married and you and your spouse together earned $300,000, you paid 10 percent on your first $7,000; 15 percent on the income over $7,000 up to $28,400; 25 percent on income over $28,400 up to $68,800; 28 percent on income over $68,800 up to $143,500; 33 percent on the income over $143,500 up to $311,950, and 35 percent on income over $311,950.. Most states have their own state income taxes, but these are not as important a contributor to state revenue as their sales taxes. The property tax is the primary source of revenue for local governments.

For all but a few years since World War II, federal government spending has exceeded the tax revenues collected. How does government make up for the **deficit** (one year's contribution to the **public debt**)? The chapter focuses on the federal government's use of debt financing. The government sells securities through its Department of the Treasury. These securities are its IOUs. People loan money to the government in return for interest payments. The securities are regarded as very safe investments because the government has never defaulted on either interest or principal. The securities come in three forms: **Treasury bills**, which mature in one year or less; **Treasury notes**, which mature in 2 to 10 years; and **Treasury bonds**, which mature in 30 years.

The **public debt** has risen enormously since 1929, particularly since the 1980s, but so has GDP. The debt/GDP ratio was lower in 1996, by about half, than at the end of World War II. Big spurts in the debt/GDP ratio occurred in the decades of the 1930s, the 1940s, and the 1980s. The debt/GDP ratio for the United States is lower than the same ratio in other industrialized countries.

Government debt, like government deficits, is a contentious political issue. How long can a government finance its deficits by selling IOUs before it goes bankrupt? Does such a government place a terrible financial burden on future generations?

Economists distinguish between an **internally financed debt** (its securities are purchased by its own population) and an **externally financed debt** (its securities are purchased by foreigners). An internal debt neither adds to nor subtracts from the nation's income. If 100 percent of the U.S. government debt is held internally (by U.S. citizens), then all the interest that the government pays goes to Americans. Where does the government get the money to pay for the interest? By taxing its citizens. In a sense then, Americans tax themselves to pay themselves. What about future generations? If future generations are forced to pay for the debt, they pay it only to themselves.

An external debt is different. The people who are taxed to pay the interest on the debt are not the same people who receive the interest payments. An external debt can burden future generations.

Internally financed debt can still cause problems. If the debt is held by few people, then everybody is taxed to pay the interest that goes to the few. In this way, the debt contributes to greater income inequality. It can also create over consumption because people view their securities holdings as real wealth and save less than they perhaps should. Finally, excessive debt can contribute to inflation and crowding out of private investment.

Deficits and debt are not inevitable. A **balanced budget** exists if tax revenues match government spending. The extraordinary rise in the deficits and debt in the 1980s resulted from the tax reform acts of 1981 and 1986 that overhauled our tax rates and brackets, and with them, tax revenues. The Gramm-Rudman-Hollings Act of 1985 was intended to introduce discipline to the budgetary process by setting targets for deficit reduction. This act failed to achieve its goals. A constitutional amendment that would mandate a year-by-year balanced budget was seriously considered by Congress but failed. However, during the late 1990s, what many thought was impossible actually happened. The deficit shrank to zero. As a result of rising tax revenues due to increasing national income, coupled with cuts in government spending, the budget was briefly in surplus. However, deficit spending has risen to new heights due to a combination of tax cuts, a downturn in the economy, and increase spending on national security since September 11, 2001.

After studying this chapter, you should be able to:

- Describe the various ways that governments have financed their activities over time.
- Discuss different systems of **income taxation**.
- Explain why an **excise tax** is a tax on consumption.
- Compare the magnitudes of **federal, state, and local tax revenues**.
- Describe how government spending can be financed through the sale of **government securities**.
- Evaluate the danger of a large **public debt** to our economic health.
- Recount the debate over the **federal budget deficit** during the 1980s and 1990s.

Concept Check — See how you do on these multiple-choice questions.

How do we distinguish among regressive, proportional, and progressive taxes?

1. A **regressive income tax** is one where the poor
   a. have a lower percentage of their income taxed than the rich
   b. pay a larger dollar amount in taxes than the rich
   c. pay a tax that varies directly with their income
   d. have a higher percentage of their income taxed than the rich
   e. are able to use tax revenue to purchase basic goods

How does the government issue debt?

2. The **public debt** is the total amount of
   a. debt held by the public
   b. government securities held by individuals, businesses, government agencies, and the Federal Reserve
   c. demand deposits held by banks
   d. outstanding commercial loans
   e. outstanding mortgages

What is the difference between internal and external debt?

3. The level of **external debt** rises when the U.S. Treasury
   a. prints more money
   b. sells securities to Americans
   c. increases the deficit
   d. decreases the deficit
   e. sells securities to foreigners

The original meaning of the word "poll" is head.

4. A **poll tax** is a tax levied
   a. on voters
   b. on those who respond to pollsters' questions
   c. per person
   d. on the value of property
   e. per village

Which levels of government levy property taxes?

5. **Property taxes** are
   a. an important source of state and local governments' revenue
   b. an important source of federal revenue
   c. proportional to income
   d. progressive
   e. consumption taxes

Am I on the Right Track?

Your answers to the questions above should be **d**, **b**, **e**, **c**, and **a**. This chapter is split into two distinct sections. The first deals with using various taxes to finance government. The array of available tax options is a tribute to the creativity of governments in need of funding. The second part of the chapter presents issues associated with

GOVERNMENT AND THE MACROECONOMY

the government's decision to borrow in order to fund spending. The decision to borrow has different implications for an economy depending on the circumstances.

Key Terms Quiz — Match the terms on the left with the definitions in the column on the right.

1. poll tax

_____ a. a tax whose impact varies inversely with the income of the person taxed so that poor people have a higher percentage of their income taxed than do rich people

2. unit tax

_____ b. a tax levied on the value of physical assets such as land or financial assets such as stocks and bonds

3. regressive income tax

_____ c. a tax of a specific absolute sum levied on every person or every household

4. sales tax

_____ d. a tax levied on a corporation's income before dividends are distributed to stockholders

5. proportional income tax

_____ e. a sales tax applied to a foreign good or service

6. customs duty

_____ f. a nonmarketable Treasury bond that is the most commonly held form of public debt

7. progressive income tax

_____ g. public debt held by foreigners

8. excise tax

_____ h. a fixed tax in the form of cents or dollars per unit levied on a good or service

9. corporate income tax

_____ i. a tax that is a fixed percentage of income, regardless of the level of income

10. public debt

_____ j. any tax levied on a good or service, such as a unit tax, a sales tax, or a customs duty

11. property tax

_____ k. a tax levied in the form of a specific percentage of the value of the good or service

12. savings bond

_____ l. the total value of government securities held by individuals, businesses, other government agencies, and the Federal Reserve

13. external debt

_____ m. a tax whose rate varies directly with the income of the person taxed so that rich people have a higher percentage of their income taxed than do poor people

True-False Questions — If a question is false, explain why.

1. Because people don't pay directly for public goods, these goods are described by economists as free goods. (T/F)

2. A poll tax is fair because every adult in a population must pay it. (T/F)

3. The difference between a deficit and the debt is that a deficit represents the accumulation of debts over many years, while a debt represents the amount by which government spending exceeds tax revenue in a single year. (T/F)

4. If the government raises interest rates on the bonds that it offers for sale, government debt may crowd out private investment. (T/F)

5. External debt is private debt and internal debt is public debt. (T/F)

6. The Gramm-Rudman-Hollings Act of 1985 called for across-the-board cuts in government spending if deficit reduction targets were not met. (T/F)

7. The largest holders of the U.S. public debt are foreigners, mainly Japanese and Saudi Arabians. (T/F)

8. The U.S. public debt in the mid-1990s was over 100 percent of GDP. (T/F)

9. When your salary bonus moves you up a bracket in a progressive income tax structure, all your income is now taxed at the new higher rate, which is why most people complain about tax increases. (T/F)

10. Compared to other industrialized countries, the tax/GDP ratio in the United States is relatively high. (T/F)

11. A principal difference between the income tax you pay and the contributions you make to Social Security is that your Social Security contributions are earmarked. (T/F)

12. The public debt consists of only one year's government securities, which must be paid back at the end of the fiscal year. (T/F)

13. If our public debt is held internally, Americans make payments on the debt to themselves. (T/F)

14. By borrowing in order to finance its spending, the government can alter the mix of goods purchased by its population to include more public goods and fewer private goods. (T/F)

15. Federal Reserve purchases of government securities issued to finance a deficit can create inflation because they cause the money supply to grow. (T/F)

Multiple-Choice Questions

1. All of the following are examples of regressive taxes **except**
   a. the poll tax
   b. excise taxes
   c. sales taxes
   d. customs duties
   e. the proportional income tax

2. The revenue from Social Security taxes is
   a. invested in a pension fund for each individual to draw on at retirement
   b. earmarked for a trust fund out of which Social Security benefits are paid
   c. never sufficient to pay all the benefits for retirees and other beneficiaries
   d. handled in the same way that other tax revenues are handled
   e. about equal to the revenue generated by gift and estate taxes

3. Crowding out is the idea that as the government finances deficit spending by borrowing, it must
   a. lower interest rates, thus diverting funds away from private investment
   b. raise interest rates, thus diverting funds away from private investment
   c. keep private borrowers completely out of the market for investment funds
   d. accept the lower growth rate in the economy that inevitably results
   e. ask for higher and higher prices on the bonds it sells

4. The national debt is a burden to future generations to the extent that a portion of the debt is held by
   a. foreigners
   b. government institutions like the Social Security trust fund
   c. insurance companies
   d. national banks
   e. pension funds

5. The primary source of revenue for general spending by the federal government is
   a. property taxes
   b. income taxes
   c. tariff revenues
   d. inheritance taxes
   e. corporate income taxes

6. The intent of President Bush's 2001 Jobs and Growth Tax Relief Reconciliation Act was to
   a. reverse defense spending cuts begun under the Clinton Administration
   b. continue the policy of welfare reform introduced under the Clinton Administration
   c. use tax cuts as a form of fiscal stimulus to reverse an economic downturn
   d. increase tax revenues in order to keep the government budget in surplus
   e. provide revenues to prepare for the increased health costs associated with aging of the baby boomers

7. Until the 1980s, most of the federal debt accumulated as a result of
   a. natural disasters
   b. government spending that was grossly out of line with spending in other countries
   c. wars and recessions
   d. tax cuts
   e. the absence of a balanced budget amendment to the Constitution

8. The argument that the U.S. public debt is not a burden to future generations of Americans is correct insofar as the debt is held by
   a. the very rich
   b. Americans, with ownership of the debt spread evenly over the population
   c. foreigners who are paid in dollars
   d. international financial institutions like the World Bank
   e. the Social Security trust fund

9. One reason that the federal budget is so difficult to balance is that
   a. the Treasury is always issuing new securities
   b. people enjoy the benefits associated with government spending programs, so that cuts are unpopular
   c. there is very little wasteful spending that could be cut
   d. even minor spending cuts and tax increases would be disastrous for the economy
   e. the budget is far too complicated to expect balance to be achieved

10. The largest owners of the U.S. public debt are
    a. individual U.S. citizens
    b. commercial banks
    c. state and local governments
    d. foreigners
    e. federal agencies and trust funds

11. Tax revenues in the United States calculated as a percentage of GDP are
    a. about the same as other industrialized countries
    b. lower than most other industrialized countries
    c. higher than other industrialized countries
    d. less than 20 percent
    e. greater than 50 percent

12. A progressive income tax is one in which
    a. everyone pays the same rate
    b. everyone must pay a fixed amount
    c. the poor pay a larger percentage of their income than do the rich
    d. the rich pay a larger percentage of their income than do the poor
    e. consumption is discouraged

13. The primary source of tax revenue for state and local governments is
    a. state income taxes
    b. estate and gift taxes
    c. sales and excise taxes and customs duties
    d. property taxes
    e. lottery revenues

14. The national debt can be a problem for all of the following reasons **except**
    a. the interest payments on the debt are mostly paid to Americans
    b. the debt may promote overconsumption
    c. the debt can create inflation
    d. the debt can crowd out private investment
    e. some of the debt is held externally

15. Deficit financing is most likely to be inflationary when the debt is purchased by
    a. the public
    b. foreigners
    c. state governments
    d. the Fed
    e. private banks

16. When the government's countercyclical fiscal policy to combat a recession creates a deficit that is financed by sales of government securities to the Federal Reserve, it can cause all of the following to happen **except**
    a. an increase in the money supply
    b. lower interest rates
    c. higher rates of unemployment
    d. higher inflation
    e. higher consumption spending

17. Arranged from shortest to the longest time to maturity, the government securities are
    a. Treasury bills, Treasury notes, Treasury bonds
    b. Treasury notes, Treasury bills, Treasury bonds
    c. Treasury bonds, Treasury notes, Treasury bills
    d. Treasury bonds, Treasury bills, Treasury notes
    e. Treasury bills, Treasury bonds, Treasury notes

18. The Gramm-Rudman-Hollings Act of 1985 called for
    a. a balanced budget amendment to the Constitution
    b. a steep tax increase in order to eliminate the large deficit
    c. across the board cuts in government spending to reduce the deficit to zero
    d. discretionary cuts in spending for less important budget items
    e. a government shut-down if spending cuts were not implemented voluntarily by Congress

19. A property tax is described as a flat-rate tax on wealth, so it is an example of a
    a. poll tax
    b. proportional tax
    c. income tax
    d. progressive tax
    e. regressive tax

20. One way that the United States' external debt could be reduced is for
    a. taxes to be decreased
    b. investment to increase
    c. the government to buy up bonds that are held by foreigners
    d. government spending to increase
    e. the government to sell bonds in foreign markets

The following questions relate to the applied, interdisciplinary, and global perspectives in the text.

21. Measured as a percentage of GDP, tax revenues in the United States are _____ compared to most other industrialized countries.
    a. higher
    b. lower
    c. about the same
    d. rising
    e. decreasing

22. A lesson that those contemplating cheating on their taxes might take from Al Capone's experience is
    a. if you cheat on your taxes, don't commit other felonies, especially violent ones
    b. that it is better to underreport your income than to not report your income at all
    c. to never purchase assets like an expensive home in Florida if your reported income could not support it
    d. that to be successful requires paying expensive bribes to IRS officials
    e. income from criminal activity must be hidden behind apparently legitimate business activities

23. Which of the following statements about tax collection around the world is **incorrect**?
    a. The rate at which taxes that are owed to the government are actually collected is very low in the United States.
    b. Russian tax collectors are armed
    c. Tax collection is more expensive in Britain, Japan, and Canada than in the United States
    d. Chinese citizens who pay their taxes voluntarily are considered to be fools.
    e. In Sweden, the government calculates citizens' tax bills for them.

Fill in the Blanks

1. The federal income tax structure is _____ with _____ tax brackets that

   range from _____ percent to _____ percent.

2. The federal debt represents the _____ of federal _____.

3. The 1997 federal budget deficit is zero due to a combination of _____ cuts and rising

   _____.

4. The government creates and sells _____ to finance its _____.

Discussion Questions

1. How does a progressive income tax differ from a proportional tax and a regressive tax? Which type of tax is the fairest? Why?

2. a. Suppose you are a debater and the topic is "The United States was correct in using public debt financing, rather than higher taxes, to finance its World War II effort." You take the affirmative. Make your case.

   b. Suppose you are given the negative. Make the case.

3. Why is the U.S. public debt not a burden when it is held by Americans? How does your answer depend on the distribution of the debt in the United States?

4. What did the Gramm-Rudman-Hollings Act of 1985 call for? Did it work? Why or why not?

5. Why was the commandeering of resources replaced by taxation as a way for governments to acquire the means to provide public goods?

Everyday Applications

A major topic for debate during the last presidential election campaign was what should be done with the growing federal budget surpluses. Several options exist including paying down the national debt, increasing government spending, and cutting taxes. These measures could be undertaken in a variety of combinations. What would you do with the surplus? Why?

Economics Online

The U.S. Treasury is responsible for financing the deficit through the creation and sale of government securities. The Treasury has a Web page (*http://www.ustreas.gov/*). Visit the page to learn more about what happens in the Treasury Department.

Answers to Questions

Key Terms Quiz

a. 3	**f.** 12	**k.** 4
b. 11	**g.** 13	**l.** 10
c. 1	**h.** 2	**m.** 7
d. 9	**i.** 5	
e. 6	**j.** 8	

True-False Questions

1. False. Public goods are not free because an opportunity cost is associated with their provision by government. The resources used to purchase public goods could have been used to purchase private goods.
2. False. A poll tax can be considered unfair because it is regressive.
3. False. The deficit is the amount by which government spending exceeds tax revenue in one year while the debt is accumulated deficits over the years minus surpluses.
4. True
5. False. External debt is owned by foreigners and internal debt is owned by Americans.
6. True
7. False. Federal agencies and trust funds hold most of the debt.
8. False. The U.S. public debt was approximately 69 percent of GDP in 1996.
9. False. Only the amount earned over the bracket is taxed at the higher rate.
10. False. The U.S. tax/GDP ratio is relatively low compared to other countries.
11. True
12. False. Different types of government securities have different lengths to maturity.
13. True
14. True
15. True

Multiple-Choice Questions

1. e	**6.** c	**11.** b	**16.** c	**21.** b
2. b	**7.** c	**12.** d	**17.** a	**22.** c
3. b	**8.** b	**13.** c	**18.** c	**23.** a
4. a	**9.** b	**14.** a	**19.** b	
5. b	**10.** e	**15.** d	**20.** c	

Fill in the Blanks

1. progressive; 5; 15; 39.6
2. accumulation; deficits minus any surpluses
3. spending; tax revenues
4. securities; deficits

Discussion Questions

1. A progressive income tax is one such that the rich are taxed a higher percentage of their income than are the poor. A proportional tax is one where rich and poor are taxed the same percentage of their income. A regressive tax is one where the poor are taxed a higher percentage of their income than are the rich. The progressive tax may be considered the fairest because the enjoyment loss from paying taxes will be

approximately the same among the rich and the poor if the rich are taxed at a higher percentage rate than are the poor. If the rich and the poor were taxed at the same percentage rate, the rich would have to derive the same enjoyment from their last dollars of income taxed away as did the poor for the system to be considered fair. This seems implausible. After all, with their last dollars of income taxed away, the poor probably would have purchased goods considered to be more necessary for subsistence and would have received more enjoyment than would the rich. If taxes are to create an equal burden across income classes, then the progressive structure is the fairest.

2. a. Affirmative: The means used to finance the war is not a real issue. Getting it financed in a quick and responsive way is. If people believe that holding bonds gives them something in the future, fine! We need their money now to buy the military equipment to win the war. All we want to do is shift the economy's position along the production possibilities curve from civilian to military production. The sale of government securities accomplishes this with less opposition than, say, a tax.

   b. Negative: While the sale of securities does the job, it is more dishonest than financing the war through taxation. People ought to know what they are fighting for and what it means in terms of sacrificing civilian goods. A tax tells them that in no uncertain terms. The public debt deceptive because people think the securities they buy add to their total wealth; they fail to realize that they eventually must pay themselves.

3. The debt is not a burden when one group of Americans is paying the interest and principal on the debt to another group of Americans. However, if the debt is held by the rich and the middle class and the poor pay taxes to finance the interest payments, then the debt can make the income distribution more unequal.

4. This act called for across-the-board cuts in federal government spending if certain specific deficit-reduction targets were not met according to a timetable. However, it didn't work largely because cuts in government spending are hard to achieve when many people benefit from the spending and fight the proposed cuts. For example, some in Congress attempted to exclude defense spending from the cuts and other attempted to exclude social welfare items. The Gramm-Rudman-Hollings deficit-reduction targets were revised in 1987 and 1991 and, in the end, simply didn't work.

5. Commandeering resources is very complicated, and you may not get the resources you need by commandeering them. Therefore, commandeering resources is unlikely to be an efficient way to provide public goods. As government became more complicated over human history, it is natural that money, with its high liquidity, would be the preferred form for payment of taxes to the government. By commandeering money, a government can gain more flexibility in the kind of goods and services it can acquire.

Homework Questions

True-False Questions — If a statement is false, explain why.

1. When the government commandeers resources to produce public goods, it is taxing. (T/F)

2. Poll taxes are regressive taxes. (T/F)

3. Since 1970, the federal government budget has been in surplus every year except 1999, 2000, and 2001. (T/F)

4. Treasury bills mature in three months, six months, or 12 months. (T/F)

5. Expressed as a percentage of GDP, the federal debt was half as big in 1945 as it is today. (T/F)

Multiple-Choice Questions

1. The burden of the U.S. public debt consists primarily of that portion of the debt that is owned by
   a. all U.S. citizens
   b. U.S. commercial banks
   c. foreigners
   d. U.S. citizens who default on their share of the payments on the debt
   e. U.S. future generations who inherit the debt

2. The tax reforms of 1981 and 1986
   a. raised tax rates but led to a reduction in tax revenues
   b. lowered tax rates and resulted in a reduction in tax revenues
   c. created additional tax brackets to capture revenue from the very rich
   d. converted the income tax structure from progressive to proportional
   e. eliminated the federal sales tax, but increased federal tax rates on inheritances

3. The main problem with the accumulation of a public debt that results from running deficit budgets each year is that
   a. financing the deficit becomes more difficult each year because the nation's credit is deteriorating
   b. interest rates have to be kept low so that the government can afford to borrow
   c. the deficit is climbing to very high levels as a percentage of GDP
   d. the government must pay a high interest rate to borrow and this tends to crowd out private investment
   e. private investment is nearly always more efficient than public investment, so most government activities should be turned over to the private sector

4. Deficit finance can be inflationary if it is done by
   a. purchases of government securities by foreigners
   b. purchases of government securities by Americans
   c. purchases of government securities by commercial banks
   d. purchases of government securities by the Federal Reserve
   e. tax increases

5. As a percentage of GDP, tax revenues in the United States
   a. are about 50 percent
   b. have ballooned since 1980
   c. tend to decrease after a national emergency has been addressed
   d. are somewhat lower than in other industrialized countries
   e. have stayed constant over our history

Discussion Questions/Problems

1. During the year 2000 presidential election campaign, much discussion centered on what should have been done with the budget surplus. There were a variety of choices. Taxes could have been reduced, government spending could have been increased, or the debt could have been reduced. These options might have been undertaken in combination or singly. What would your recommendation for the budget surplus have been? Justify your answer with careful economic reasoning.

2. Explain why externally held government debt is more burdensome than internally held debt.

PART 4 — GOVERNMENT AND THE MACROECONOMY

COMPREHENSIVE SAMPLE TEST

Give yourself 50 minutes to complete this exam and see how you do. The answers follow. Don't look until you are finished.

True-False Questions — If a statement is false, explain why. Each question is worth two points.

1. Classical school economists believe that the economy adjusts to a full-employment GDP automatically. (T/F)

2. The Keynesian aggregate supply curve is upward sloping as GDP rises toward full employment. (T/F)

3. The long-run Phillips curve was downward sloping during the 1970s. (T/F)

4. Rational expectations theorists believe that a fiscal policy that attempts to close a recessionary gap will have no effect on unemployment and will cause higher inflation. (T/F)

5. The benefits from public goods are not diminished when additional people consume these goods, but the benefits can be withheld from people. (T/F)

6. Social Security contributions and benefits are examples of merit goods. (T/F)

7. Temporary Assistance for Needy Families is an example of an entitlement program. (T/F)

8. The public debt fell as a percentage of GDP from the end of World War II to the 1980s. (T/F)

9. Crowding out results in a shifting of resources from private goods production to public goods production. (T/F)

10. Tax revenues measured as a percentage of GDP are higher in the United States than in most other industrialized countries. (T/F)

Multiple-Choice Questions — Each question is worth two points.

1. One area of agreement between neo-Keynesians and rational expectations theorists is that
   a. temporary victories over unemployment through the use of fiscal and monetary policy are possible
   b. the aggregate supply curve is horizontal up to a full-employment level of GDP
   c. the Phillips curve is downward sloping and stable
   d. fiscal policy is generally more effective than monetary policy
   e. the long-run Phillips curve is vertical

2. The stabilization policy that would be promoted by a classical economist is
   a. wage and price controls to halt inflation
   b. fiscal policy for recessionary gaps and monetary policy for inflationary gaps
   c. growth in the money supply that matches real GDP growth and no intervention in the economy
   d. tax cuts for recessionary gaps and slower growth in the money supply for inflationary gaps
   e. spending increases for recessionary gaps and higher interest rates for inflationary gaps

3. The Keynesian answer to the question "Why inflation?" is
   a. excessive monetary growth
   b. too much government intervention
   c. the influence of unions and minimum wage laws
   d. excessive aggregate demand
   e. high tax rates that stifle inflation

4. According to the Keynesian school of macroeconomic thought, there would never have to be a choice between
   a. fiscal policy and monetary policy
   b. a tax cut and a government spending increase
   c. growth in the money supply and lower interest rates
   d. a cut in government spending and slower growth in the money supply
   e. combating unemployment and combating inflation

5. The main idea expressed by supply-siders using the Laffer curve is that if
   a. tax rates are lowered, GDP will grow, and tax revenue will increase
   b. tax rates are lowered, GDP will grow, but the deficit will increase
   c. government spending is cut, GDP will fall, but the deficit will decrease
   d. business is deregulated, the aggregate supply curve will shift to the right
   e. government spending is reduced, crowding out will diminish

6. Keynesians and supply-siders agree that it is possible to reduce both the rate of inflation and the rate of unemployment, but Keynesians focus on changing _____ while supply-siders focus on changing _____ to accomplish these goals.
   a. fiscal policy; monetary policy
   b. government spending; taxes
   c. aggregate demand; aggregate supply
   d. the money supply; the tax rate
   e. aggregate supply; aggregate demand

7. To be effective, an automatic stabilizer should
   a. increase aggregate demand in the downturn phase and decrease aggregate demand in an inflationary phase
   b. increase aggregate demand at full-employment GDP and increase aggregate supply during a recession
   c. reduce wages during a recession and increase wage during an inflation
   d. increase the money supply during a recession and decrease the money supply during an inflation
   e. be studied carefully before it is allowed to operate

8. If the market demand for a product falls, a classical school economist predicts that _____ and a Keynesian economist predicts that _____.
   a. price and output will fall; price will fall and output will remain unchanged
   b. price will fall and output will remain unchanged; output will fall and price will remain unchanged
   c. output will fall and price will remain unchanged; price will fall and output will remain unchanged
   d. price and output will fall; price and output will remain unchanged
   e. price and output will fall; price will remain unchanged and output will fall

9. The government provides public goods because the private market would
   a. not provide any of them
   b. not provide enough of them
   c. provide too many of them
   d. charge prices that are too low
   e. only sell exclusive and rival public goods

10. A transfer payment does not affect the mix of public and private goods produced because
    a. only the poor receive transfer payments and they cannot afford public goods
    b. transfer payments do not affect consumer sovereignty
    c. the government determines what recipients can purchase with transfer payments
    d. the transfer payments are too small to affect the mix in a significant way
    e. transfer payments are supported with tax revenues and public goods are purchased with government debt

11. Which of the following is the largest item in the federal budget?
    a. government purchases
    b. transfer payments
    c. net interest
    d. defense spending
    e. public assistance

12. The program Temporary Assistance for Needy Families replaced
    a. the Personal Responsibility and Work Opportunity Reconciliation Act
    b. Social Security
    c. Medicaid
    d. Aid to Families with Dependent Children
    e. state-run welfare programs

13. One reason to expect that Social Security taxes may increase in the near future is that
    a. more people will be working to support a larger retired population
    b. the elderly population is less healthy than it used to be
    c. fewer people will be working to support a larger retired population as baby boomers retire
    d. Congress intends for Social Security to replace private pension plans
    e. more people are opting for early retirement so they can collect benefits at an earlier age

14. Between 1970 and 1999, real government spending _____, and as a share of GDP, government spending _____.
    a. more than doubled; more than doubled
    b. increased slightly; more than doubled
    c. more than doubled; remained constant
    d. remained constant; decreased
    e. fell; dropped dramatically

15. In a society where all incomes are equal, a poll tax is
    a. a regressive tax
    b. a proportional tax
    c. a progressive tax
    d. an excise tax
    e. a property tax

16. Measured as a percentage of GDP, tax revenues in the United States
    a. have been rising rapidly since the 1980s
    b. have been falling rapidly since the 1980s
    c. are among the lowest of the industrialized countries
    d. are among the highest of the industrialized countries
    e. are about average for industrialized countries

17. A customs duty is a tax placed on
    a. a customary activity like a wedding or funeral
    b. an imported good or service
    c. an exported good or service
    d. a luxury good like alcoholic beverages
    e. a basic good like milk or medicine

18. Which of the following is the largest source of federal tax revenues?
    a. Social Security contributions
    b. income taxes
    c. sales, excise, and customs taxes
    d. estate and gift taxes
    e. property taxes

19. One problem with the public debt is that not everyone holds the debt, so
    a. the poor may pay more in taxes than they receive in interest on the debt
    b. some are crowded out of receiving interest income
    c. those who do are adversely affected by inflation
    d. underconsumption and recession are likely results
    e. payments to the handful of foreigners who hold the debt are particularly burdensome

20. The successful balancing of the federal budget during the Clinton era is due to
    a. a growing feeling in America that government can solve social problems and a willingness to pay for the solutions
    b. a balanced budget amendment to the Constitution
    c. the Gramm-Rudman-Hollings Act
    d. tax reforms during the 1980s
    e. growth in GDP, rising tax revenues, and government spending cuts

Discussion Questions/Problems — Each question is worth 10 points.

1. Why do neo-Keynesians believe that temporary victories over unemployment are possible, while rational expectations theorists believe it is impossible to lower the unemployment rate even temporarily with fiscal or monetary policy?

2. Describe the events of the 1960s and 1970s that eroded the Keynesian belief in the possibility of fine-tuning the economy.

3. Suppose that a balanced budget amendment to the Constitution is passed. How would this affect the operation of automatic stabilizers during a recession?

4. Distinguish between the impact on future generations of an internally financed government debt and an externally financed government debt.

Answers to Sample Test on Part 4

True-False Questions

1. True
2. False. The neo-Keynesian aggregate supply curve is upward sloping as GDP rises toward full employment.
3. False. The Phillips curve shifted upward during the 1970s, creating a vertical long-run Phillips curve.
4. True
5. False. Consumption of public goods cannot be withheld from people.
6. False. Social Security contributions and benefits are examples of transfer payments.
7. False. Temporary Assistance for Needy Families requires that people engage in a work activity within two years of receiving benefits and benefits are limited to five years. The program effectively ends entitlement.
8. True
9. True
10. False. Tax revenues measured as a percentage of GDP are lower in the United States than in most other countries.

Multiple-Choice Questions

1. e	6. c	11. b	16. c
2. c	7. a	12. d	17. b
3. d	8. e	13. c	18. b
4. e	9. b	14. c	19. a
5. a	10. b	15. b	20. e

Discussion Questions/Problems

1. To a neo-Keynesian, a fiscal or monetary policy designed to lower unemployment will increase aggregate demand, causing employment and real GDP to rise. However, the price level increases as well. Workers observe that their real wages are eroded by the rising price level and bargain for wage increases. In an environment of rising GDP, businesses grant these wage increases. The higher wages increase production costs and lower profits. Therefore, both production and employment are cut. The policy served to decrease unemployment only temporarily.

    To a rational expectations theorist, even this temporary decrease in the unemployment rate is impossible to achieve. Once the fiscal or monetary policy aimed at decreasing the unemployment rate is announced, workers will immediately bargain for a wage increase because they correctly anticipate that the policy will cause higher inflation and erode their real wages. Therefore, output and employment fail to increase even temporarily. The only effect of the policy is to increase inflation.

2. During the early 1960s, Keynesian economists such as Arthur Okun, Paul Samuelson, James Tobin, Robert Solow, and Lawrence Klein believed that it was possible to fine-tune the economy to operate at full employment with zero inflation. It was simply a matter of creating policies to increase aggregate demand when the economy was in recession and reduce aggregate demand during periods of inflation. These economists thought that the problem would be either unemployment or inflation, not both at once. However, the Phillips curve showed that a decrease in unemployment would be associated with an increase in inflation. Neo-Keynesians argued that this relationship between inflation and unemployment could be explained by the market power wielded by unions, monopolies, and particular resource suppliers. For example, at high levels of employment, as were experienced in the United States during the mid-1960s, unions could ask for and receive higher wages. These higher labor costs would be passed on in the form of higher prices and higher inflation. During the early 1970s, it became apparent that high rates of unemployment and high rates of inflation could coexist. At that time, the OPEC-orchestrated oil supply shock led to higher costs of production and an increase in the price level. High inflation combined with unemployment — stagflation — marked the rest of the 1970s into the 1980s.

3. An amendment to the Constitution calling for a strict, year-by-year balancing of the federal budget would interfere with the operation of automatic stabilizers. For example, consider a year when the economy slips into a recession. As real GDP and employment decline, government spending increases automatically in the form of increased unemployment insurance payments and welfare benefits, so aggregate demand is propped up somewhat. At the same time, people slide into lower tax brackets as their incomes decline, so the government's tax revenues are automatically lower. Both of these phenomena boost aggregate demand, but cause the budget deficit to increase. With a balanced budget amendment, government would be required to increase taxes, reduce spending, or some combination of the two in order to balance the budget. The effect of a tax increase and spending cut would be to decrease aggregate demand, making the recession worse.

4. An internally financed government debt is one that is held by Americans. Therefore, interest payments are made to Americans with tax dollars paid by other Americans. For a period of time, government spending rises, corresponding to the initial increase in the debt. A good example is the decision to use debt in order to

finance a war effort, such as World War II. However, once the crisis passes, government spending returns to normal levels, and the interest on the debt is paid to one group of Americans by taxing another. As long as the debt is owned by a wide range of citizens, overconsumption is not promoted, inflation is not created, and the problem of crowding out is avoided, an internally financed debt is not a burden for future generations.

However, if the debt is externally financed — held by foreigners instead of Americans — then the debt will be a burden for future generations because the interest payments will be made by our children to people in other countries, causing a drain on American resources. Consumption levels in this country will decline as a result. One solution to this problem is for the government to buy back the debt that it issues.

CHAPTER 16

INTERNATIONAL TRADE

Chapter in a Nutshell

In the second chapter of the text, you were introduced to the concepts **absolute advantage** and **comparative advantage** that are the principles on which international trade is based. You may recall from Chapter 2 that by specializing in production activities that offer absolute and comparative advantages, a country can realize gains from trade. The benefits from **international specialization** and **free trade** are explored in more detail in this chapter. You will learn that free trade benefits some groups in the economy and hurts others. Competition from **imports** can drive down prices and profits, hurting some domestic producers and their employees. Entire industries in a country may be destroyed due to international competition. However, consumers benefit from the lower prices of the imported products. In addition, exporting firms and their employees can benefit from free trade and the resulting higher prices and profits. A persuasive case for free trade can be made because the gains from specializing and trading outweigh the costs.

Still, international trade is frequently limited by government policy. The principal barriers used to limit free trade are **tariffs** and **quotas**. However, the trend over the last few decades has been toward reducing these barriers. We'll examine some of the institutions and agreements involved in international trade, such as the **General Agreement on Tariffs and Trade**, the **European Economic Community**, and the **North American Free Trade Agreement**.

After you study this chapter, you should be able to:

- Explain the difference between **absolute and comparative advantage**.
- Make the case for **free trade**.
- Calculate the **terms of trade** for different countries.
- List the United States' major trading partners.
- Evaluate arguments against free trade.
- Describe how **tariffs** and **quotas** can be used to limit free trade.
- Distinguish between **customs unions** and **free trade areas**.

Concept Check — See how you do on these multiple-choice questions.

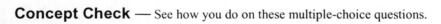

Why do countries trade? Why don't they produce all of the goods they need domestically?

1. The advantages associated with **international specialization** in production result from
   a. cheaper labor in some countries than in others
   b. differences in the competitive strengths of countries
   c. reduced transportation costs
   d. differences in the opportunity costs of production among countries
   e. differences in demand among countries

This question focuses on a concept that was presented in Chapter 2.

2. If Sweden has an **absolute advantage** over Ireland in the production of automobiles, then this results from
   a. its ability to sell automobiles in Ireland for less than the cost of production in Ireland
   b. its ability to produce automobiles using fewer resources than Ireland
   c. the size of the Swedish market relative to the Irish market
   d. competitive free trade in automobiles
   e. its effective use of tariffs over many decades

The terms of trade are the ratio of export prices to import prices. What kinds of goods do less-developed countries export? What kinds of goods do they import?

3. Changes in the **terms of trade** typically put less-developed countries at a disadvantage because
   a. they specialize and trade in agricultural goods rather than manufactured goods
   b. they have higher labor costs
   c. industrialized countries practice unfair trade with less-developed countries
   d. they specialize and trade in services like tourism
   e. tariffs and quotas are used more often in less-developed countries

What is the logic behind the imposition of a quota on imported goods?

4. The main reason for imposing a **quota** on imports of a good is to
   a. lower the price of domestic goods
   b. lower the costs of production of domestic goods
   c. encourage lower costs of production for foreign goods
   d. create a larger market share for domestic goods
   e. avoid the use of a tariff

How does a customs union differ from a free trade area?

5. If a **customs union** were established for all of South America, then these countries would
   a. raise tariffs on imports from non-South American countries
   b. practice complete free trade
   c. practice free trade within South America and have a common trade policy for other countries
   d. have a common trade policy within South America and free trade for other countries
   e. practice free trade within South America and let each South American country pursue an independent trade policy with other countries

Am I on the Right Track?

Your answers to the questions above should be **d**, **b**, **a**, **d**, and **c**. Understanding the economic principles of international trade requires that you apply what you have learned about opportunity costs and demand and supply analysis. If you find yourself confused or stuck on a question or problem, it might be a good idea to review what you learned in Chapters 2 and 3 of the text. The concepts of opportunity cost and demand and supply don't change when we use them to examine international trade, but the context is quite different.

Key Terms Quiz — Match the terms on the left with the definition in the column on the right.

1. free trade

_____ a. goods and services bought by people in one country that are produced in other countries

2. tariff

_____ b. international trade that is not limited by protectionist government policies such as tariffs and quotas

3. international specialization

_____ c. a country's ability to produce a good using fewer resources than are used by the country it trades with

4. quota

_____ d. a country's ability to produce a good at a lower opportunity cost than the country with which it trades

5. absolute advantage

_____ e. exporting a good or service at a price below its cost of production

6. reciprocity

_____ f. a trade agreement to negotiate reductions in tariffs and other trade barriers

7. comparative advantage

_____ g. the use of a country's resources to produce specific goods and services

8. General Agreement on Tariffs and Trade

9. imports

_____ i. a limit on the quantity of a specific good that can be imported

10. customs union

_____ j. goods and services produced by people in one country that are sold in other countries

11. exports

_____ k. a set of countries that agree to free trade among themselves but are free to pursue independent trade policies with other countries

12. European Economic

_____ l. an international organization dealing with the rules of trade between nations

13. terms of trade

_____ m. a free trade area consisting of Canada, the United States, and Mexico

14. free trade area

_____ n. a group of countries that agree to free trade among themselves and a common policy for all other countries

15. dumping

_____ o. a customs union comprised of 16 European countries

16. North American Free Trade Agreement (NAFTA)

_____ p. the amount of a good or service (export) that must be given up to buy a unit of another good or service (import)

17. European Union

_____ q. a tax on an imported good

18. World Trade Organization Community (EEC)

_____ r. an agreement between countries in which trading privileges granted by one to the others are the same as those granted to it by the others

Graphing Tutorial

The impacts of free trade and tariff policies on a domestic market can be represented in a demand and supply graph. The graph on the following page shows the demand and supply for wine in the United States assuming free trade. The intersection of the demand curve and the United States' supply curve gives the equilibrium quantity and price for the domestic market. The price of a case of wine would be $50, and U.S. consumers would purchase 300 million cases if no wine were imported. However, the world price for wine, shown in the graph at $30 per case, is lower than the domestic price, so the United States will import wine. Assuming free trade, domestic producers of wine supply 200 million cases to the U.S. market. At a $30 world price for wine, the United States will import 200 million cases since the total quantity demanded is 400 million cases. The world supply curve for wine is represented on the graph as a horizontal line at the $30 world price.

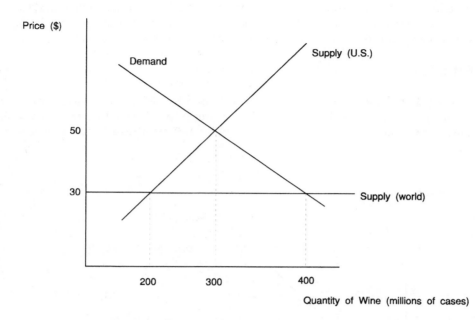

Suppose that U.S. wine producers demand protection from international competition and the government obliges them with a $10 per case tariff. The demand and supply graph shown below illustrates the effects of the tariff policy.

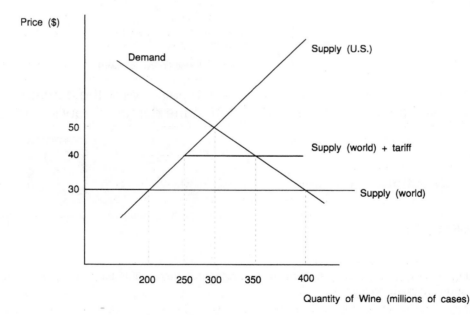

The tariff increases the price of imported wine by $10 per case to $40. The horizontal line at $40 per case starting at 250 million cases shows the effect of the tariff on the world supply curve. U.S. wine producers benefit because they are able to produce 250 million cases of wine at the $40 price. Imports are cut from 200 million cases to 100 million cases. The amount of wine consumed in the United States falls from 400 million cases to 350 million cases. The tariff will generate revenue equal to 100 million cases multiplied by the $10 per case tariff, or $1 billion.

When you draw a graph to show the effect of a tariff, first locate the position of the world supply curve, then shift it up by the dollar amount of the tariff to find the new quantity supplied and quantity demanded. The revenue generated by the tariff is equal to the tariff multiplied by the quantity of imports.

Graphing Pitfalls

A tariff is a tax on an imported good, and a tax on a good raises its price. However, it raises the price of the good from the world price, which is below the domestic equilibrium price, and not from the domestic price itself. So don't make the mistake of trying to show the effect of a tariff by increasing the domestic price by the amount of the tariff as shown in the graph below.

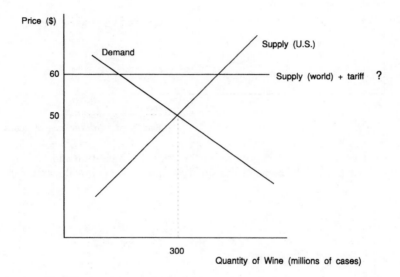

A tariff shifts the world supply up from a point below the domestic equilibrium price and quantity, not from the domestic equilibrium.

True-False Questions — If a statement is false, explain why.

1. If the opportunity costs of producing two goods differ between two countries, then specialization and free trade will benefit both countries. (T/F)

2. If all countries were endowed with the same natural resources, there would be fewer opportunities for specialization and trade. (T/F)

3. When two countries engaged in free trade benefit, this means that everyone in both countries benefits. (T/F)

4. If Italy uses fewer resources to produce wine than California, then Italy has a comparative advantage over California in wine production. (T/F)

5. The cheap foreign labor argument is a legitimate argument against free trade because the cheap labor leads to low costs of production. (T/F)

6. Political power was a more prevalent force influencing international prices and the distribution of gains from trade during the era of European colonialism in the 17th through the 19th centuries than today. (T/F)

7. The terms of trade equation for Mexico is the index of Mexican export prices divided by the index for Mexican import prices multiplied by 100. (T/F)

8. The world's industrialized countries buy most of their imports from less-developed countries because labor costs there are so much lower. (T/F)

9. The terms of trade have improved radically for most less-developed countries in recent years. (T/F)

10. Japan has a larger volume of imports and exports than any other country. (T/F)

11. NAFTA created a customs union between Canada, the United States, and Mexico while the European Economic Community is a free trade zone. (T/F)

12. The national security argument against free trade is that goods vital to the nation's security should be produced domestically. (T/F)

13. The infant-industry argument holds that protection should be withdrawn once an industry has had sufficient time to acquire expertise and experience. (T/F)

14. Dumping refers to a firm selling its goods in foreign markets below its domestic cost in order to drive competitors out of those markets. (T/F)

15. If a country is a most-favored nation under GATT, then tariff rates for that country are zero. (T/F)

Multiple-Choice Questions

1. If it takes Mexico 40 labor-hours to produce a barrel of wine and 30 labor-hours to produce a bushel of corn, then
   a. Mexico could not benefit from international trade
   b. Mexico has an absolute advantage in wine production
   c. Mexico has a comparative advantage in wine production
   d. the opportunity cost of 1 barrel of wine is 4/3 bushel of corn
   e. the opportunity cost of 1 bushel of corn is 4/3 barrel of wine

2. One difference between a tariff and a quota that both limit imports to the same quantity is that a
   a. quota gives more encouragement to domestic producers to become more competitive than the tariff
   b. quota raises the price by less than the tariff
   c. quota generates more revenue for the government than the tariff
   d. tariff generates tax revenue and the quota does not
   e. tariff raises the price by less than the quota

3. A country's terms of trade is the ratio of
   a. the quantity of its exports to the quantity of its imports
   b. the value of its exports to the value of its imports
   c. the index of its export prices to the index of its import prices, multiplied by 100
   d. domestic prices to international prices, multiplied by 100
   e. prices protected by tariffs to those prices subject to free trade

4. An arrangement that permits free trade among member countries and sets a common tariff policy for the rest of the world is called
   a. reciprocity
   b. a free trade area
   c. a trading bloc
   d. NAFTA
   e. a customs union

5. The infant-industries argument is used to
   a. promote indiscriminate free trade
   b. protect a new industry that employs unskilled labor
   c. protect textiles, especially children's wear, in most countries
   d. promote lower tariff rates on imports
   e. support the protection of newly established industries from foreign competition

Questions 6 and 7 refer to the table presented below showing the number of labor hours required to produce cloth and wine in England and Portugal.

	Cloth (100 yards)	Wine (1 barrel)
England	100	120
Portugal	90	80

6. From the table it is clear that
   a. England has a comparative advantage in cloth production and Portugal has a comparative advantage in wine production
   b. the opportunity cost of 100 yards of cloth in England is 9/10 what it is in Portugal
   c. England has an absolute advantage in both activities
   d. England has a comparative advantage in wine production and Portugal has a comparative advantage in cloth production
   e. neither country can gain from specialization and trade

7. The opportunity cost of 100 yards of cloth in England is _____ barrel of wine, and the opportunity cost of 100 yards of cloth in Portugal is _____ barrel of wine.
   a. 6/5; 8/9
   b. 10/9; 3/2
   c. 9/10; 2/3
   d. 5/6; 9/8
   e. 1; 1

8. Because the less-developed countries were never really happy with GATT, they were allowed to
   a. impose stringent quotas on imports from industrialized countries
   b. practice dumping manufactured goods in industrial economies' markets
   c. enjoy the industrial economies' tariff concessions without having to reciprocate
   d. improve their terms of trade with additional tariffs
   e. improve their terms of trade with additional quotas

9. The argument for trade protection that supports the existence of a wide array of different industries is known as
   a. cheap labor industries
   b. infant industries
   c. specialization and division of labor
   d. economic development
   e. the diversity of industry argument

10. A country's ability to produce a good at a lower opportunity cost than the country it trades with gives a(n)
   a. superiority
   b. absolute advantage
   c. international specialization
   d. comparative advantage
   e. profit equal to the difference between the prices in the two markets

11. All of the following are arguments for trade restrictions **except**
   a. retaliation
   b. specialization
   c. cheap labor
   d. diversity of industry
   e. national security

12. Suppose that Brazil's terms of trade change from .9 to 1.2. Which of the following must be true?
   a. Brazil gets fewer real goods for a unit of its exports
   b. the index of import prices has increased
   c. Brazil gets more real goods for a unit of its exports
   d. the index of export prices has decreased
   e. Brazil's economy is primarily agricultural

13. If Chile increases its average tariff rate by 50 percent,
   a. Chilean customs duties will fall
   b. Chile's terms of trade equation will increase
   c. imports will be more expensive in Chile
   d. employment in Chile will increase due to increased exports
   e. Chilean imports will rise because import prices will fall

14. If the opportunity cost of producing onions is lower in Montana than in Ohio, then
   a. Montana has a comparative advantage in onions over Ohio
   b. Montana has an absolute advantage in onions over Ohio
   c. Ohio has an absolute advantage in onions over Montana
   d. Montana has more highly skilled onion farmers than Ohio
   e. Ohio has an absolute advantage in onion production over Montana

15. Free trade between Canada and the United States
    a. helps every Canadian and American
    b. generally hurts one country and helps the other
    c. allows for production specialization in Canada and the United States
    d. is more beneficial to the larger country, United States
    e. is more beneficial to the smaller country, Canada

16. The North American Free Trade Agreement (NAFTA)
    a. protects the United States from production that uses cheap labor in Mexico
    b. created free trade between Canada and the United States, but protected both from Mexican cheap labor production
    c. created a customs union, similar to the European Economic Community, in Canada, the United States, and Mexico
    d. created a customs union, similar to the European Economic Community, in Canada and the United States
    e. created a free trade area that includes Canada, the United States, and Mexico

17. Most international trade takes place
    a. among the industrially developed countries, which trade primarily with each other
    b. between the industrially developed countries, which export, and the less-developed countries (LDCs), which import
    c. between the LDCs who export raw materials and the industrialized countries which import raw materials
    d. among the LDCs because they are mostly young, dynamic economies, such as Korea and Hong Kong
    e. among the LDCs because they have the largest populations, such as India, China, and Brazil

18. If the U.S. government places a quota on wheat, it is to
    a. restrict the quantity of wheat U.S. wheat producers can sell abroad
    b. raise government revenues from imports of wheat to the United States
    c. restrict the quantity of wheat that can be imported
    d. shift the domestic supply curve to the right in order to lower domestic wheat prices
    e. shift the domestic supply curve to the left in order to raise domestic wheat prices

19. With the exception of the 1920s and early 1930s, the trend in U.S. tariff rates since 1860 has been
    a. increasing
    b. decreasing
    c. constant
    d. increasing until the 1920s and decreasing after the early 1930s
    e. decreasing until the 1920s and increasing after the early 1930s

20. The main difference between a free trade area and a customs union is that
    a. the former includes all countries in the western hemisphere and the latter includes only France, Germany, Italy, Holland, Belgium, and Luxembourg
    b. the former requires tariffs for all members and the latter does not
    c. the former does not require tariffs for all members while the latter does
    d. the former allows free trade among members and individual tariff policies to be applied to nonmembers, while the latter allows free trade among members and a common tariff policy for nonmembers
    e. the former uses quotas for members and tariffs for nonmembers, and the latter uses tariffs for members and quotas for nonmembers

The following questions relate to the interdisciplinary, global, and applied perspectives in the text.

21. An unintended consequence of increasing and freer international trade
    a. is a blending of different cultures in unexpected and, perhaps to some people, undesirable ways
    b. has been the abandonment by the French of such cultural icons as the Eiffel Tower
    c. a move by all of Canada's NHL hockey teams to the United States
    d. a decrease in standards of living for people in industrialized countries
    e. an increase in unemployment in countries that trade the most with each other

22. One way for a small developing economy to benefit rapidly from a freer trade environment is to
    a. make certain that tariffs remain high on imports that compete with domestically produced goods
    b. impose strict quotas on imports that compete with domestically produced goods
    c. encourage foreign multinationals to enter the economy to speed capital formation and spur exports
    d. use tax revenues to subsidize exports
    e. provide tax cuts to firms that export

23. Although NAFTA created more jobs in the United States than it destroyed in the period from 1994 through 1998, the extent to which American workers benefitted or were harmed is unclear because
    a. the jobs created may have been low-paying jobs and the ones destroyed high-paying
    b. illegal immigration to the United States surged during these years driving down wages
    c. profits declined in most industries during these years
    d. few firms engaged in increased trade with Mexico
    e. nontariff barriers were erected in both countries to protect domestic industries

Fill in the Blanks

1. Differences in the _____ a specific good between two countries present

   opportunities for _____ which, when taken, result in _____.

2. In a two-country, two-goods world, each country will have a _____ advantage in a

   different good, and this will form the basis for _____.

3. The terms of trade for less-developed economies tend to deteriorate because changes in relative prices favor

   _____ over _____.

4. The practice followed under GATT whereby a tariff _____ offered to one member must be

   offered to all is known as _____.

Discussion Questions

1. List and critique the arguments opposed to free trade.

2. Why are less-developed countries at a disadvantage in the terms of their trade with industrialized countries?

3. What's the difference between a customs union and a free trade area?

4. Describe the pattern of U.S. tariffs from 1870 to the present.

Problems

1. The table presented below shows the number of labor-hours needed to produce an automobile or a computer in the United States and France.

	United States	France
Automobile	120	100
Computer	60	55

a. Which country has an absolute advantage in computer production? Comparative advantage? Explain.

b. If these countries specialize and trade, which country will specialize in automobiles? Computers? Explain.

c. If free trade exists between the United States and France, then what are the highest and lowest levels for the price of an automobile (expressed in terms of computers)? Which level favors the United States? France? Why?

2. Suppose that in one hour the United States can produce 180 computer microprocessors or 220 bushels of rice and that Japan in one hour can produce 160 microprocessors or 120 bushels of rice. (Note that in this problem the numbers refer to physical units, that is, microprocessors and bushels of rice, rather than labor-hours.)

a. What is the opportunity cost of a microprocessor in the United States? In Japan? Who should specialize in microprocessor production? In rice production? Show your work.

b. Suppose that these two countries begin to trade and that the price of one computer microprocessor is equal to one bushel of rice after trade. If the United States and Japan specialize according to their comparative advantages and trade, what are the potential gains from trade for each country?

c. Identify which groups win and which groups lose as a result of trade in each country.

3. The following questions refer to the demand and supply diagram below showing the market
   for bananas in the United States.

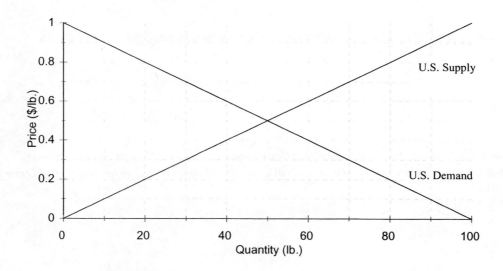

a. What are the equilibrium price of bananas and the equilibrium quantity before trade?

b. Let's now introduce free trade. Suppose banana producers from Honduras are willing to supply any
   quantity of bananas at a price of $.20 per pound. Draw the Honduran supply curve on the U.S.
   banana market in the diagram above. How many bananas will the U.S. producers supply? How many
   will the Honduran producers supply to U.S. consumers? How many bananas will U.S. consumers
   purchase?

c. Now suppose the United States imposes a $.20 per pound tariff on Honduran bananas. What is the new
   price for bananas in the United States? How many bananas will U.S. producers supply? How many will
   Honduran producers supply? How many bananas will U.S. consumers purchase? How much revenue
   will the tariff generate? Illustrate your answers in the graph.

Everyday Applications

Consider how the reduction of barriers to free trade in recent years has affected your economic well-being. Are you a net beneficiary, or have you and your family suffered as a result? Do you have close relatives who work in industries that feel the pressure of increasing international competition? How would you go about calculating the benefits and costs to yourself from freer international trade?

Economics Online

For a look into the latest developments in international trade and trade policy, visit the World Trade Organization's home page (*http:/www.wto.org/*).

Answers to Questions

Key Terms Quiz

a. 9	**f.** 8	**k.** 14	**p.** 13
b. 1	**g.** 3	**l.** 18	**q.** 2
c. 5	**h.** 17	**m.** 16	**r.** 6
d. 7	**i.** 4	**n.** 10	
e. 15	**j.** 11	**o.** 12	

True-False Questions

1. True
2. True
3. False. Those in nonspecialized lines of production will be hurt by competition from international trade as the prices of goods they produce fall.
4. False. Italy has an absolute advantage because it uses fewer resources to produce wine than California. Comparative advantage refers to lower opportunity cost.
5. False. Cheap labor may be cheap, but it may also be less productive, so the per unit cost of producing a good may be relatively expensive.
6. True
7. True
8. False. Industrialized countries trade mostly with each other. Their labor forces are typically more productive.
9. False. The terms of trade have deteriorated for many less-developed countries in recent years.
10. False. The volume of trade is highest for the United States followed by Germany and Japan.
11. False. NAFTA created a free trade area and the EEC is a customs union.
12. True
13. True
14. True
15. False. Most-favored nation status means that a tariff concession offered to one member of GATT is offered to all members of GATT.

Multiple-Choice Questions

1. d	**6.** a	**11.** b	**16.** e	**21.** a
2. d	**7.** d	**12.** c	**17.** a	**22.** c
3. c	**8.** c	**13.** c	**18.** c	**23.** a
4. e	**9.** e	**14.** a	**19.** b	
5. e	**10.** d	**15.** c	**20.** d	

Fill in the Blanks

1. costs of producing; geographic specialization; more total goods produced
2. comparative; specialization
3. manufactured goods; agricultural goods
4. concession; reciprocity

Discussion Questions

1. The **national security argument** holds that goods essential to the national security should be produced domestically. The problem with this argument is that the list of goods deemed essential to national security tends to grow over time as industry lobbyists draw connections between their industries and national security.

    The **diversity of industry argument** holds that a wide range of industries should exist in a country to increase economic stability. The problem with this argument is that although it may apply to some highly specialized less-developed countries, it hardly applies to the diversified industrial economies, such as the United States, Canada, and France.

    The **antidumping argument** states that foreign competitors sell their goods in markets below their domestic cost of production in order to drive competitors out of the industry. Although dumping is illegal in many countries, including the United States, it is difficult to prove, which makes the legislation difficult to enforce.

    The **infant industry argument** support trade protection for industries that are just beginning in a country to afford them time to learn the industry and gain expertise. The problem is how to determine when the period of infancy is over.

    The **cheap labor argument** holds that industries cannot compete with other countries producing the same goods with much lower labor costs. However, the higher cost of labor in a country often stems from its labor being more productive. This means the higher-cost labor may actually result in lower production costs.

    The **retaliation argument** holds that the restriction of access to a country's markets is justified if it is in retaliation for trade restrictions on the other side. If the threat of retaliation or actual retaliation opens up foreign markets, then it is beneficial. But if retaliation doesn't work, it can make a country worse off by restricting the purchases of goods that were beneficial.

2. Less-developed countries are at a disadvantage because their exports are typically agricultural goods and natural resources. The prices of manufactured goods, produced primarily by industrialized countries, have risen relative to the prices of agricultural goods and natural resources. Therefore, the terms of trade, defined as the ratio of an index of export prices to an index of import prices, have declined for less-developed countries.

3. A customs union, like the European Economic Community, has a policy of free trade for members and a common tariff policy with respect to nonmembers. A free trade area, like NAFTA, requires free trade among members and allows each member to establish its own trade policy with respect to nonmembers.

4. From 1860 to 1870, tariff rates rose from less than 20 percent to over 45 percent. From 1870 to 1920, the average tariff rate fell gradually to a low point in 1920 of about 5 percent. Tariff rates climbed during the 1920s to about 20 percent in the early 1930s, but have fallen steadily since to an average rate of 5.9 percent in the early 1990s.

Problems

1. a. France has an absolute advantage in both computer and automobile production. It takes only 55 hours to produce a computer in France versus 60 hours in the United States and only 100 hours to produce an automobile in France versus 120 hours in the United States. However, the United States has a comparative advantage in computer production because the opportunity cost of producing 1 computer is .5 automobile whereas the opportunity cost of 1 computer in France is .55 automobile.

   b. In this case, the United States will specialize in computer production, and France will specialize in automobiles because the opportunity cost of producing computers is lower in the United States than in France, while the opportunity cost of producing automobiles is lower in France than in the United States. France gives up 1.82 computers to produce an automobile, and the United States gives up 2 computers to produce an automobile.

   c. The price for an automobile would range from the U.S. price of 2 computers to the French price of 1.82 computers. The U.S. consumer prefers the French price. The French producers prefer the U.S. price. Each country can sell its specialty for more in the other country.

2. a. The opportunity cost of a microprocessor in the United States is 11/9 bushels of rice. The opportunity cost of a microprocessor in Japan is 3/4 bushel of rice. The United States should specialize in rice production, and Japan should specialize in microprocessor production.

   b. Before trade, in one hour, the United States could have produced either 180 microprocessors or 220 bushels of rice. If the United States specializes in rice production, it can trade at the 1-to-1 rate for 220 microprocessors, 40 more than it could before trade. Similarly, before trade, in one hour, Japan could produce either 160 microprocessors or 120 bushels of rice. By specializing in microprocessor production, Japan can trade at the 1-to-1 rate for 160 bushels of rice, 40 more than it could before trade.

   c. In the United States, rice farmers gain an immediate advantage as a result of trade, while microprocessor producers are hurt. In Japan, rice farmers lose and microprocessor producers gain.

3. a. The equilibrium price of bananas prior to trade is $.50 per pound, and 50 pounds are sold.

   b. The Honduran supply curve of bananas shows as a horizontal line at $.20 per pound. U.S. producers will supply 20 pounds of bananas in competition with Honduran suppliers, who export 60 pounds of bananas to satisfy the 80 pounds of bananas that are demanded at $.20 per pound by U.S. consumers. The graph on the following page shows the Honduran supply at $.20 per pound.

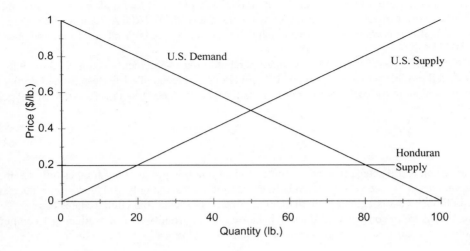

c. The new price for bananas in the United States will be $.40 — the price of Honduran imports plus the
    $.20 per pound tariff. Now U.S. suppliers will supply 40 pounds of bananas to U.S. consumers, and
    Honduran suppliers will export 20 pounds of bananas to satisfy the 60 pounds of bananas that U.S.
    consumers demand at a price of $.40 per pound. The graph below shows the situation
    with the tariff. The Honduran supply is raised by the amount of the tariff to the horizontal line at $.40
    per pound. Tariff revenue is the area corresponding to the 20 pounds of bananas that are imported with a
    $.20 per pound tax. Tariff revenue is 20 x $.20 or $4.00.

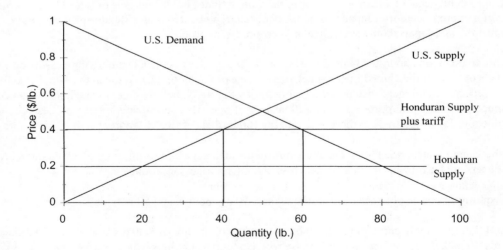

Homework Questions

True-False Questions — If a statement is false, explain why.

1. If two countries specialize and trade according to comparative advantage, they each will produce more of all goods than they did before. (T/F)

2. A country that has a comparative advantage will use fewer resources to produce a good than its trading partner. (T/F)

3. Japan has routinely applied nontariff barriers to limit imports over time. (T/F)

4. A customs union allows its members to pursue independent trade policies with countries outside the union. (T/F)

5. Tariff rates have increased and the volume of trade decreased worldwide since the early 1970s. (T/F)

Multiple-Choice Questions

1. The terms of trade for a country are deteriorating if the ratio of
   a. import prices to export prices is falling
   b. import prices to export prices is constant
   c. comparative advantage increases
   d. export prices to import prices is rising
   e. export prices to import prices is falling

2. A tariff is good for the protected industry because it allows
   a. greater competition from imports
   b. the protected industry to produce less at a higher price
   c. consumers to pay a lower price for the good and buy more
   d. inefficient firms to leave the industry
   e. firms to produce more than they would if they faced foreign competition

3. If the opportunity cost of producing chocolate is lower in Pennsylvania than in Kansas, then
   a. Pennsylvania has a comparative advantage over Kansas in chocolate production
   b. Pennsylvania has an absolute advantage over Kansas in chocolate production
   c. Kansas has an absolute advantage over Pennsylvania in chocolate production
   d. Pennsylvania has more highly skilled chocolate producers than Kansas
   e. Kansas has a comparative advantage over Pennsylvania in chocolate production

4. All of the following are examples of arguments for restricting trade *except*
   a. the infant industries argument
   b. the cheap labor argument
   c. the diversity of industry argument
   d. the income equality argument
   e. the national security argument

5. If Mexico can produce can produce a bushel of corn in 10 labor hours and a computer chip in
    20 labor hours, then we know that
    a. Mexico has a comparative advantage in corn production
    b. Mexico has an absolute advantage in corn production
    c. Mexico should specialize in corn production
    d. the opportunity cost of one bushel of corn is 0.5 computer chip
    e. the opportunity cost of one bushel of corn is 2 computer chips.

Discussion Questions/Problems

1. The following table shows the number of labor hours required to produce an automobile in the United
    States and England.

Labor hours to produce:	United States	England
1 automobile	70	150
1 computer	100	120

    a. What is the opportunity cost of an automobile in the United States? In England? Which country has a
        comparative advantage in automobile production? How do you know?

    b. Suppose each country has 1000 labor hours to use for either automobile production or computer
        production. What is the maximum quantity of autos and computers that each country can produce?

    c. Now suppose the two countries begin to trade. Suppose the price ratio of automobiles to computer
        equalizes at one to one. How does each country benefit from trade?

2. How do economists define the "terms of trade" among nations? Why have the terms of trade deteriorated
    for many developing countries?

CHAPTER 17

EXCHANGE RATES, BALANCE OF PAYMENTS, AND

INTERNATIONAL DEBT

Chapter in a Nutshell

Along with the flows of goods and services being traded between countries, there are corresponding flows of money. For example, in order to buy goods from Japan, we must acquire yen, the Japanese currency. In order for the Japanese to buy American goods, they must acquire dollars. Americans who want yen, Japanese who want dollars, and other traders buy and sell national currencies in **foreign exchange markets**. The price of one currency in terms of another country's currency is called the **exchange rate,** which is determined by the interaction of demand and supply for the currency in a floating exchange rate system. Fluctuations in a nation's exchange rate can have a significant impact on the nation's ability to import or export goods. A rise in the price of a nation's currency, called appreciation, can cause its exports to fall and imports to rise. Similarly, a decline in the price of a nation's currency, called depreciation, can cause its exports to rise and imports to fall.

The financing of a nation's international trade and its other financial transactions with the rest of the world are recorded in its **balance of payments**. The **balance on current account** itemizes the nation's imports and exports, its income receipts and payments on investment, and its unilateral transfers of funds. The **balance on capital account** itemizes changes in foreign asset holdings in the nation and the nation's asset holdings abroad. A deficit in the current account balance is matched by a surplus in the capital account balance. What defines a balance of payments problem? A current account deficit can be a problem for a country if it is forced to pay for the deficit by running down its stocks of foreign currencies, selling its assets to acquire other currencies, or borrowing other currencies excessively. Borrowing creates **international debt**. Moreover, interest must be paid on international debt. When the interest payments on the debt become too high a percentage of a nation's exports, the debt can become burdensome, resulting in a significant depreciation of the country's currency and a decline in living standards.

After studying this chapter, you should be able to:

- Explain how currencies are bought and sold on **foreign exchange markets**.
- Describe the factors that affect the demands for currencies and their supplies.
- Show how floating exchange rates allow currencies to **appreciate** and **depreciate**.
- Give an example of **arbitrage** in foreign exchange markets.
- Explain how **fixed exchange rates** work.
- Relate the **balance on current account** to the **balance on capital account** in the **balance of payments**.
- Present a set of options that a country might employ to service its **international debt**.

Concept Check — See how you do on these multiple-choice questions.

What is being traded in a foreign exchange market?

1. The purpose of **foreign exchange markets** is to allow people to
   a. practice arbitrage
   b. increase their country's current account balances
   c. increase their country's capital account balances
   d. finance international debt
   e. buy and sell different currencies

It makes sense to purchase a good (or a currency) where its price is low and sell it where its price is high.

2. **Arbitrage** creates mutually consistent exchange rates because
   a. it causes a currency to appreciate to balance imports with exports
   b. it causes a currency to depreciate to balance exports with imports
   c. floating exchange rates are always in a state of flux
   d. when a currency is purchased at a low price in one market and sold at a high price in another, the prices converge
   e. when a currency is sold at a low price in one market and purchased at a high price in another, the prices converge

Think about problems that countries encounter when trying to maintain fixed exchange rates.

3. One potential problem for a country with **fixed exchange rates** is that
   a. a decrease in the demand for its currency can create a drain on foreign exchange reserves used to maintain the exchange rate
   b. the currency is probably prone to depreciation
   c. exchange rates are fixed as a result of the devaluation of the currency
   d. a current account deficit will result
   e. merchandise imports will exceed merchandise exports

How do households typically handle temporary cash flow problems? How do countries do the same?

4. The **International Monetary Fund** was created to aid countries that have foreign exchange reserves problems by
   a. devaluing the country's currency
   b. lending the country foreign exchange reserves through purchase-and-resale agreements
   c. helping to re-establish the country's exchange rate at a higher level
   d. purchasing the country's assets abroad and converting them to foreign currencies
   e. helping the country find new markets for exports

Remember that the ultimate long-run solution to a balance of trade problem is for a country to become more productive.

5. A negative **balance of trade** for a country will not be a long-run problem if
   a. the country's foreign exchange reserves are depleted in order to finance it
   b. the country imports new capital equipment to improve its competitiveness in world markets
   c. the IMF stops lending the country foreign exchange reserves
   d. the country can sell important national assets to finance it
   e. the country also imports large quantities of services from the rest of the worl

Am I on the Right Track?

Your answers to the questions above should be **e**, **d**, **a**, **b**, and **b**. Foreign exchange rates are determined by the interaction of demand and supply in foreign exchange markets, just as prices of other goods are determined in markets. The impact of erratic fluctuations in exchange rates can undermine the advantages of international trade because they contribute to uncertainty about the prices of imports and exports. Fixed exchange rates may appear to be a solution to floating exchange rates. However, fixed exchange rates create problems of their own, not the least of which is the possibility of accumulating excessive international debt in order to maintain the exchange rate. There are many key terms for this chapter. A key to your success in the chapter is understanding the new key terms and how they are used to explain the determination of exchange rates, the balance of payments, and international debt.

Key Terms Quiz — Match the terms on the left with the definitions in the column on the right.

1. foreign exchange market

_____ a. a rise in the price of a nation's currency relative to foreign currencies

2. balance of payments

_____ b. a rate determined and maintained by government by buying and selling its own currency on the foreign exchange market

3. exchange rate

_____ c. an itemized account of a nation's foreign economic transactions

4. balance on current account

_____ d. transfers of currency made by individuals, businesses, or the government of one nation to individuals, businesses, or governments in other nations without anything being given in exchange

5. floating exchange rate

_____ e. tariffs and quotas used by government to limit a nation's imports

6. balance of trade

_____ f. a market in which currencies of different nations are bought and sold

7. appreciation

_____ g. an exchange rate determined strictly by the demands and supplies for a nation's currency

8. unilateral transfers

_____ h. a category that itemizes changes in foreign asset holdings in a nation and that nation's asset holdings abroad

9. depreciation

_____ i. interest payments on international debt as a percentage of a nation's merchandise exports

10. balance on capital account

_____ j. a system in which the government, as the sole depository of foreign currencies, exercises complete control over how these currencies can be used

11. arbitrage

_____ k. the stock of foreign currencies held by a government

12. international debt

_____ l. a category that itemizes a nation's imports and exports of merchandise and services, income receipts and payments on investment, and unilateral transfers

13. fixed exchange rate

_____ m. the practice of buying a foreign currency in one market at a low price and selling it in another at a higher price

14. debt service

_____ n. the number of units of foreign currency that can be purchased with one unit of domestic currency

15. foreign exchange reserves

_____ o. government policy that lowers the nation's exchange rate, i.e., fewer units of foreign currency for a unit of its own currency

16. import controls

_____ p. the difference between the value of a nation's merchandise exports and its merchandise imports

17. devaluation   _____ q. an international organization formed to make loans of
                                                   foreign currencies to countries facing balance of
                                                   payments problems

18. exchange controls   _____ r. the total amount of borrowing a nation is
                                                   obligated to repay other nations and international
                                                   organizations

19. International Monetary Fund (IMF)   _____ s. a fall in the price of a nation's currency relative to
                                                   foreign currencies

Graphing Tutorial

Foreign exchange markets can be represented using demand and supply graphs. Buyers and sellers of different
nations' currencies make exchanges in these markets, just as buyers and sellers of other goods make exchanges
in markets. The equilibrium price in a foreign exchange market is called the exchange rate. The demand and
supply graph presented below shows the foreign exchange market for zaps, the currency for the imaginary
nation Zapland, priced in dollars. On the vertical axis we show the price of zaps in dollars — dollars per zap.
On the horizontal axis we measure the quantity of zaps. The demand and supply curves are drawn to show the
exchange rate — the equilibrium price of zaps measured in dollars — equal to $5 per zap.

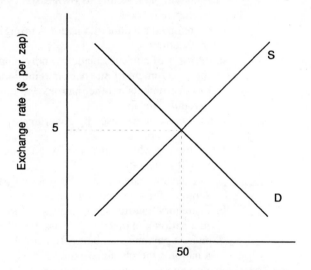

Why is the demand for zaps downward sloping? As the price of zaps measured in dollars decreases,
goods from Zapland become more attractive to American consumers, and the quantity demanded of zaps
increases. Why is the supply of zaps upward sloping? People in Zapland supply zaps in order to buy goods
produced in the United States. As the price of zaps measured in dollars increases, U.S. goods are relatively
cheaper for Zaplanders, so they supply larger quantities of zaps for dollars.

What causes the demand curve for zaps to shift? Suppose incomes in the United States increase. With
higher incomes, Americans will buy more goods from Zapland; hence they will demand more zaps at all
exchange rates. The demand for zaps shifts to the right, and the exchange rate for zaps increases from the $5
per zap level. A change in tastes would also shift the demand curve for zaps. If goods from Zapland become
more fashionable, the demand for zaps will increase, causing the demand curve to shift to the right and the
exchange rate to rise. Changes in interest rates in the United States and Zapland will influence the demand for
zaps. If the interest rate in Zapland rises relative to the interest rate in the United States, then the demand for
zaps increases as U.S. savers take advantage of the higher return in Zapland.

The supply curve of zaps is shifted by changes in the same factors in Zapland. If incomes in Zapland increase, they will demand more goods from the United States, and the supply of zaps shifts to the right. If Zaplanders' tastes change so that U.S. goods are more appealing, the supply of zaps shifts to the right. If interest rates in the United States rise relative to interest rates in Zapland, the supply curve shifts to the right as Zaplanders take advantage of saving opportunities in the United States.

A floating exchange rate is one determined strictly by the demand for and supply of a nation's currency. The factors that determine the demand for zaps and the supply of zaps would naturally change over time, causing the exchange rate of dollars per zaps to fluctuate. If the exchange rate increases from $5 per zap to $7 per zap, we say the dollar has depreciated (or weakened) relative to the zap because more dollars are required to purchase a zap. If the exchange rate decreases from $5 per zap to $3 per zap, the dollar has appreciated (or strengthened) relative to the zap because fewer dollars are required to purchase a zap. Erratic fluctuations in free-floating exchange rates can cause problems for businesses that import and export because unexpected changes in exchange rates result in unexpected changes in the price of goods being traded internationally.

Suppose that to avoid the problems of uncertainties associated with floating exchange rates, the U.S. government fixes the exchange rate at $5 per zap. Suppose further that the demand for zaps increases from D to D' as shown in the graph below.

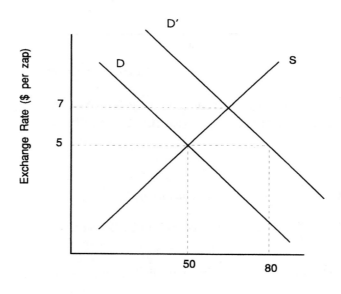

Quantity of Zaps (1,000s)

If the exchange rate were floating, it would rise from $5 per zap to $7 per zap — the new equilibrium exchange rate. However, the fixed exchange rate policy mandates that all exchanges of dollars for zaps occur at the $5 per zap rate. The graph shows an excess demand for zaps equal to 30,000 zaps at $5 per zap. The U.S. government must come up with its own supply of zaps — 30,000 in this case — to satisfy the excess demand. Problems with the fixed exchange rate policy could arise if the U.S. government runs out of zaps. These are described in detail in your text.

Graphing Pitfalls

Problems with labeling the axes sometimes arise when graphing foreign exchange markets. Remember that if the exchange rate measured along the vertical axis is dollars per zap, then zaps are being measured on the horizontal axis. Recall the fish market we examined in Chapter 3. The price of fish is measured in dollars per fish. Therefore, fish are measured on the horizontal axis. Don't make the mistake shown in the graph below of putting the exchange rate of dollars per zap on the vertical axis and dollars on the horizontal axis.

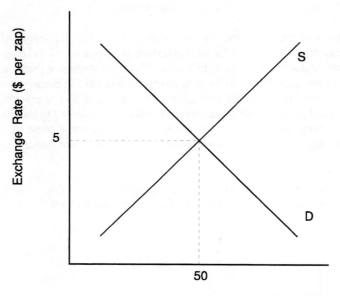

If the exchange rate on the vertical axis is dollars per zap, then the horizontal axis measures zaps, not dollars as shown above

True-False Questions — If a statement is false, explain why.

1. The foreign exchange market is where the international trade of goods and services takes place. (T/F)

2. An exchange rate is the number of units of one currency required to purchase one unit of another currency. (T/F)

3. As a nation's income increases, its demand for imports increases, creating an increase in its demand for foreign currencies. (T/F)

4. A currency depreciates if less of that currency is required to buy one unit of another currency. (T/F)

5. The supply curve of a currency will shift to the right when interest rates in that country fall relative to interest rates in other countries. (T/F)

6. If exports of merchandise are greater than imports of merchandise, then a favorable balance of trade exists. (T/F)

7. Arbitrage is the process whereby currencies are purchased in markets with low prices and sold in markets with high prices, creating mutually consistent exchange rates. (T/F)

8. One problem with a fixed exchange rate is that if the demand for imports continually increases, an excess demand for foreign currency will be generated at the fixed exchange rate that may deplete foreign currency reserves. (T/F)

9. An exchange control system requires exporters to convert any foreign exchange earned by trade into the domestic currency in order to replenish the government's supply of foreign exchange. (T/F)

10. The balance of payments account is an itemized account of a country's exports and imports of merchandise. (T/F)

11. Exports of goods and services and income receipts on investments from the rest of the world represent dollar inflows in the balance on current account. (T/F)

12. Low productivity contributes to a favorable balance of trade by making the domestic producers' goods relatively cheaper than goods from other countries. (T/F)

13. An American taking a vacation in Cancun has the same effect on Mexico's balance on current account as a Mexican businessperson exporting goods and services to the United States. (T/F)

14. The balance on capital account shows changes in the capital stock of all industries within a country. (T/F)

15. Foreign investment in the United States represents a capital inflow to the United States. (T/F)

Multiple-Choice Questions

1. One effect of an appreciation of the U.S. dollar is that
   a. it increases the demand for U.S. labor
   b. Americans can buy imports more cheaply
   c. American incomes decrease
   d. foreigners will demand more U.S. exports
   e. U.S. labor will become less productive

2. An increase in income in the United States will
   a. increase the demand for foreign currencies
   b. cause United States exports to increase
   c. cause the value of the dollar measured in foreign currencies to increase
   d. decrease the demand for foreign currencies
   e. shift the supply curve of dollars to the left

3. All of the following are useful options for the government to pursue to bolster foreign exchange reserves **except** to
   a. impose exchange controls
   b. impose export controls
   c. adjust the exchange rate
   d. borrow foreign currencies
   e. permit a free floating exchange rate

4. An example of dollar inflows on the balance on current account is
   a. the export of services
   b. unilateral transfers of dollars to U.S. students in Europe
   c. changes in U.S. assets abroad
   d. the payments on foreign investments in the United States
   e. the import of services

5. The balance of trade is given by
   a. income receipts minus income payments on investments
   b. the balance of unilateral transfers
   c. merchandise exports plus service exports minus the sum of merchandise and service imports
   d. merchandise exports minus merchandise imports
   e. the balance on current account

6. If the U.S. dollar appreciates relative to the Japanese yen, then
   a. more yen will be required to purchase one dollar
   b. fewer yen will be required to purchase one dollar
   c. the dollar has weakened relative to the yen
   d. Japan's demand for U.S. goods will increase
   e. the Japanese supply of yen will increase

7. The balance on current account includes all of the following items **except**
   a. merchandise exports minus merchandise imports
   b. exports of services minus imports of services
   c. income receipts minus income payments on investments
   d. changes in U.S. assets owned abroad and foreign assets owned in the U.S.
   e. unilateral transfers of currency by individuals

8. A persistently unfavorable balance on current account would represent a balance of payments problem if
   a. it were the result of declining productivity in the economy and an inability to compete in international markets
   b. it were the result of large imports of basic goods such as oil
   c. a strengthening of the nation's currency increased the price of its exports to foreign buyers
   d. reserves of foreign currencies increased
   e. the government pursued a surplus budget

9. People who practice arbitrage will create mutually consistent exchange rates if
   a. they operate in a country that practices exchange controls
   b. exchange rates are set properly by government
   c. productivity increases in the economy of the country whose currency is being traded
   d. they buy a currency in one market at a low price and then sell at a high price in another market
   e. the currency being traded appreciates

10. The impact of an Indonesian businessman purchasing a U.S. bond is to
    a. increase the current account deficit in the United States
    b. increase the balance on capital account in the United States
    c. increase the U.S. government budget deficit
    d. cause U.S. interest rates to rise
    e. contribute to a balance of payments problem in the United States

11. One consequence of a depreciation in a country's exchange rate is that
    a. its demand for foreign currencies increases
    b. its exports decrease
    c. its imports decrease
    d. other countries, in response, must depreciate theirs
    e. its government cannot borrow from the IMF

12. The demand for U.S. dollars on the foreign exchange market will increase when
    a. U.S. incomes increase
    b. foreign incomes decrease
    c. interest rates in the rest of the world rise dramatically while U.S. rates remain unchanged
    d. U.S. interest rates rise dramatically while those in the rest of the world remain unchanged
    e. U.S. exports increase

13. In an economy's balance of payments account,
    a. the capital and current accounts must add to one
    b. the current account is always greater than the capital account
    c. both the balance on current account and the balance on capital account are zero
    d. the capital plus current account balances must equal zero
    e. capital outflows must equal capital inflows

14. Floating exchange rates refer to
    a. the ability of exchange rates to even out when displaced by shocks to the foreign exchange market
    b. new issues of foreign exchange offered on the market
    c. an exchange rate determined by the demand for and supply of a nation's currency
    d. an excess demand for a nation's currency that causes its devaluation
    e. an excess supply of a nation's currency that causes its appreciation

15. If the current account for a country is in deficit, then there must be
    a. a surplus in the government budget
    b. low interest rates
    c. high productivity
    d. a capital account surplus
    e. the presence of attractive investment opportunities

16. If Elrod is a student at the University of Toronto in Ontario, Canada, and his parents in Fresno, California, send him $75, the money is a
    a. private unilateral transfer, shown as a U.S. dollar outflow in the U.S. balance of payments account
    b. private unilateral transfer, shown as a Canadian dollar outflow in the Canadian balance of payments account
    c. current account transfer, shown as a U.S. dollar inflow in the U.S. balance of payments account
    d. capital account payment, shown as a U.S. dollar inflow in the U.S. balance of payments account
    e. capital account payment, shown as a Canadian dollar outflow in the U.S. balance of payments account

17. If the International Monetary Fund provides a loan of yen to the United States to help finance its unfavorable balance of trade, the
    a. IMF's supply of foreign reserves will increase
    b. United States balance on capital account will increase
    c. IMF will expect the U.S. to repurchase the dollars used to acquire the yen at a later date
    d. U.S. balance on current account will increase
    e. Japanese balance on current account will decrease

18. Debt service refers to
    a. interest payments on international debt as a percentage of a nation's merchandise exports
    b. the outflows from a nation's capital account to pay for its imports of foreign services
    c. the outflows from a nation's current account to pay for its imports of foreign services
    d. debt owed to a nation for the export of its services
    e. international debt representing all the services transacted on all nations' balance of payments accounts

19. A potential problem with free floating exchange rates is that
    a. people who practice arbitrage may gain from the losses of others
    b. uncertainty in exchange rate fluctuations may hinder international trade
    c. exchange rates may never reach equilibrium
    d. the currency markets may become monopolized
    e. less-developed countries may issue too much currency

20. Some countries may not worry about an unfavorable balance on current account because
    a. they know they can always borrow to cover the deficit
    b. they import capital goods to build up export industries that will eventually eliminate the deficit
    c. deficits are always a stimulant to economic growth, which is a higher priority
    d. they can, if necessary, fix the exchange rate to wipe out the deficit
    e. their capital account will be favorable since the balance of payments always ends up at zero

The following questions relate to the applied and global perspectives in the text.

21. If a tourist from Canada and a tourist from Japan compare notes on the cost in Canadian dollars and Japanese yen, respectively, of trips to the United States in 1960 and 2000 they will find that
    a. the trip was more expensive in 2003 in Canadian dollars and less expensive in Japanese yen in 2003
    b. the trip was less expensive in 2003 in Canadian dollars and more expensive in Japanese yen in 2003
    c. the trips cost exactly the same in both currencies in 2003 as they did in 1960
    d. both the Canadian dollar and the Japanese yen appreciated relative to the dollar
    e. both the Canadian dollar and the Japanese yean depreciated relative to the dollar

22. One effect of a currency devaluation in a developing country intended to help reduce a chronically unfavorable balance of trade is
    a. an increase in the prices of goods and services made with domestic labor and materials
    b. an increase in the inflation rate because imports become more expensive
    c. an increase in the unemployment rate
    d. a decrease in inflation because imports become less expensive
    e. a decrease in the number of people in poverty

23. Which of the following assertions regarding the economic impact of the euro is **incorrect**?
    a. The euro will increase Europe's global economic power.
    b. Trade among European countries will be simplified.
    c. The euro will quickly replace the dollar as the international currency.
    d. Countries within the European Union will be unable to pursue their own national economic interests.
    e. National central banks in Europe are replaced by the European central bank.

24. Because debts in many LDCs to foreign creditors are beyond repayment, one approach that is being discussed to deal with the problem is
    a. to forgive the debts and to lend more to the LDCs in order to finance development projects
    b. to forgive the debts but not to lend any more
    c. forgive the debt and insist on policies to improve education and reduce poverty
    d. seize land in the LDCs as payment for the debts
    e. impose tariffs on LDC exports in order to punish them for not paying their debts

Fill in the Blanks

1. If the dollar-for-Mexican peso exchange rate falls, then Mexican goods are _____ for Americans, and the quantity demanded of pesos will _____.

2. The _____ for Mexican pesos reflects the U.S. demand for Mexican goods and services, and the _____ of Mexican pesos reflects the Mexican demand for U.S. goods and services.

3. If a government finds it difficult to maintain a fixed exchange rate, the government can resort to policies such as _____, _____, _____, or

   _____.

4. If foreigners find attractive investment opportunities in the United States, the effect will be to cause the dollar to _____ relative to foreign currencies; hence foreign goods will become relatively _____ for Americans, and foreigners will find American goods relatively

   _____.

5. The debt service that is associated with a country's international debt is defined as the percentage of _____ that is accounted for by _____ payments on the debt.

Discussion Questions

1. a. Why is the demand curve for Mexican pesos downward sloping?

   b. Why is the supply curve of dollars priced in pesos upward sloping?

2. Describe the circumstances that led to the rise of the U.S. current account deficit during the 1980s.

3. Why is borrowing to finance an unfavorable balance on current account so dangerous for a less-developed country? Explain the nature of the long-run adjustment that will correct a current account deficit. Is this adjustment process painless for the less-developed country? Explain.

4. Under what circumstances would a country face a shortfall in its foreign exchange reserves? Discuss the role the International Monetary Fund plays in stabilizing a country's currency in times of crisis.

Problems

1. Graph the supply and demand for the foreign exchange market, expressed in terms of pesos per dollar. Show the equilibrium price at 5 pesos per dollar. Suppose the demand for dollars increases so that the new exchange rate is 7 pesos per dollar. Has the peso appreciated or depreciated? Which currency has strengthened? Is this good or bad for the United States? For Mexico?

2. Suppose the following data represent Mexico's international transactions measured in pesos.

Merchandise exports	15		Merchandise imports	10
Change in foreign assets in Mexico	12		Change in assets abroad	8
Exports of services	7		Imports of services	5
Income receipts on investment	5		Income payments on investment	10
			Unilateral transfers	6

   a. What is Mexico's balance of trade?

   b. What is its balance on current account?

   c. What is its balance on capital account?

Everyday Applications

An appreciation or depreciation in a country's currency can dramatically affect the finances of the country's citizens who are studying at universities and colleges in other countries. For instance, a decline in the value of the yen relative to the dollar can make it much more costly for Japanese students to study and live in the United States. Do you know any foreign students (perhaps you are one!) who have been affected by recent exchange rate changes? If their (or your) parents are assisting by sending money from home, do they have to spend more or less of their domestic currency to maintain the same level of assistance?

Economics Online

The IMF has a Web site (*http://www.imf.org/*). Visit the site to find out more about the structure of the IMF and its activities.

Answers to Questions

Key Terms Quiz

a. 7	**f.** 1	**k.** 15	**p.** 6
b. 13	**g.** 5	**l.** 4	**q.** 19
c. 2	**h.** 10	**m.** 11	**r.** 12
d. 8	**i.** 14	**n.** 3	**s.** 9
e. 16	**j.** 18	**o.** 17	

True-False Questions

1. False. The foreign exchange market is a market for foreign currencies, not goods and services.
2. True
3. True
4. False. The currency depreciates if more of it is required to purchase one unit of another currency.
5. True
6. True
7. True
8. True
9. True
10. False. The balance of payments is an account of a country's entire international transactions.
11. True
12. False. Low productivity contributes to an unfavorable balance of trade because domestic goods are relatively more expensive than goods from other countries.
13. True
14. False. The capital account itemizes changes in foreign asset holdings in a nation and a nation's asset holdings abroad.
15. True

Multiple-Choice Questions

1. b	**6.** a	**11.** c	**16.** a	**21.** a
2. a	**7.** d	**12.** d	**17.** c	**22.** b
3. e	**8.** a	**13.** d	**18.** a	**23.** c
4. a	**9.** d	**14.** c	**19.** b	**24.** c
5. d	**10.** b	**15.** d	**20.** b	

Fill in the Blanks

1. cheaper; increase
2. demand; supply
3. devaluation; import controls; exchange controls; borrowing foreign currencies
4. appreciate; expensive; cheaper
5. merchandise exports; interest

Discussion Questions

1. a. Suppose a Mexican hat sells in Mexico for 1 peso and the exchange rate is $5 per peso. If you buy that hat, you think of it as a $5 hat. If the exchange rate falls to $2 per peso, that same hat becomes a $2 hat. At that price, you may choose to buy more hats. As the exchange rate falls — U.S. dollars per peso — the Mexican good becomes cheaper, and therefore, the quantity demanded of pesos increases.

   b. Think of Mexicans buying U.S. goods. At $5 per peso, Javier Herrera can buy a VCR tape priced in the United States at $5 for only a peso. Suppose Javier buys 4 tapes. If the exchange rate falls to $2 per peso, then the $5 tape now costs him 2½ pesos. That's more expensive so he buys fewer tapes. As a result, the quantity supplied of pesos decreases as the exchange rate falls.

2. The strength and stability of the U.S. economy compared to other economies were an important factor contributing to the current account deficit. Foreigners perceived that the United States was a good place to invest, given the investment security and reasonable rates of return. Demand for U.S. dollars increased. Another factor was the relatively high interest rates in the United States. That, too, shifted the demand curve for U.S. dollars to the right, driving up the exchange rate for the dollar. A stronger dollar made foreign goods and services relatively cheaper for U.S. consumers.

3. Borrowing to finance an unfavorable balance on current account becomes problematic when the debt service rises to levels that are difficult to sustain. Exports must earn enough foreign exchange to pay the interest on the debt. A country cannot continually borrow if the debt service keeps rising because it simply won't be able to meet the interest obligations. Potential lenders will be unwilling to lend or will do so only at very high interest rates. However, there is an automatic correction mechanism that will reduce the unfavorable balance on current account. As a country imports more than it exports, its exchange rate will fall (currency depreciates) relative to others, making imports more expensive. At the same time, the country's exports become more attractive, so the trade gap will tend to shrink. This adjustment process may be very painful for a less-developed country, particularly if it depends on imports of food. As the exchange rate falls, food imports become more expensive, and living standards decline.

4. Suppose the U.S. government fixes the exchange rate at 3 euros per dollar, and following this, the demand for European goods and, therefore, euros increases to create an excess demand of 20 million euros at the fixed 3 euro per dollar rate. The government is forced to use 20 million of the euros it held in reserve to buy $6.67 million on the foreign exchange market to maintain the fixed rate at 3 euros per dollar. But how deep are the government's pockets? How many euros does it need to have in reserve to continue to use them to buy U.S. dollars to support the fixed rate of exchange? What if it runs out of euros? Wouldn't the

excess demand for francs undermine the fixed rate? If the government runs out of euros and still wants to maintain the fixed rate, it can appeal to the IMF for a loan of reserves, buying euros for dollars with the promise of later repurchasing its dollars with euros.

Problems

1.

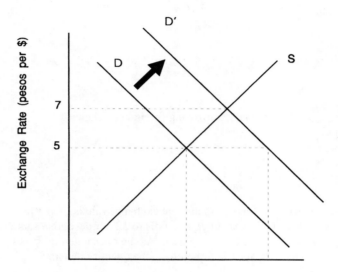

The peso has depreciated because it requires more pesos to buy one dollar. A depreciation of the peso means that the dollar has strengthened relative to the peso. One dollar buys more pesos — 7 rather than 5. Whether this is good or bad depends entirely on who you are. If you are a Mexican exporter to the United States, this is good because the prices of your exports have fallen in dollars. If you are a consumer in the United States, this is good because Mexican goods are cheaper. However, it is bad for Mexican importers of U.S. goods who must pay more in pesos for a given amount of American goods.

2. a. Mexico's balance of trade is equal to merchandise exports minus merchandise imports = 15 - 10 = 5. Mexico has a positive or favorable balance of trade.

   b. Mexico's balance on current account is equal to merchandise exports + exports of services + income from investments - (merchandise imports + imports of services + income payments on investments + unilateral transfers) = 15 + 7 + 5 - (10 + 5 + 10 + 6) = 27 - 31 = -4. Mexico has a negative or unfavorable balance on current account.

   c. Mexico's balance on capital account is the difference between changes in foreign assets in Mexico and changes in Mexican assets in foreign countries = 12 - 8 = 4. This positive or favorable balance on capital account offsets the negative balance on current account.

Homework Questions

True-False Questions — If a statement is false, explain why.

1. To an American, the exchange rate between the British pound and the dollar is the number of pounds that can be purchased with one dollar. (T/F)

2. If the dollar depreciates relative to the Japanese yen, then more yen are required to purchase one dollar. (T/F)

3. A surplus on the current account means that the amount of capital flowing into a country exceeds the amount of capital flowing out of a country. (T/F)

4. An increase in the debt service as a percentage of exports is a positive sign for a developing country. (T/F)

5. One advantage to fixed exchange rates is a reduction in the level of uncertainty associated with international trade. (T/F)

Multiple-Choice Questions

1. Given an unfavorable balance of trade, the current account can still be favorable if
   a. there is a larger value for merchandise imports
   b. exports of services are less than imports of services
   c. unilateral transfers of dollars out of the United States exceed unilateral transfers of dollars into the United States
   d. sales of U.S. assets to foreigners increase
   e. exports of services are greater than imports of services by enough to offset the unfavorable trade balance

2. The supply curve of U.S. dollars on the foreign exchange market reflects the
   a. willingness of people in the United States to supply goods and services on the international market
   b. willingness of foreigners to demand U.S. goods and services on the international market
   c. willingness of people in the United States to demand foreign goods and services on the international market
   d. willingness of foreigners to demand U.S. dollars on the foreign exchange market
   e. the net exports (exports minus imports) that U.S. producers sell on the international market

3. If the United States fixes its exchange rate for the euro ($s per euro) below the market exchange rate such that a chronic excess demand for euros exists, in order to maintain the exchange rate, the United States government must
   a. fix the exchange rate further below the market rate in order to strengthen the dollar
   b. raise United States interest rates
   c. sell euros in currency markets in order to maintain the exchange rate
   d. take steps to increasee European exports
   e. lend its reserves of euros to developing countries

4. The difference between the value of a nation's merchandise exports and its merchandise imports is its
   a. external debt
   b. balance on capital account
   c. balance of trade
   d. foreign exchange reserves
   e. foreign exchange rate

5. Fixed exchange rates were designed to
   a. increase a nation's exports, if the fixed rate is low enough
   b. reduce a nation's imports, if the fixed rate is high enough
   c. reduce the uncertainties of international trade associated with floating exchange rates
   d. strengthen the nation's currency by curtailing the import of other currencies
   e. provide government with revenues

Discussion Questions/Problems

1. Discuss the problems associated with floating and fixed exchange rates.

2. Is international debt always a problem for a less-developed country? Explain.

CHAPTER 18

THE ECONOMIC PROBLEMS OF LESS-DEVELOPED ECONOMIES

Chapter in a Nutshell

Why do many people in the countries of Asia, Africa, and Latin America endure standards of living that barely support physical subsistence? Obviously, these people don't choose to remain poor. But the world they inhabit seems to afford them little choice. What can be done to improve their circumstances? Since the early 1950s, economists have focused some attention on the problem of persistent national poverty. Poor countries face challenges that are fundamentally different from those faced by the world's industrialized economies. For example, most poor countries are qualitatively different from industrialized countries. They lack a basic **infrastructure** — institutions and public facilities to support modern ways of producing goods and services. People in industrialized countries often take their economies' infrastructures for granted. Over the last 30 years, some **less-developed countries (LDCs)** have made considerable progress in modernizing their economies with accompanying increases in their per capita incomes, but many others haven't.

This chapter explores the characteristics of less-developed countries and the different approaches that they might take toward successful development. The pattern of low per capita incomes among LDCs is outlined. Rapid population growth in LDCs can contribute to slow growth in per capita incomes. **Economic dualism** — the coexistence of two separate and distinct economies within an LDC, one modern and the other traditional — is observable in many LDCs. Frequently, the basic prerequisites for economic development, such as political stability and infrastructure, are missing in LDCs. Two strategies for development, the **big push** and unbalanced development with **forward and backward linkages**, are compared. Finally, the roles played by foreign direct investment and foreign economic aid in economic development are considered.

After studying this chapter, you should be able to:

- Explain how the term **less-developed countries** came to be used by economists.
- Describe the variety of circumstances that exist in LDCs.
- Show how rapid population growth can slow down per capita income growth in LDCs.
- Discuss **economic dualism**.
- Contrast the **big-push** and the **unbalanced** strategies for economic development.
- Present arguments for and against **foreign direct investment** in LDCs.
- Contrast **foreign direct investment** and **foreign economic aid**.

Concept Check — See how you do on these multiple-choice questions.

Could the term "underdeveloped" be construed as pejorative language?

1. The term **less-developed countries** is used instead of "underdeveloped countries" to describe the situations faced by economies in Asia, Africa, and Latin America because
   a. progress toward development has been significant in all of these countries
   b. per capita income in these countries is approaching per capita income in industrialized countries
   c. the term underdeveloped is too prejudicial and LDCs are the equals of industrialized countries on grounds other than economic
   d. the United Nations passed a resolution to use the term "less-developed"
   e. the term underdeveloped countries masked differences among them

Can you recall the definition for human capital?

2. All of the following are examples of investments in **human capital except**
   a. productivity gains due to better education
   b. improved bridges and highways
   c. free vaccinations against polio for all children
   d. on-the-job training for newly hired factory workers
   e. a retraining program for unemployed workers

In some LDCs, two distinct economies seem to exist alongside one another.

3. **Economic dualism** means that
   a. the world consists of industrialized countries and less-developed countries
   b. an LDC has distinct modern and traditional economies
   c. some LDCs are politically stable and some are unstable
   d. infrastructure development is prevalent is some LDCs and absent in others
   e. two approaches to economic development exist — the big push and unbalanced development

Some economists believe that capital formation on a massive scale is necessary for development to begin in certain LDCs.

4. The **big-push** development strategy depends on
   a. backward and forward linkages
   b. first undertaking an unbalanced growth strategy
   c. foreign direct investment
   d. an integrated network of government-sponsored and financed investments
   e. generous foreign economic aid

Learn the distinction between forward and backward linkages.

5. **Forward linkages** refer to
   a. investments in one industry that create opportunities for profitable investments in other industries
   b. investments in one industry that create demands for inputs, thereby inducing investment in other industries
   c. connections between LDCs and industrialized countries created by foreign direct investment
   d. connections between LDCs and industrialized countries created by foreign economic aid
   e. connections between LDCs and industrialized countries that result from the colonial past

Am I on the Right Track?

Your answers to the questions above should be **c**, **a**, **b**, **d**, and **a**. Addressing the problems of less-developed economies requires that we first identify the most pressing of these problems and then arrive at strategies to remedy these problems. While there are many similarities among the problems facing LDCs, significant differences exist as well. The strategies appropriate for one LDC may or may not be appropriate for another. The problems associated with economic develoment are complex, making generalizations difficult. The questions that follow will help you begin to appreciate how difficult it can be for LDCs to realize successful development strategies.

Key Terms Quiz — Match the terms on the left with the definitions in the column on the right.

1. less-developed countries   _____ a. the investment in workers' knowledge, acquired through education and/or experience that enhances their productivity

2. big push   _____ b. the basic institutions and public facilities upon which an economy's development depends

3. human capital   _____ c. the development strategy that relies on an integrated network of government-sponsored and financed investments introduced into the economy all at once

4. forward linkage   _____ d. investments in one industry that create demands for inputs, inducing investment in other industries to produce those inputs

5. economic dualism   _____ e. economies of Asia, Africa, and Latin America

6. backward linkage   _____ f. investments in one industry that create opportunities for profitable investments in other industries, using the goods produced in the first as inputs

7. infrastructure   _____ g. the coexistence of two separate and distinct economies within an LDC, one modern and the other traditional

Graphing Tutorial

Demand and supply diagrams can be used to represent the labor markets in the traditional and modern sectors of an LDC characterized by economic dualism. The demand and supply graphs in Panel A and Panel B below show the labor markets in the traditional and modern sectors, respectively.

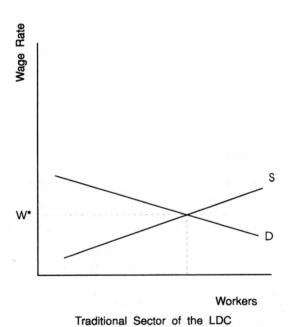

Traditional Sector of the LDC

A

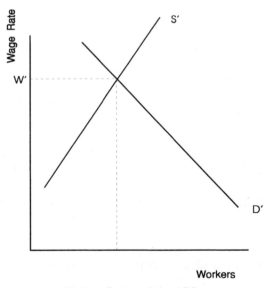

Modern Sector of the LDC

B

    In the traditional sector, the supply of labor is plentiful, as shown by the supply curve drawn far to the right, and the demand for labor is relatively low, reflecting traditional technology and weak prices. This combination yields a low wage level at W*. In comparison, in the modern sector, the demand for labor is higher, reflecting industrial technology applied to the export market where productivity and prices are higher.

However, the supply of labor is limited, and the curve is relatively steep, reflecting the scarcity of technical skills in the LDC. This combination of demand and supply yields a much higher wage rate at W'.

The problem with economic dualism is its tendency to persist. The skills of those in the traditional sector are inadequate for the modern sector. A large percentage of the population may be virtually trapped in poverty conditions.

Graphing Pitfalls

It is critical to position the supply curve for labor properly in graphs showing the labor market under conditions of economic dualism. Suppose we switch the supply curves for labor between the two sectors. Graphs with the supply curves switched are shown below.

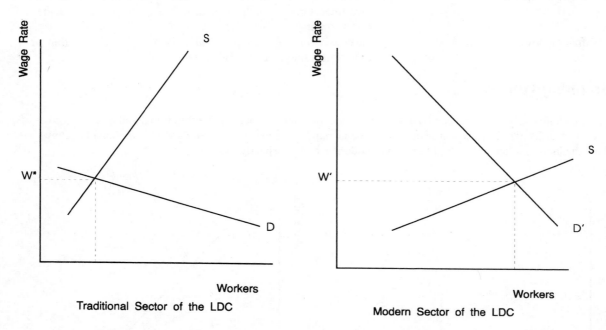

It should be apparent immediately that these graphs are drawn incorrectly because the wage rates in the two labor markets are approximately equal. That is because the supply curves have been switched. The supply curve for labor in the traditional sector should lie to the right, while the supply of labor in the modern sector is pushed up to the left, reflecting the scarcity of technical skills in the population. Be certain that your graphs make economic sense once you draw them.

True-False Questions — If a statement is false, explain why.

1. Economists have determined specific levels of per capita income and specific rates of output growth that identify countries as LDCs. (T/F)

2. Prior to the 1960s, LDCs were prejudicially described as economically backward and underdeveloped. (T/F)

3. Per capita income levels among many of the LDCs are at or near subsistence. (T/F)

4. The success of an economy in raising its per capita income depends not only on how well it generates economic growth, but also on how well it contains population growth. (T/F)

5. LDCs are characterized by an age distribution profile that loads the population in the under-15-years-old group. (T/F)

6. Investments in human capital have low payoffs, but they are realized very quickly. (T/F)

7. LDCs would be able to make larger investments in capital goods if production levels were further above subsistence. (T/F)

8. A characteristic of all LDCs is the complete absence of a modern, urban, export-driven sector. (T/F)

9. Economic dualism refers to the coexistence of both a modern and a traditional sector in an LDC. (T/F)

10. The labor demand and supply curves in the traditional sector of an LDC both tend to be relatively flat. (T/F)

11. Political instability in LDCs leads to uncertainty about property rights, which interferes with economic decision making. (T/F)

12. The power of traditionalism in an LDC is reflected in the way people in LDCs quickly adopt new technologies for producing goods. (T/F)

13. A country's infrastructure consists of its basic institutions and the public facilities, like transportation and communication systems, upon which development depends. (T/F)

14. A big-push development strategy relies on coordinated increases in investment in several industries at once in order to create interlocking markets for output. (T/F)

15. The unbalanced development strategy relies on private entrepreneurs to undertake investment projects that become profitable as a result of government-sponsored investment in infrastructure. (T/F)

Multiple-Choice Questions

1. People in LDCs are poor because
   a. they choose to be
   b. of their colonial legacies
   c. of slow population growth
   d. the world they inhabit affords them little choice
   e. of economic dualism

2. Levels of income have jumped dramatically in recent years in all of the following countries **except**
   a. Brazil
   b. Korea
   c. Hong Kong
   d. Ethiopia
   e. Taiwan

3. All of the following are characteristics of less-developed countries **except**
   a. low levels of human capital
   b. political instability
   c. low levels of infant mortality
   d. the absence of infrastructure
   e. the persistence of powerful traditionalism

4. The vicious circle of poverty in LDCs means that
   a. people are poor because they can't invest in capital goods and they can't invest in capital goods because they are poor
   b. their production possibilities curves are bowed-out from the origin
   c. investments in human capital have long payoff periods, so they aren't undertaken even though they are essential for economic growth
   d. investments in infrastructure have long payoff periods, so they aren't undertaken even though they are essential for economic growth
   e. the large fraction of an LDC's population that is poor and below the age of 15 ensures that the population will remain poor for years to come

5. Economic dualism in LDCs is reflected in the fact that most people live in the traditional sector where
   a. their skills allow them dual careers in both the traditional and the modern sectors
   b. most employment is in low-productivity agriculture or marginal service-related jobs
   c. some jobs pay high wages and some jobs pay low wages
   d. demand curves for labor are flat and supply curves of labor are steep
   e. the rich and the poor live side by side

6. It is possible to add significantly to a country's stock of human capital by
   a. investing in physical capital
   b. ending political instability
   c. improving the infrastructure
   d. ensuring that children receive primary education
   e. adopting the big-push strategy instead of the unbalanced strategy for economic development

7. Economic dualism would be best demonstrated in a country where
   a. some 20 percent of the population works for high wages in the modern sector and the rest work
      in the traditional sector
   b. the population is 80 percent urban and 20 percent rural
   c. production is virtually all agricultural compared to the industrialized countries nearby
   d. production is carried out with high-tech and low-tech methods in industry
   e. many people have jobs in both agriculture and industry

8. Political instability in an LDC interferes with economic development by causing
   a. uncertainty in economic decision making
   b. economic dualism
   c. the rise of single-party regimes
   d. the big-push strategy to be more difficult to adopt
   e. the unbalanced strategy to be more difficult to adopt

9. If a peasant in an LDC follows traditional methods of agriculture instead of adopting modern technology,
   it is likely that
   a. production will fluctuate more from year to year
   b. growth rates in output will be slower
   c. growth rates in output will be more rapid
   d. investment in agriculture will be high
   e. foreign direct investment will be higher

10. Even though the payoffs to investments in human capital are relatively high, these investments may not be
    made in an LDC because
    a. the LDC will not be able to compete internationally
    b. it is impossible for people in the traditional sector to take advantage of them
    c. the gains in productivity are realized gradually over a long period of time
    d. population growth will then increase
    e. only those in the modern sector can benefit from them

11. Although it is possible to transplant a modern Detroit automobile plant to an LDC such as Chad, the plant
    is unlikely to contribute much to Chad's economic development because
    a. Chad lacks the skilled personnel necessary to run the plant
    b. an adequate energy system to power the plant is lacking
    c. a system of good roads does not exist
    d. the Chadian banking system is still embryonic
    e. all of the above

12. A key difference between the big-push strategy and the unbalanced development strategy is that
    a. the big-push strategy focuses on a few key industries
    b. the big-push strategy is less expensive
    c. the unbalanced development strategy is an integrated network of government investments
    d. the big-push strategy relies mainly on private entrepreneurs
    e. the unbalanced development strategy relies on forward and backward linkages while the big-push
       strategy involves all sectors of the economy

13. Government investment is emphasized by advocates of the big-push strategy because
   a. only government has the resources to finance the large investments required
   b. private investment is already fully utilized
   c. the government is likely to have a longer time horizon than private investors, making it possible for government to wait for the results of investment that come in the long run
   d. private investors are incompetent
   e. only the government has the personnel to implement and manage the big push in highly technical industries

14. The unbalanced development strategy is unbalanced because
   a. governments that undertake this approach are unstable
   b. forward linkages are stronger than backward linkages
   c. backward linkages are stronger than forward linkages
   d. an imbalance results between supply capacity and the creation of new demands
   e. government's role is completely eliminated so the process is completely private

15. Backward linkages in the unbalanced development strategy relate to increases in
   a. demands for inputs produced in other industries
   b. demands for the products of the backward traditional sector
   c. traditional practices that emerge in opposition to modernization
   d. links between businesses in the traditional sector
   e. links with government agencies that used to sponsor fledgling private-sector businesses

16. Undertaken successfully, foreign direct investment in an LDC should lead to
   a. an outward shift in the production possibilities curve
   b. a flattening of the production possibilities curve since resources are more easily substitutable in production
   c. a return to conditions similar to those experienced by LDCs under colonial rule
   d. high levels of international debt for LDCs
   e. greater need for foreign economic aid

17. U.S. foreign economic aid since 1970 has consisted mostly of
   a. arms exports
   b. direct food relief
   c. grants for development
   d. low-interest loans
   e. high-interest short-term loans

18. One reason that the big-push strategy might be necessary for a developing country is that
   a. private investors may be unwilling to undertake the projects necessary for development
   b. LDC governments have ample resources to support the big-push strategy
   c. few LDCs have the human capital necessary to allow the unbalanced development strategy to work
   d. the big-push is required to raise wages in the traditional sector
   e. the big-push creates more human capital than any other strategy

19. The main reason for the existence of forward linkages in the unbalanced development strategy is that investments in one industry will result in
   a. lower interest rates for other investors in other industries
   b. savings that can be transmitted to other industries
   c. opportunities for investment in new industries that use the output of the first as inputs
   d. the gradual replacement of the traditional economy by forward-looking entrepreneurs
   e. the expansion of infrastructure investment in the traditional sector

20. All of the following are explanations for the low level of development in the traditional sector of an LDC **except**
    a. low levels of literacy
    b. low levels of capital per person
    c. poor infrastructure
    d. attitudes opposed to modernization
    e. the absence of low-wage labor

The following questions relate to the applied and global perspectives in the text.

21. The economic success of China's one couple, one child policy can be measured by
    a. the number of couples who are caught and punished for attempting to have two children
    b. the extent of the decrease in China's population over the coming decades
    c. a shift along the production possibilities curve toward investment goods production
    d. a shift inward of the production possibilities curve
    e. a decrease in the rate of growth of China's GDP since fewer goods and services need to be produced

22. Narrowing the Internet access gap between developed and less-developed countries may be difficult for LDCs because
    a. the advantages in international commerce of widespread Internet use are limited for LDCs
    b. the Internet has not helped even the developed countries to grow faster
    c. the Internet is likely to be replaced with a new technology soon, so any investment will be wasted
    d. investment in Internet access in a LDC requires highly-skilled labor and considerable capital
    e. their economies are already growing at the maximum rate possible

23. A symbiotic linkage exists between the pineapple industry and the cattle industry in Indonesia where
    a. pineapple canning results in pulp to use in cattle feed and cattle produce manure for fertilizer
    b. cattle ranchers rotate land from cattle pasture to pineapple production from year to year
    c. beef and pineapple are favorite items in Indonesian cuisine
    d. cattle graze among the pineapple plants keeping weeds down
    e. trucks used to transport cattle can also be used to haul pineapples

Fill in the Blanks

1. Economic dualism is the _____ of two separate and distinct economies within an LDC, one _____ , primarily urban, and export driven, the other _____, agricultural, and self-sustaining.

2. Foreign direct investment allows an LDC to create _____ goods production without having to sacrifice_____ goods production.

3. Many LDCs are caught in the vicious _____ — they are poor because they are unable to invest in _____, and the reason they don't is because they are _____.

4. The big-push strategy emphasizes investment in many projects _____ to create both _____ capacity and markets for the production.

5. The unbalanced strategy emphasizes private-sector development in key areas of the economy to create

_____ and _____ linkages to new projects.

Discussion Questions

1. Why is rapid population growth considered to be a problem for many LDCs?

2. Contrast the role of government in the big-push development strategy and the unbalanced strategy.

3. List and discuss some basic prerequisites for economic development that may be absent in an LDC.

4. Why would an LDC welcome foreign direct investment? Why might an LDC be reluctant to allow foreign direct investment?

Everyday Applications

Often, a state government provides financial support for economic development within its borders. For example, it may offer tax incentives to new businesses thinking of relocating to the state or to established businesses thinking of leaving the state. Does your state engage in these types of efforts? In what ways is this process similar to the efforts of LDCs that wish to engage in economic development? In what ways is it different?

Economics Online

The World Bank supports development projects in many LDCs. Find out more about the World Bank's activities at its Web site (*http://www.worldbank.org*.

Answers to Questions

Key Terms Quiz

a. 3   f. 4
b. 7   g. 5
c. 2
d. 6
e. 1

True-False Questions

1. False. Although specific levels for income and growth that can be used to label countries as less developed have not been identified, some levels are so low that economists have no trouble agreeing that these countries are LDCs.
2. True
3. True
4. True
5. True
6. False. The payoffs from investments in human capital are relatively high, but they are realized in the long run.
7. True
8. False. Economic dualism, the coexistence of a modern economy and a traditional economy in an LDC, frequently occurs.
9. True
10. True
11. True

12. False. Traditionalism is reflected in the slow pace at which new techniques are adopted.
13. True
14. True
15. True

Multiple-Choice Questions

1. d	**6.** d	**11.** e	**16.** a	**21.** c
2. d	**7.** a	**12.** e	**17.** c	**22.** d
3. c	**8.** a	**13.** c	**18.** a	**23.** a
4. a	**9.** b	**14.** d	**19.** c	
5. b	**10.** c	**15.** a	**20.** e	

Fill in the Blanks

1. coexistence; modern; traditional
2. capital; consumer
3. circle of poverty; capital goods; poor
4. all at once; productive
5. backward; forward

Discussion Questions

1. The main problem associated with rapid population growth in many LDCs is that it makes the achievement of per capita income growth more difficult. Per capita income growth is defined as income growth divided by population growth. If population grows faster than income, per capita income falls. In many LDCs, population growth is rapid and income growth is slow. Such LDCs face a double-whammy problem. Population growth rates in excess of 2.5 percent per year are not uncommon among LDCs, meaning that economic growth must exceed 2.5 percent per year in order for per capita income to grow at all.

    Another problem associated with rapid rates of population growth in LDCs is that the country's age distribution profile is weighted heavily in the under-15-years-old group. Even though children living in poverty in an LDC consume meagerly, they still consume more than they produce. The consumption requirements of the large numbers of children in LDCs make it more difficult for these countries to shift resources from consumption goods production to capital goods production in order to accelerate growth rates. So, high rates of population growth contribute to the vicious circle of poverty — people are poor because they can't invest in capital goods and they can't invest in capital goods because they are poor.

2. The role of government in the big-push development strategy is extensive. The idea behind the big-push strategy is that by pursuing a large all-at-once investment commitment in many different industries, ready markets for the interlocking projects will be created. Furthermore, the growing markets in the economy make many other investment projects attractive. Economists who advocate the big-push strategy believe that government is best suited to initiate, finance, and manage the set of infrastructure and development investments that comprise the big push. The main reason for relying on government to undertake the big push is that government has a sufficiently long time horizon to make the kinds of investments where payoffs may lie some time in the future.   Once the big push is underway, the private sector is expected to participate because the big push creates a set of new, profitable investment opportunities.

    The unbalanced strategy relies less heavily on government investment in the economy. The unbalanced strategy is based on the idea that every investment will have its own set of backward and forward linkages. A backward linkage results when investment in one industry creates demands for inputs in another industry, inducing investment in it to produce those inputs. An example would be the construction of a railroad that creates a demand for steel rails, causing the steel industry to expand. A forward linkage is investment in one industry that creates opportunities in other industries that use the goods produced in the first as inputs.

Continuing with the railroad example, a forward linkage from railroad construction might be the expansion of agricultural production for export to distant markets. The railroad provides transportation, an input critical to the expansion of agricultural exports. The unbalanced strategy emphasizes reinforcing imbalances caused by the continuous creation of new supplies and new demands in the economy. The emphasis on government investment is minimal. However, government funding and putting in place some of the economy's key infrastructure investments are still important for the unbalanced strategy to be successful.

3. Political stability is a basic prerequisite for development that is absent from many LDCs. If governments are routinely overthrown and replaced by new regimes in a country, people become very uncertain about their legal systems and their property rights. Economic decision making becomes difficult in such an uncertain environment.

   Another basic prerequisite for development is a modern view of the world. Traditionalism may prevail in much of an LDC's population. People in LDCs may rely on custom in their economic relationships. They may be reluctant to part with traditional ways of producing goods for new and more productive ways. Economic modernization is very difficult if a country is tradition-bound in its economic relationships.

   Finally, infrastructure is a necessary prerequisite for development that is absent in many LDCs. A country's infrastructure consists of the basic institutions and public facilities upon which production and development depend. Examples of infrastructure include an education system, a legal system, a financial system, as well as transportation, communication, and energy networks. It is virtually impossible to start using modern technologies in production without an infrastructure in place.

4. Foreign direct investment can be a boon to an LDC because it allows the country to expand economic development at zero opportunity cost. Instead of sacrificing consumption goods production in order to invest more in capital goods production, foreign capital is infused into the LDC. Thus, no consumption goods are sacrificed, and production increases due to the infusion of foreign capital. Typically, foreign direct investment brings new expertise to an LDC along with the new capital goods.

   However, most LDCs hold some reservations about a development program based heavily around foreign direct investment. Some of these reservations are the result of lingering images from the LDCs' colonial pasts. Such LDCs may have been raw material supply bases for countries in the West. Their entrepreneurs may have had little freedom to operate except in restricted traditional production and retail activities. The best industries were reserved for the colonial power. The prospect of inviting back in the very colonial powers that the LDC threw off with independence is ironic indeed.

   To avoid problems associated with their colonial legacies and foreign direct investment, LDC governments typically impose stringent regulations on foreign investors. For example, foreign investors may be excluded from certain fields of activity. They may be required to hire nationals in managerial positions and/or meet employment quotas. Finally, ceilings may be imposed on the amount of profit a foreign investor can take out of the LDC.

Homework Questions

True-False Questions — If a statement is false, explain why.

1. Per capita income growth has been difficult for LDCs to achieve because most of these countries have high population growth rates. (T/F)

2. Economic dualism is a term that describes the presence of extremely rich countries alongside very poor countries around the world. (T/F)

3. The Internet is an example of a consumption good for people in LDCs. (T/F)

4. One advantage to the big-push strategy of development is its relatively low cost for LDCs. (T/F)

5. Backward linkages are investments in industries that create demands for inputs that are produced in other industries causing investment in them. (T/F)

Multiple-Choice Questions

1. Foreign direct investment has the advantage that _____, which has to be weighed against the disadvantage that _____.
   a. growth is much faster; the environment is destroyed
   b. investment is financed by foreigners; images of the colonial past may be rekindled
   c. investment in foreign countries is profitable; domestic investment may languish
   d. domestic firms get funding; foreign firms lose employment
   e. LDCs profit enormously; industrialized nations suffer

2. A big-push development strategy emphasizes investment in
   a. one key industry
   b. the production of consumer goods for immediate marketing
   c. several industries at once that have interlocking markets
   d. the oil industry
   e. industries that require the most investment (big push) to get going

3. LDCs face a "double-whammy problem" when
   a. population growth rates are low and income growth is high
   b. population growth rates are low and income growth is low
   c. the modern sector and the traditional sector both fail to expand
   d. population growth rates are high and income growth is high
   e. population growth rates are high and income growth is low

4. The unbalanced development strategy relies heavily on
    a. the existence of extensive forward and backward linkages with investment projects
    b. private sector investment in infrastructure to get the process started initially
    c. an inflow of foreign direct investment
    d. the development of both the modern and traditional sectors simultaneously
    e. the emergence of ready markets for new investment projects

5. One effect of China's "one couple, one child" policy is
    a. greater reproductive freedom for women
    b. delayed retirements as the supply of younger workers declines
    c. greater ease in raising per capita incomes as population growth slows
    d. a shift of resources away from investment goods to consumption goods
    e. an inward shift of the production possibilities curve

Discussion Questions/Problems

1. Why is economic dualism a problem for a less-developed country? Consider the impact of dualism on the distribution of income in an LDC? Does dualism increase or decrease inequality in the income distribution?

2. Should an LDC fund all of its development efforts internally, that is to say, completely avoid foreign loans and foreign direct investment? Discuss.

PART 5 — THE WORLD ECONOMY

COMPREHENSIVE SAMPLE TEST

Give yourself 50 minutes to complete this exam. The answers follow. Don't look until you are finished!

True-False Questions — If a statement is false, explain why. Each question is worth two points.

1. If two countries trade according to comparative advantage, then more goods will be available in both countries for consumption. (T/F)

2. A quota will restrict imports at the same time that it generates tax revenues for the government. (T/F)

3. A country's terms of trade will improve when the ratio between an index of export prices and an index of import prices increases. (T/F)

4. The most valid argument for trade restrictions is the cheap foreign labor argument. (T/F)

5. The exchange rate is the number of units of foreign currency that can be purchased with one unit of domestic currency. (T/F)

6. A depreciation of the yen relative to the dollar means that more yen are required to purchase a dollar. (T/F)

7. A negative balance on current account will be matched by a negative balance on the capital account. (T/F)

8. A massive, interlocking strategy of investments in infrastructure, manufacturing industries, and services is consistent with the big-push strategy. (T/F)

9. Economic dualism is the coexistence of two separate and distinct economies within an LDC, one modern and the other traditional. (T/F)

10. Foreign direct investment consists primarily of money for development that is granted to LDCs by the governments of industrialized countries. (T/F)

Multiple-Choice Questions — Each question is worth two points.

1. The table below shows the number of hours required to produce either one ton of steel or one bushel of grapes in the United States and Chile.

Labor-Hours to Produce:		
	1 ton of steel	1 bushel of grapes
United States	100	160
Chile	200	180

   The United States has an absolute advantage in _____ and a comparative advantage in _____.
   a. both activities; grape production
   b. both activities; steel production
   c. steel production only; grape production
   d. grape production only; both activities
   e. steel production; both activities

2. Using the data presented in the table for question 1, the opportunity cost of one bushel of grapes is _____ in the United States and _____ in Chile.
   a. one-half ton of steel; 9/10 tons of steel
   b. 10/9 ton of steel; 9/10 ton of steel
   c. 8/5 tons of steel; 9/10 ton of steel
   d. 5/8 ton of steel; 9/10 ton of steel
   e. 5/8 ton of steel; 10/9 tons of steel

3. A country could benefit from protection against free trade based on the infant-industries argument if
   a. its labor is cheaper than in foreign countries
   b. the protected industry successfully learns the trade
   c. the protected industry pays for the protection through higher taxes in the future
   d. the protected industry gains the expertise necessary to compete and accepts removal of protection
   e. the industry employs large numbers of workers

4. Suppose that a tariff equal to $2 per pound is imposed on imported sugar. The revenue from this tariff will be
   a. 0
   b. $100 million
   c. $200 million
   d. $400 million
   e. $600 million

5. The graph below shows the market for sugar in the United States, including imports.

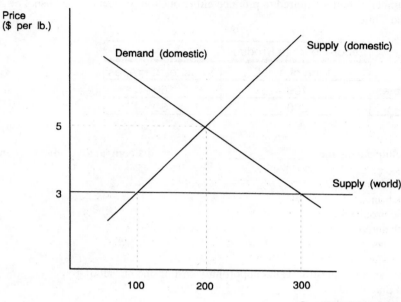

The graph shows that the world price for sugar is _____ and, with free trade, the United States will consume _____ million pounds of sugar per week.
a. $5 per pound; 200
b. $3 per pound; 200
c. $5 per pound; 100
d. $3 per pound; 100
e. $3 per pound; 300

6. Suppose that the terms of trade for a country specializing in gold exports have deteriorated due to a decline in gold prices. The best advice for this country would be to
a. impose a tariff on gold imports in order to raise the price
b. hold gold off the world market to raise its price
c. continue to export gold as long as it has a comparative advantage in gold production
d. stop trading in international markets because specialization is no longer beneficial
e. begin dumping gold in the world market

7. The key difference between GATT and the WTO is that
a. the WTO has been more aggressive in enforcing compliance with its ruling than was GATT
b. GATT was more effective at settling disputes between trading partners
c. reciprocity no longer applies under the WTO
d. the WTO has fewer members
e. the European Union has rejected the WTO

8. If incomes increase in the United States, the demand for foreign currencies in the United States will be expected to
   a. decrease
   b. increase
   c. remain unchanged
   d. depend on tastes for foreign goods
   e. depend on the exchange rates

9. Suppose a decision is made by the U.S. government to fix the exchange rate between the dollar and German mark at $3/mark. An increase in the demand for German goods will force the United States to
   a. purchase marks in foreign exchange markets to make up the excess demand for marks
   b. purchase marks in foreign exchange markets to make up the excess supply of marks
   c. borrow marks from the IMF to make up the excess supply of marks
   d. supply marks at the $3/mark rate in order to satisfy the excess demand for marks
   e. supply marks at the $3/mark rate in order to satisfy the excess demand for dollars

10. Suppose the exchange rate between the dollar and German mark is fixed by the U.S. government at $3/mark. The equilibrium exchange rate in foreign exchange markets is $5/mark. Under these circumstances, there is a
    a. chronic excess demand for marks that could be eliminated by devaluing the dollar to $5/mark
    b. chronic excess supply of marks that could be eliminated by devaluing the dollar to $5/mark
    c. chronic excess demand for dollars that could be eliminated by devaluing the dollar to $5/mark
    d. reason to think the dollar will appreciate
    e. reason to think the mark will depreciate

11. The International Monetary Fund was created in 1944 to provide
    a. funds for development projects in newly independent LDCs
    b. advice on fixing currency exchange rates between members of GATT
    c. a forum for discussions on lowering tariffs around the world
    d. low-interest loans for entrepreneurs in LDCs
    e. temporary loans of foreign currencies to countries to help stabilize their currencies

12. When a country imposes import controls through tariff and quota adjustments, the purpose is to
    a. expand imports so that new capital equipment essential for development can be obtained
    b. eliminate the negative balance on current account
    c. eliminate the positive balance on capital account
    d. decrease the volume of imports so that the demand for foreign currencies is reduced
    e. increase the volume of imports so that the demand for foreign currencies is increased

13. The balance of trade is
    a. positive if the capital account balance is positive
    b. the difference between merchandise exports and merchandise imports
    c. the difference between service exports and service imports
    d. negative if the capital account balance is negative
    e. the same as the balance of payments

14. A balance of payments problem exists for the United States when
    a. currency reserves are run down to low levels to obtain the balance
    b. too many U.S. assets are sold to obtain the balance
    c. the United States borrows excessively in foreign exchange markets to obtain the balance
    d. the United States is unable to increase exports over time to eventually obtain the balance
    e. all of the above

15. Successful economic development could be represented on a production possibilities curve by
    a. a shift along the curve toward production of more consumption goods followed by an outward shift of the curve
    b. a shift along the curve toward production of more capital goods followed by an outward shift of the curve
    c. a change in the shape of the curve so that it is less bowed-out from the origin
    d. an inward shift of the curve as a result of foreign direct investment
    e. a move along the curve to a point where enough consumption goods are produced to meet subsistence needs

16. All of the following are possible results from rapid population growth in an LDC **except**
    a. slower per capita income growth
    b. an age profile that loads the population in the under-15-years-old group
    c. the need for the LDC to invest more in education
    d. an increase in wages over time as labor becomes scarcer
    e. greater investments in housing

17. In order for economic dualism to exist in an LDC,
    a. rates of per capita income growth must be negative
    b. a modern sector and a traditional sector must operate as two distinct economies in the country
    c. population growth rates must exceed 2.5 percent per year
    d. the terms of trade must deteriorate
    e. about half the population must be illiterate

18. The main reason for the emphasis on massive investments in the big-push development strategy is to
    a. establish a role for government in the economy
    b. demonstrate to private entrepreneurs that development is possible
    c. create ready markets for the new projects thereby inducing investment in other projects
    d. appear more receptive to foreign direct investment
    e. attract aid from foreign governments

19. A good example of backward linkages in an LDC would be
    a. an expansion of the country's fertilizer industry in response to expanded agricultural production
    b. an increase in the demand for teachers due to population growth
    c. the creation of a market for computer software due to growth in the computer manufacturing industry
    d. trade relationships that are established with poorer LDCs
    e. foreign direct investment coming from countries that were once colonial powers in the LDC

20. All of the following are basic prerequisites for successful economic development in an LDC **except**
    a. a colonial past
    b. political stability
    c. infrastructure
    d. a modern view of the world
    e. enough human capital to undertake modern investment projects

Discussion Questions/Problems — Each question is worth 10 points.

1. The table from question 1 in the multiple-choice section is reproduced below.

	Labor-Hours to Produce:	
	1 ton of steel	1 bushel of grapes
United States	100	160
Chile	200	180

    a. Suppose that the United States and Chile each have 1,000 hours to devote to either steel production or grape production. Before trade, how much steel and how many bushels of grapes could each country produce if it devoted all its resources to producing one or the other?

    b. Now suppose that the United States and Chile each have 1,000 hours of labor available and they specialize and trade freely according to comparative advantage. Suppose that the international price is established at one ton of steel per one bushel of grapes. Show how both the United States and Chile can be better off as a result of specializing and trading according to comparative advantage at this price.

2. The graph from question 5 in the multiple-choice section is reproduced below.

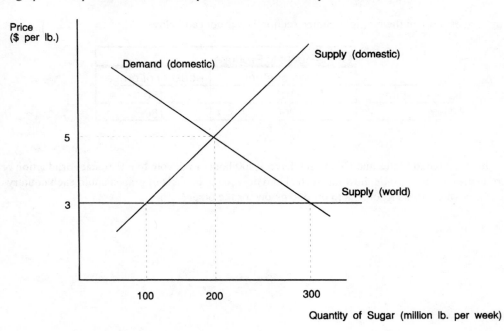

a. Suppose that a $1 per pound tariff is imposed on sugar imports. Sketch in the effect of this tariff on the graph above. Carefully label the new quantity supplied by domestic producers and the new quantity demanded. About how much sugar is imported now?

b. Approximately how much revenue does the tariff generate? Explain how you arrived at your answer.

3. Discuss the advantages and disadvantages of fixed exchange rates.

4. What is meant by the term human capital? What kinds of investments can an LDC make that will increase human capital? Why might an LDC be reluctant to make these investments?

Answers to the Sample Test on Part 5

True-False Questions

1. True
2. False. A quota will restrict imports, but it will not generate tax revenues because it is not a tax. A tariff both restricts imports and generates tax revenue.
3. True
4. False. If foreign labor is cheaper, it is because the labor is less productive. It makes more sense to buy goods where they are priced the lowest because that way the maximum amount of real goods can be purchased.
5. True
6. True
7. False. A negative balance on current account will be matched by a positive balance on the capital account.
8. True
9. True
10. False. Foreign direct investment is carried on by private businesses, not government.

Multiple-Choice Questions

1. b	**6.** c	**11.** e	**16.** d
2. c	**7.** a	**12.** d	**17.** b
3. d	**8.** b	**13.** b	**18.** c
4. a	**9.** d	**14.** e	**19.** a
5. e	**10.** a	**15.** b	**20.** a

Discussion Questions/Problems

1. a. If the United States devoted all 1,000 hours to producing steel, it could produce 1,000 hr./100 hr./ton = 10 tons of steel. If the United States devoted all 1,000 hours to producing grapes, it could produce 1,000 hr./160hr./bushel = 6.25 bushels.

   If Chile devoted all 1,000 hours to producing steel, it could produce 1,000/200 = 5 tons of steel. If Chile used all of its labor to produce grapes, it could produce 1,000/180 = 5.55 bushels of grapes.

   b. The United States has a comparative advantage in steel production. A ton of steel costs 5/8 bushel of grapes in the United States. In Chile, a ton of steel costs 10/9 bushels of grapes. The United States will specialize in steel and Chile in grapes.

   Suppose the United States uses the 1,000 hours to produce 10 tons of steel. At the 1:1 price ratio, the United States can trade those 10 tons of steel for up to 10 bushels of grapes. It can obtain 10 bushels instead of only 6.25 bushels. By the same logic, if Chile uses all of its labor to produce 5.55 bushels of grapes, it can trade for up to 5.55 tons of steel. This is greater than its no-trade amount.

2. A graph with the tariff and the new quantities supplied and demanded is shown on the following page.

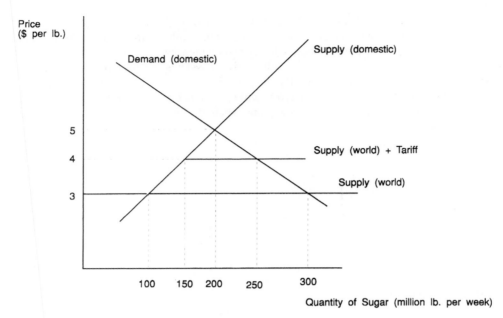

a. The tariff raises the price of imported sugar to $4. Domestic suppliers will increase their output by 50 million pounds per week to 150 million pounds per week. Consumption of sugar will fall from 300 million pounds per week to 250 pounds per week. The amount of sugar imported will drop to 100 million pounds per week.

b. Tariff revenue is equal to $1 per pound multiplied by the 100 million pounds imported, or $100 million.

3. The main advantage to fixed exchange rates is that they eliminate the uncertainty associated with flexible exchange rates. For example, suppose that a U.S. importer has contracted to purchase goods from Germany, and between the contract agreement and delivery, the German mark appreciates relative to the dollar (the dollar depreciates). The German goods become more expensive for the American importer as a result.

The disadvantage to fixed exchange rates is that if the exchange rate is set incorrectly, a chronic excess demand for or excess supply of foreign currencies will result. For example, suppose the United States sets the exchange rate between the mark and the dollar at $3/mark. Suppose the exchange rate for marks and dollars in foreign exchange markets is $5/mark. Under these circumstances, there will be an excess demand for marks in the United States, so the United States will be forced to cope with the excess demand. This can be done by supplying marks from U.S. foreign exchange reserves. Another alternative is for the United States to adjust the exchange rate to $5/mark (a depreciation of the dollar relative to the mark). The United States could impose import controls and adjust tariffs and quotas in order to limit imports and decrease the demand for marks. Exchange controls could also be imposed whereby exporters are required to turn over their earnings of foreign currencies at the fixed rate. Finally, the United States could go to the IMF to borrow marks to cover the excess demand for them.

However, problems are associated with each of these solutions to the problem of chronic excess demand for foreign currencies. For example, reserves of currencies might be drawn down to dangerously low levels. Currency depreciation makes imports more expensive for U.S. consumers. Import controls risk retaliation from other countries. Exchange controls limit the freedom of exporters in the United States. Borrowing from the IMF must be done with the expectation that the loan will be paid off after the currency crisis is over.

4. Human capital is the investment in workers' knowledge acquired through education, training, and/or experience, along with investments in the health of workers that enhance their productivity. An LDC can make investments in human capital by building new schools, training teachers, introducing job training, increasing the number of physicians, and expanding health delivery systems such as clinics and hospitals. Even though these investments may have high payoffs, the payoffs may not be realized until far in the future. An LDC that is anxious for quick, visible payoffs will be less inclined to invest in human capital than in other forms of capital, like a big manufacturing plant, where the payoff is relatively quick and highly visible.